MANAGING YOUR BAND
PERSONAL MANAGEMENT: THE ULTIMATE RESPONSIBILITY

2nd Edition

ISBN 0-9651250-2-5

For information:

HiMarks Publishing Co.
P. O. Box 2083
Wayne, NJ 07474-2083
Fax: 973.720.2217
marcones@wpunj.edu

HiMarks Publishing Co.

Exclusively Distributed By

HAL•LEONARD®
CORPORATION
7777 W. BLUEMOUND RD. P.O. BOX 13819 MILWAUKEE, WI 53213

MANAGING YOUR BAND

ARTIST MANAGEMENT:
THE ULTIMATE RESPONSIBILITY

By
Dr. Stephen Marcone

2nd
EDITION

For every musician who, against unbelievable odds, was given the chance to play in the major leagues and blew it!

MANAGING YOUR BAND
ARTIST MANAGEMENT: THE ULTIMATE RESPONSIBILITY
by
Dr. Stephen Marcone
Second Edition

CONTENTS

ACKNOWLEDGMENTS

This book took a long time to write. It became more a labor of love as the years went on. I started it when my son was learning how to talk and finished it during the tail end of my divorce. Like I said, the book took a long time to write.

I started the project by hooking up with Mark Spector, then manager of 38 Special. We met for a while, but I guess that neither of us had the interest or perseverance to see it through. I put it down for several years and then got the itch not to give up on it.

A while later a former student and attorney, Jeffrey Aber, put a bug in my ear to collaborate. I must thank him for the tedious work he did on Chapter Six. He was very helpful. He explained the details and put up with my ignorance. Jeff became busy and then moved to L. A. . I put the book down again.

A colleague of mine, Karl Guthrie, is a practicing entertainment attorney and a great talker. During several of his weekly visits to the college to teach Law and Ethics in the Music and Entertainment industry, we would talk (sometimes, I might confess, through a good deal of the class period) about the current state of affairs in the industry. Karl enjoys my insights about current events. Karl kept asking about the book and stirred my interest to move it along. He also was very willing to share most of the agreements found in this book with me and I am thankful.

Lastly, as a [former] boardmember of the Music and Entertainment Industry Educators Association I am in contact with most of the industry educators throughout the country. There is an expressed need for a text that can be used in a personal management/entrepreneurship course. They too helped me find the energy to finish.

I purposely left the acknowledgements from the first edition in this edition as well. Although this edition is more comprehensive it still deals with the basic issues of entrepreneurship and artist representation. For this edition, I thank a former student, Adam Kornfeld of Q.B.Q. Entertainment, for the updated contracts in chapter nine, and my students who completed my personal management course, for their proofreading, contributions to chapters one and twelve, and general insight into what is expected in a text.

S. M.

February , 1998
Wayne, NJ

INTRODUCTION

With barely a music graduate degree in hand, I was given the opportunity to play in the major leagues. As a band that wrote and performed its own material, we somehow generated some interest at Epic Records to give us a chance and sign us. The group was holding down a six nights a week, six sets a night summer gig at **THE** club in Lake George New York and packing the place. We rehearsed almost everyday and were probably as tight as any band could be. We sounded great and people paid to hear (and see) us. Things were happening pretty fast and it was all exciting (and foreign) to the six of us.

As we began our first tour of arenas (as an opening act) we were told on numerous occasions to concentrate on the music and let "them" worry about the business. This was the fall after the summer of Woodstock 69, and it was obvious to many that there was now big money to be made from rock 'n' roll. We had management. A friend of ours who could be trusted, a doctoral student at Syracuse University, had been booking the band and had the intestinal fortitude to put up with us. He could swim, and although we didn't know it, but not with the barracudas!

A short time later, while we were still in demand, we realized his shortcomings and decided to try another manager. We found one, or I should say, he found us, and had his attorney draw up an agreement. He came to us with experience, and we all liked him. After all, he was hipper than our friend, lived in NYC, and had gotten high with us on several occasions. What was not to like!

We received the contract that the attorney composed, read it and were shocked that this guy, our new found friend, would demand what was written on the pages. In fact, we were so appalled (and green) that instead of asking our attorney to respond with an equally outrageous counteroffer, we decided to run (not walk) back to our original manger/friend and ask his forgiveness.

Basically this is where the story ends. In fact, we committed industry mortal sin number two and went on to manage ourselves. After all, The Beatles did it (without success), so why couldn't we. Well, this is how I learned what not to do.

Only a few years later I realized that musicians are being short changed. That, for the most part, the record business is not controlled by the players. With the right education and information, musicians could be in control of their own destinies. However, it would take time. Today the more successful musicians understand the business, make decisions, and some control their own careers, production and record companies.

This book has been written to help the cause. Personal management is still the weakest link in a business that operates by fragmenting its product. That is, an artist must give pieces of his/her product to several people that control different fragments of the business. Holding on to all of it doesn't work. **ONE HUNDRED PERCENT OF NOTHING =NOTHING,** no matter how you slice it. An artist must understand and learn to live within this concept. The trick is to give it to the right people for the shortest amount of time possible. I hope this book helps artists choose the right people to give it to, and right people learn how to do it right!

INTRODUCTION TO SECOND EDITION

As soon as I started using the first edition of this text in class, I noticed some gaping holes. So in this edition, along with updating the statistical material, I have tried to fill in some of those spaces. Throughout the book, the web is discussed as a tool for many of the artist's needs.

In Chapter One, I included an example of project management. It is an example of a few of my student's work, students I believe will be future leaders of this industry. Another addition to chapter one is the stages of an American artist's career, that Simon Frith complied. It really is another way of examining the maze that is included on the back the front cover.

Chapter Five, The Multinationals, is new. It discusses the Big Six and their relationship to the world industry.

In Chapter Nine a sample tour budget is included, which can be used as a tool for both costing out a show and settling with the promoter.

Chapter Eleven includes two examples of artists who have been misguided financially but are on the road to recovery.

In Chapter Twelve additional case studies have been added, and of course, updates.

The Instructor's Companion has also been updated accordingly.

The subject of how to remain fair to both genders was never an issue to me. Throughout the book I tried to use s/he and his/her when either applied. My intention was (and is) to emphasize equality.

CHAPTER ONE

PERSONAL MANAGEMENT

"Management is the most complex area of the record business . . ."
Michael Lippmann. Billboard Magazine, Vol. 98#52

By the end of this chapter you should be able to:

1. Discuss the role of a personal manager
2. List eight characteristics a manager should have
3. Discuss the three characteristics a potentially successful artist should have
4. Discuss how an artist should choose a manager
5. List the artist's "team" and discuss their individual roles and how they are chosen
6. Discuss two key points found in an artist-personal manager agreement
7. Manage a project in an organized manner
8. Define talent and success as it relates to the industry.

DO I NEED A MANAGER?

At one time or another, most artists/musicians ask the $64 question of do I need a manager. The answer isn't always as obvious as one might expect. In fact, it may even be more complicated than first imagined, because there are several types of managers, and a big difference between two types most often employed in the entertainment industry: a personal manager and a business manager.

The second question that is asked is when do I need management? Is the role of the manager most important when: an artist is looking for a record deal; a new artist has reached the status of Celine Dion or Puff Daddy; an artist has become a veteran performer (ie: Mick Jagger); or an artist has reached the residual stage of Jimi Hendrix?

The answer to all of the above is that at each stage the artist may not recognize that s/he needs a manager, but it is clear that s/he needs **management**. And unless the artist is committed to giving the 24/7 (a term that is used to mean 24 hours a day, 7 days a week) to the business side of the career, someone must take the responsibility.

WHAT IS IT?

The role of the personal manager in the music and entertainment business can be compared to the role of a football coach. Short range strategy plays an important part of every possession in every quarter of the game. Long range strategy plays a role in determining a successful season. Each play is determined by the team's strengths versus the opponent's weaknesses. During a losing game, it must be extremely frustrating to watch from the sidelines and not be able to play.

The personal manager coaches the artist and his or her team. Every musical set of every gig is important in winning over an audience. Each gig has an effect on the long range game plan. How much can the team do to insure the success of the next performance? During a weak concert, it must be extremely frustrating to watch from the wings and not be able to play.

Most managers will confess that when they got their first client, they thought they knew a great deal more about managing then they really did. Most managers will also confess that they learned management by "doing it." Furthermore, managers that have survived in this business will confess that the most crucial aspect to surviving was ADMITTING that they neither knew the CORRECT answer to certain questions, nor did they know WHAT the correct information was that they SHOULD HAVE known. Some managers will even admit that they STILL don't know everything they should know.

SO WHAT IS IT?

Personal management means being responsible for every part of the artist's career . . . twenty-four hours a day, seven days a week. It involves making decisions you and your artist can live with, and developing a trusting relationship with an artist that allows you to make decisions without consulting him or her. It's a relationship that matures over time and grows out of mutual respect. This respect may be gained in two ways: by maintaining a record of not "screwing up," and by truly considering the artist's opinion about his or her career. A personal manager should never let the artist feel that his or her opinion is worthless. In fact, the artist's opinion can be and should be an integral part of the decision making process.

AN ART OR A CRAFT?

Well it's both! The mechanics of the job can be learned, so the craft isn't very mysterious. Learning the fundamentals and routines is easy. The creative or artistic side of the job is more complex.

A successful manager has the ability to motivate people, and generate excitement about a project. A successful manager senses other people's needs, not only the artist's, but the needs of the other people who are part of the "army" that works for and with the artist. This part of the creative aspect is seldom learned. A person either does them or doesn't. Personalities play a major role in the business, and at times personal relationships are even more important than talent.

WHO SHOULD TRY IT?

Anyone who wants to. However, Figure 1.1 lists eight characteristics that contribute to success. A discussion of some of the points follows.

A good personal manager is

1. a self-starter
2. patient
3. organized
4. able to make decisions and take responsibility
5. able to recognize creativity and talent
6. able to recognize uniqueness
7. able to recognize the potential value of an artist in the marketplace
8. knowledgeable about the music business

Figure 1.1

PATIENCE

A successful manager is a patient one. The creative process takes time. Composing songs or developing a concept for an album cannot be rushed. Deadlines and timetables constantly need readjustment. Truly creative people cannot turn on creativity precisely at a designated time. The manager must feel comfortable with the unpredictability - - with changing schedules and unanticipated cost overruns.

A manager must also wait for information to be collected. Being "ultra" busy in this business seems to be a status symbol. It takes days and repeated phone calls before decisions are finalized. Many record executives (decision makers) divide their time between NYC, LA, and London, and even some very successful and prominent managers have trouble pinning them down.

Developing careers evolve through many levels. However, they don't always appear to be moving in the right direction (or any direction). Stars must "pay their dues," and a manager must wait for each level of success to be reached before another level can be attained.

In this business, success does not provide instant gratification. An audience may go wild during a concert or a critic may write a positive review of a recording, however, success is measured **quantitatively**. How many tickets were sold? How much airplay did the record receive? How high on the charts did the record go? It takes time for these measurements to be made. And it takes patience by the record company to allow time for success to happen. "Patience **is** a virtue" . . . a necessary virtue for success.

ABILITY TO RECOGNIZE CREATIVITY AND TALENT

How does one develop the ability to recognize creativity, talent, or uniqueness? Does one either have a feel for it or not? Can it be developed? Can it be taught?

Everyday, successful personal managers receive many demo tapes from new artists. (One manager said that his office receives up to 200 tapes each week!) It's hard to explain how a manager reaches the conclusion that someone has a unique talent. Record company a&r people use their personal judgement when deciding who will be permitted to record. They say it's a feeling that one instinctively gets when they hear or see it. The late John Hammond, indisputably Columbia Records' greatest talent scout, had the ability. (Hammond brought, among others, Benny Goodman, Bob Dylan, and Bruce Springsteen to the label.) If someone has potential to recognize talent, it can probably be developed with practice, but it can't really be taught. (In this industry, two-thirds to three-quarters of the albums released never even regain their recording costs!)

A personal manager must possess the ability to recognize the talent in undiscovered artists. Related experience in the industry may help, but the confidence must come from within. No one is infallible. Every successful manager and record company have "passed" on at least one successful artist. But the ability to recognize creativity and unique talent plays a major role in all aspects of this business.

RECOGNIZING THE TRUE ARTIST

Every successful performer has true artistry, or some combination of artistry and craftsmanship with market value. However, given this ingredient, what other characteristics are essential when choosing an artist with success potential? Consider the following.

1. Desire, determination, and patience

Serious determination is essential in order to survive in this business. Most artists have ALMOST quit more than once. Since success is seldom instant, an artist must have the maturity to wait for the industry and the audience to react.

2. Credibility

On stage or off, an artist must have a clearly focused image in order to succeed. (Image is discussed in a later chapter.)

3. Potential to withstand changes in the marketplace

A manager should ask him/herself if this person has the potential to make recordings that will last a generation. Also, will the artist's personality mature with his or her craft? Every artist should strive to be a classic.

It's also true that many "artists" make a great deal of money for only a short time. When managing such an artist, one correct strategy is to find a reason why the public would want to buy the act on a short term basis rather than for the lasting potential. Although money has been made with both kinds of artists, most managers would choose to handle the "classic" artist.

When asked why he chose to work with a particular artist, one manager summed up her qualities by saying, "her personality is clearly defined . . . she articulates a sense of self . . . with the proper guidance, she has the potential to sellout arenas."

CHOOSING A MANAGER

Every artist would like to be managed by a person with strong industry contacts and a proven track record. These elements improve the chance of success. Credibility is as important for a manager as it is for an artist. However, given these qualities, what should an artist look for when choosing a manager?

A management agreement is essentially a legal contract to enter into a relationship. **Mutual trust** is crucial to a successful working relationship. The artist and manager must have **compatible personalities**. When describing their managers, most artists will list the positive qualities and conclude by saying "and I like him or her."

CHOOSING THE "TEAM"

Typically, an artist's team is composed of a manager, an attorney, an agent, a publicist, and an accountant or a business manager. The artist must feel comfortable with the team members that are directly involved with the financial aspects of the career; namely, the manager, attorney, and accountant. However, the manager must be able to work with all of the team members. A good manager will offer the artist suggestions as to who should play certain roles, and will specifically chose who will play others. The following are guidelines that maybe helpful when choosing the team.

Attorney

Attorneys plays a major role in the music business. Sometimes it seems as if there is a contract for every aspect of a career. Therefore, the manager should offer an artist at least three names of attorneys with whom the artist would feel comfortable doing business with. Three who have exhibited sound judgement and distinguished experience . . . and leave the responsibility of choosing one with the artist. The artist should interview them and actually choose the attorney him/herself. The legal documents have the final word in business, so why should the manager take full responsibility in an area that could sour and lead to mistrust?

Booking Agent

A manager must maintain a close relationship with the artist's booking agent. They will converse on the phone several times on any given day. This relationship is far more important than the booking agent's relationship with the artist. As always, the artist should offer input into this decision, but the manager should make the final choice.

When choosing an agent, and before signing an exclusive agreement, the manager should evaluate the degree of enthusiasm that exists **throughout the entire agency** for the artist. Large agencies usually divide the country (or world) into territories, and assign an agent to each territory. Agents will also be assigned to specific categories of the business, such as concert promoters in the northeast, or midwest colleges. Therefore, overwhelming support by one agent and no interest displayed by other agents, could present booking problems at a later date. Broad support by the agency is more beneficial in the long run.

Publicist

The proper creation of publicity and handling of an image are crucial to a successful career. Most often publicists are hired to manage specific campaigns, projects, events, or tours. It is the manager's responsibility to hire the right person or agency for the job, and artist's leave this to the manager.

Accountant (Business Manager)

The accountant holds the fiscal responsibilities, and controls all collections and disbursements. This allows the manager to concentrate on the more creative endeavors. When choosing an accountant, again, several names should be suggested, and let the artist make the final decision.

THE DAILY ROUTINE

In this business, each day brings a new offer or a new crisis. Some days the mail is opened in the morning and some days it sits until late afternoon. Some days the phones light up before the office is opened, and some days things unravel in an orderly fashion.

However, there are certain constants. Each day the manager should ask these questions: "Am I making as much money for my artist as I possibly can? Are as many records, concert tickets, T-Shirts, etc. being sold as possibly can? What could I be doing to make more money for my artist?"

Asking these questions on a daily basis ensures that certain "career maintenance" routines are completed. The manager will be certain to talk to the record company everyday. If the artist is touring, he or she will converse with the agent several times during the day; contact will be made with every individual that can increase the amount of money being made.

Even though it seems like business can be maintained by fax, e-mail, the net, etc., managers who are not located in one of the centers of the industry (NYC, LA, Nashville, or London) are at a distinct disadvantage. Personal contacts are of great importance. In this business, absence does NOT make the heart grow fonder. In fact, "out of sight,- out of mind" fits this business more closely. Daily contact is the key.

Everyone must work towards clearly defined short range and long range career goals. Musicians are conditioned to live from job to job (gig to gig). Most wonder if the phone will ring again. Most don't approach their lives in a career-oriented manner. Artists talk about what's happening today, where as every day the manager must adjust the career plan to focus on the long range objectives.

This author visited a prominent manager to witness the activities of a routine business day. Rob Kos, manager of *Art Garfunkel*, *Rusted Root*, and others, was kind enough to allow me to spend a few hours hanging and talking with him. What follows are my observations of the day.

Mr. Kos is a reserved kind of guy that feels he is effective because he is persistent. At times, he must ask various people connected with an artist to do something they might not be particularity interested in doing. He persuades them to complete what is asked rather than scream at them. Because he graduated from college as a music major, he feels he can connect with an artist on a creative level, and will participate in the artist's creative activities if asked to do so. He does get excited about his artists' music, and probably wouldn't be in the business if he didn't.

Kos' daily routine is as follows. He is in the office (at Metropolitan Entertainment in New York City) before 9 AM and sets up the activities of the day by creating a "to do" list. He then opens the mail and checks the faxes, which will consist of artist fan mail, offers, contracts, tour itineraries, bills, and other correspondence. He attends to any European business next because of the time zone difference. England and Ireland are six hours ahead of Eastern Standard Time so their business day is almost complete when the New York business day is just beginning (forget about trying to do business between England and Los Angeles, and thanks God for fax machines). After he completes his European business, he tackles L.A.

While this author was present, a series of phone calls were made. Kos wears a headset phone for comfort . Besides the usual calls, the following calls were made. During the first call, Kos explains the deal he has personally setup with China Records. He has been appointed American President of China, an independent English alternative label, that has given him the power to sign acts and distribute a&r budgets. Next he makes his weekly call to Polygram asking for a fax of the latest BDS Report . Each week he disseminates the report to all concerned parties informing them of the record's progress. Rob comments on how the business has become information based, not unlike any other business. The final unusual phone call was to a marketing company that is performing merchandising responsibilities for *Rusted Root* who is signed with Polygram. The group sells a good deal of merchandise each night, and Rob has made a mail order deal with the marketing company, and has been able to keep merchandising out of record contract negotiations. As this author was leaving, I could see that the day's activities were heating up.

THE CONTRACT

(A full discussion of the contract appears in **Chapter Two.**)

Several industry sourcebooks listed in the bibliography include artist-personal management agreements with appropriate comments (see Shemel & Kravilovsky, 1985 or Passman, 1991). When it all boils down, these are key points that are important to both parties.

1. Term

Both parties must agree on the length of the contract, option periods, which party has the right to extend the agreement. Contingencies concerning extending the agreement must also be agreed upon, as some contracts include a minimum gross income the artist must make for the manager to continue.

2. Compensation

How much should the manager be paid? Is the commission based on gross earnings, net earnings, or some formula that represents a mixture of both?

Most or the remainder of the agreement contains fairly standard clauses that are negotiated in a routine manner. However, the artist MUST be represented by his or her own attorney throughout the negotiations.

PROJECT MANAGEMENT

Career Plan

Stages of an American Career

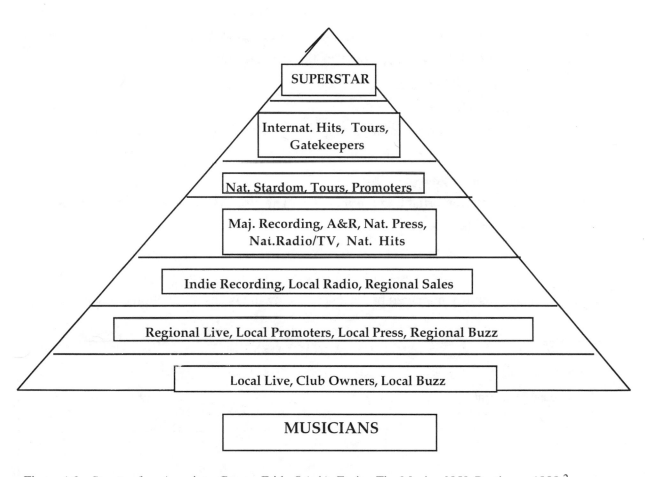

Figure 1.2   Stages of an American Career. Frith, S.(ed.) Facing The Music. N.Y. Pantheon. 1988.[2]

Figure 1.2 illustrates the various stages of an American artist's career. While the lower levels of the hierarchy are fondly known as "paying your dues," it is the graduating up to the third level, **indie recording and regional sales,** that is the step that is considered a major goal and is more easily attained with sound project management and a career plan. It is the level that most driven musicians attain but unfortunately never leave. Crossing the bridge from level three to level four is what stumps even the most assertive. It is here that the well thought out career plan is essential.

The artist's career plan may be completed in several ways. It's true that long range and short range goals are important, however, only the more successful managers follow a set procedure and budget. Setting goals is simple, attaining them is difficult.

A successful career includes talent, organization, and planning. Given that the artist has a certain amount of talent (or at least appeal), it's the manager's responsibility to oversee the organization and planning. Invariably the "plan" is the weakest link.

A successful plan includes:

a) preparation,

b) securing the proper information,

c) having the proper attitude, and

d) establishing goals.

The goals should motivate the artist and the manager. The strategy for reaching them should be flexible. A timetable should be set and tactics developed. This planning is needed to successfully complete any project. Projects are developed to solve specific problems or complete specific tasks, and once they are completed, they end (and another begins). Figure 1.3 lists eight ingredients that are important to a successfully managed project. The following is an explanation of each point.

PROJECT MANAGEMENT
1.   Problem Statement
2.   Background Statement
3.   Objectives
4.   Procedures
5.   Plan
6.   Schedule
7.   Budget
8.   Success Indicator

Figure 1.3

1. **Problem Statement**

The problem statement is an explanation of what is perceived to be needed, therefore creating a problem. For example, if the artist wants to change record companies, an investigation into why this is perceived to be a need should be made. Exactly what is the problem that the artist believes a new record company will solve? The solution may really be another producer or songwriter. A manager must be certain that if there is a real problem, it's clearly stated, and the perceived solution (project) is the correct one.

2. **Background Statement**

Information about the background and significance of the problem is very useful in determining the value of a project. For example, if the artist wishes to record with a specific producer, the producer's track record may include significant information pertinent to attaining a certain goal.

3. **Project Objectives**

Are there many objectives or only one? If there are many, a prioritized list is essential. One method of writing objectives is to put each objective in a behavioral form. For example, instead of listing an objective as "learn" three new songs, in behavioral form it might read "perform" or "arrange" or "memorize" three new songs. This form makes it more obvious when an objective is completed.

4. **Project Procedures**

What steps must be completed to meet the objectives? Each step should be listed in chronological order (the project's critical path). **Creative** and **organizational** tasks should be listed. For example, if the stated project is to complete another recording, then all the creative and organizational tasks that need to be completed before arriving at the studio, during the recording process, and after its completion must be listed. Obviously, some tasks occur simultaneously, but a chronological list is still important.

5. **Project Plan**

Who will complete which tasks? Who will make certain each task is completed? What strategy will be used to complete each task? For example, who will write the new songs? Who will search for an outside writer? Who will hire the producer? Specific tasks must be assigned to specific people. This is what makes a plan work.

6. **Schedule**

Realistic timetables work best. Set realistic deadlines and don't require tasks to be completed long before they are needed. Activity schedules with a natural flow help to complete the project.

7. <u>Budget</u>

What is the money needed for, when is it needed, and where will it come from? These three questions need to be answered. Also, remember to include a 10-15% miscellaneous expense category for unforeseen expenses.

8. <u>Success Indicator</u>

How will the success of the project be determined. Realistic goals should be set. If an artist's second recording sells 2 million copies, 3 million short of the first record's sales, is it not successful?

Career planning is one of the most important functions a personal manager performs. Being organized is also important. Preparing a well-organized plan greatly improves the artist's chances of success.

What follows is an example of a class project. It has been included here with the permission of future industry leaders David Allu and John Landieri.

YOU WERE SPIRALING
by
David Allu and John Landieri

I. Problem Statement:

A.   The perceived problem:

The manager of *You Were Spiraling,* Michael Kahn, believes that more exposure is needed. He would like us to obtain more exposure for the band. The way he would like us to do so this is by getting airplay for the band at college radio stations throughout the northern New Jersey, New York City, and eastern Pennsylvania area.

1.   Why is this perceived to be needed?

The band and Kahn want more people to be aware of the band. There are some other ways of getting the name and sound of the band heard: performing, print, tv, and the web, to name a few. Our group chose to focus on airplay to meet the need of getting exposure for a number of reasons. **Firstly,** print media is being covered by the other group in the class. **Secondly**, the band can not perform this month. All of their time and energy is going toward the recording of a new demo. When the recording process is completed they will resume performing. **Thirdly**, obtaining airplay on college radio stations will reach the most people. The only tv programs that the band might be able to perform on are public access tv programs. We think a college radio station will reach more consumers than a public access program.

II. Background Statement:

Why would a band want to have their music played on a radio station? Radio has been and still is a crucial form of promotion for a recording artist. Throughout the history of rock 'n' roll, and even years before rock emerged, the radio has played an integral role in promotion. Other means of publicity such as MTV, VH-1, Letterman and The Tonight Show have also been important. However, at the level that *You Were Spiraling* is performing, music videos and national tv exposure are not possible. As a form of promotion, radio is number one. So, at our level, radio remains the medium that has the greatest exposure. Furthermore, radio play is free (discounting the cost of the promo CD, the paper the bio is printed on and postage). Many other forms of marketing tools and advertisements require money that the band does not have.

Why did we choose college radio? The perceived market for *You Were Spiraling* is the college age group. Many college radio stations are central to the campus' music scene. Colleges have traditionally been a place to "brake" new music and artists. We will persuade college radio stations to play the CD to increase the awareness of the group on each campus.

III.   Project Objectives:

A.   **Have as many college radio stations as possible in the area put a *You Were Spiraling* song in rotation**

IV.   Project Procedures:

1. Choose ten college radio stations in the north Jersey, New York City and PA. Area.

2. Make telephone contact with the program director at each station informing him/her of *You Were Spiraling*. Ask his/her permission to send a CD and Bio.

3. Send a CD and Bio (make note of the date sent) to each station that we have spoken with and have granted us permission. Compose a letter to enclose in the package. The letter should thank the individual for his/her time and inform him/her of the songs we are pushing. These songs are "Your New Boy" and "Crisis @ 92 Credits".

4. Call the program director 4-5 working days after the package is sent. Ask if s/he has had a chance to listen to the CD. If s/he has, ask what they thought. Ask if s/he preferred either of the suggested songs. Persuade to add a song(s) to the playlist.

5. If the program director has not listened to the CD, call back in another 1-2 days (proceed with #4).

6. Have friends and band members call station and requests the song.

7. Call each station every three days to get feedback.

NOTE: On occasion, the DJs of college radio station will choose which records the station will air. Many DJs have their own shows and choose the material for the show themselves. In this case, speaking with the program director may be pointless or only mildly helpful. As a result, we should substitute the DJ of the program director as the person addressed in our phone calls.

V.   Project Plan:

1. Dave and John have five CDs each. Each will be responsible for his CDs.

2. Dave will contact the following five rradio stations:

       a. WFDU 91.3 FM   Fairleigh Dickinson College

       b. WGLS 89.7 FM   Rowan College of NJ

       c. WFMU 91.1 FM   formerly Upsala College

     d. WRSU 88.7 FM   Rutgers University

     e. WPRB 103.3 FM Princeton University

3. John will contact the following five radio stations:

     a. WLFR 91.7 FM   Stockton State College

     b. WMCX 88.9 FM Monmouth University

     c. WPSU 91.1 FM   Penn State University

     d. WKDU 91.7 FM Drexel University

     e. WTSR 91.3 FM   located in Trenton

4. Each member will follow the project procedures.

5. John and Dave will inform each other and Michael of each task as it is completed and the stations that add the song(s).

VI. Schedule:

10/27/97	All materials are sent out.
10/31/97	All stations have been contacted.
11/7/97	Each team member should have airplay on at least **one** station.
11/21/97	Each teacm member should have airplay on at least **three** stations.

VII. Budget:

The group will be reimbursed for the following expenses incurred:

     gas

     postage

     telephone

     mileage

VIII. Success Indicator(s):

A. Airplay

In order for the project to be deemed successful Michael Kahn will be happy with airplay on five of the ten stations. As a manager for a band, he feels that any support is appreciated. So, even radio play on one station will make him more content than none. However, the challenge is to have as many spins as possible.

B. The Conditions for a Successful Project:

1. The band feel as though they have benefitted from the group's work.

2. The group has participated in a positive successful learning experience.

3. The band song(s) will be in rotation **2-3 times** per day at least **one** but preferably **five** college radio stations in the area.

SO WHAT'S THE SECRET

Well there really isn't a secret. How big of a star the artist becomes will be determined by many factors, the least of which is how well the manager keeps the artist a **priority** among the industry gatekeepers. If there was a secret, that's what it would be.

In his book <u>Tarnished Gold,</u> the late R. Serge Denisoff defines two concepts in relationship to this industry; **talent and success.** He states, "Talent is the *commodity* that has economic potential."[1] In other words, creating an original musical presentation that is marketable to record buying audiences. And it's the industry gatekeepers, namely, club owners, agents, radio programmers, promoters, and record company "ties" (personnel) that define the talent. They make the decision as to who gets the chance to be seen and heard.

Talent alone does not guarantee success however, "Success," Denisoff writes, "is the artist's *ability* to persuade the industry gatekeepers to recognize the talent."[2] This persuasion not only comes in the form of music, but in stage presence and overall excitement and charisma as well. Furthermore, the artist must then choose the industry leader whose evaluation of his/her talent is correct.

So there's the formula, now go to it. Play in the major leagues. It's a tough road to stardom. Not many that try make it. Again, according to Denisoff, "only 17 new artist per year, it is believed, ever record a Top 40 hit, while in the same year 23 persons are statistically likely to be struck dead by lightning."[3] If you have what it takes, those odds shouldn't stop you!

SUMMARY

1.   A key to successful artist management is obtaining the proper information.

2.   The artist's opinion should be part of the decision making process.

3.   Management is an art and a craft.

4.   The most important characteristic a manager can have is patience.

5.   Artists striving for success should have talent, desire, determination, and patience.

6.   An artist must have a clearly focused image.

7.   The artist's and the manager's personalities must be compatible.

8.   The artist's team is composed of the personal manager, attorney, booking agent, publicist, and accountant.

9.   In this business, there is no such thing as a typical day.

10.   Each day, the manager should ask: "Am I making as much money for the artist as possible?"

11.   The artist and manager must agree on the length of the contract and manager's compensation.

12.   An organized career plan is essential for success.

13.   Talent is the commodity that has economic potential.

14.   Success is the artist's ability to persuade the industry leaders to recognize the talent.

15.   The manager must keep his/her artist a priority with the industry leaders.

PROJECTS

1.   Using the outline for project management, create a fictitious project and complete a detailed plan.

2.   Role play an initial artist and manager meeting.

3.   Negotiate a fair artist - manager agreement.

NOTES

1.   R. Serge Denisoff. <u>Tarnished Gold</u>. Transaction Books. New Brunswick, N.J.   1986.   pg. 37.
2.   Ibid.
3.   Robert Burnett. <u>The Global Jukebox.</u> Routledge Press. London, U.K. 1996. p. 126
4.   Op. Cit. Pg. 38.

CHAPTER TWO

THE CONTRACT

"Fellows, forget about the contract. If it's not working like a marriage, the contract is not going to help!" Anonymous

---

By the end of this chapter you should be able to:

1. Discuss why a **written** agreement between an artist and personal manager is typically used in the industry.
2. Discuss the four basic parts of a legal contract.
3. Discuss what it means to act in a fiduciary manner for the artist.
4. Discuss all the parts of a typical artist/personal manager contract, identifying a fair deal for both sides on each point.
5. List the areas where advice and counsel should be offered by the manager that are in accordance with the American Federation of Musicians' guidelines.
6. Compose a fair artist/personal manager agreement.

On several occasions, as a royalty artist in a group, the author was involved in negotiations with prospective managers and was given artist/personal management contracts to read. Depending upon where we were in the negotiations, some contracts were more elaborate than others. Some contracts also favored the manager more than others. Regardless of the situation, when various members of the group inquired about the language in different sections of the contracts, the various attorneys representing the managers invariably used the marriage analogy. They assured us, in each case, that the contracts would not bind us to managers we no longer wanted to represent us. They also assured us that we, as artists, were truly "the boss."

"The manager works for the artist, and it's never the other way around. So if the manager isn't performing to the artist's satisfaction, he or she should be fired." My response was always the same. If this is true, why do we need to sign a written agreement? If the relationship is supposed to work like a marriage and the artist is the boss, why should any problems arise? The answer is simply that problems do arise.

It's been reported that Elvis and Colonel Parker never had a written contract. Their deal was consummated with only a handshake. Unfortunately, the estate on behalf of Elvis' daughter, Lisa Marie, has sued the Colonel for a number of misappropriations (see Chapter 12). Seldom is an issue of <u>Billboard Magazine</u> published without an artist/manager suit reported.

The contract is there for protection. It's signed by both parties so that each is protected from each other. It's signed with the understanding that although it is a relationship, it's first a business. And the business is more important than either party individually. In this way it works like a marriage should work.

Another reason for a contract is that a manager, as an employee of the artist, acts in a fiduciary capacity. This means that the relationship is one involving a confidence or a trust. For this reason, the manager should never have an unfair economic advantage, and reputable managers refuse to enter into agreements where the artist is employed by a company in which they have a vested interest. For example, if a manager also owns a concert promotion company, s/he would have an unfair economic advantage if that company booked the artist, and s/he also collected a commission from the artist on the date.

Acting in a fiduciary manner implies that the artist's interest must come first, and the manager's interest second. The manager is obliged to operate in the artist's interest, and this has been the basis of many artist/manager disputes.

Most people believe that a contract must be in writing and signed by both parties to be valid. The truth is that the terms of most contracts only have to be agreed upon by both parties, and if the agreement is witnessed then it is a valid agreement. Contracts are put in writing to avoid any situation whereby one party denies that they agreed to something. Besides, as more time passes, people have different recollections as to what actually occurred. So even though it may take a long time to negotiate, it's easier in a long run if the contract is in writing.

There are **four basic parts** to any legal contract of this type. They are: **mutual assent, consideration, capacity, and legality.**

mutual assent-- This is the offer and acceptance by both parties. For example, John Jones wants to manage the "Dumbbells." The "Dumbbells" want a manager. This is the section of the contract that begins with "Whereas."

consideration-- This is the trading process. Something of worth changes hands when services are performed. For example, if Jones manages the "Dumbbells," they agree to perform and appear where they are told to.

capacity-- This means that both parties are of sound mind and body, and have the legal capacity to perform the necessary functions to carry out the terms of the contract.

legality-- The contract must be for a legal purpose. A contract for a deal to buy a car that you know has been stolen, is not legal.

The following is a typical artist/personal management contract. The term "typical" is used because there is no such thing as standard contract. Although the language may vary, the items addressed in all contracts are common. For educational purposes, comments that address each issue in terms of its fairness to both parties have been inserted.

AGREEMENT made this day of _____ by and between _____ (hereinafter referred to as "Manager") and _____(hereinafter referred to as "Artist").

> *The artist should make certain that the individual manager's name appears in the opening statement and not the name of a business or corporation, thereby making the manager personally responsible. The same holds true for the manager. The manager should insist that each member of the performing group have personal contracts with the manager.*

The parties named above hereby agree as follows:

1. The Manager hereby agrees to act as exclusive personal representative, manager and adviser in the entertainment industry, including but not limited to vaudeville; motion pictures; theaters; television (including cable and pay television); radio; recording; records; personal appearances; sale, lease or other disposition of literary, dramatic, poetic, lyrical or musical material which the Artist may create, compose, write or collaborate in the creation, composition or writing, in all fields of the entertainment industry; commercial tie-ups or endorsements; and any act, unit or package show of which the Artist may be an owner or part owner, directly or indirectly. The Manager will exert reasonable efforts to develop and advance the Artist's professional career in Artist's best interest and to confer with, counsel and advise artist in all matters relating to thereto. The Manager will advise and guide the artist in the best use of Artist's talents and services and will endeavor to exploit such talents and services fully, either personally or by arrangement with third parties.

> *Section One defines the responsibilities of the manager in specific terms. This section is meant to be all-inclusive as the artist is accepting the manager as the exclusive personal representative. According to the American Federation of Musicians (the union), the artist's representative should offer advise and counsel in five specific areas, and most contracts include these areas in various forms. They are:*
>
> *1.   the selection of literary, artistic, and musical materials*

1.   the selection of literary, artistic, and musical materials
2.   all matters relating to public relations
3.   adoption of a proper format for the best presentation of artist's talents
4.   selection of a booking agent
5.   the types of employment the artist should accept.

The section is written for the manager to exert "reasonable" efforts and not necessarily "best" efforts. The artist should ask for a definition of the word "reasonable" and then negotiate in his or her best interests. The last sentence states that the manager can assign the work of managing the artist to another party. Although this does not constitute an assignment of the agreement to a third party, the artist should be very careful about what responsibilities the manager can delegate to others and who can actually perform the management service. The artist must also be certain that the manager is always considered the responsible party.

Sometimes a "key man" clause is inserted here, which means that the manager must remain the responsible party or the artist has the option of getting out of the contract.

2.   The Artist hereby agrees to render services to the Manager upon the terms herein contained for a period of __ years from the date of this agreement, and for such additional period as the Manager shall be entitled to in accordance within any options contained below. During the term hereof, and any extension, the Manager shall be entitled to the exclusive services of the Artist throughout the area named below in all branches of the entertainment industry, and any fields of endeavor related thereto, including without limitation, performance, promotion, advertising, music, creative arts, recording, commercials, endorsements, and merchandising.

Contracts are written from either of two perspectives; the artist has all the obligations or the manager has all the obligations. This agreement is written with the artist having the obligations. In the second sentence, the manager shall be "entitled" to the exclusive services of the artist. "Entitled" is a very strong word and the artist may seek a substitution.

The section defines the term of the agreement. Most contracts are for a minimum of three years excluding the option periods. To enable the artist to get out of a bad deal some contracts are written with a clause that states that after a certain amount of time, usually 18 months or so, the manager must have secured a recording contract, or the artist must have earned a certain amount of money for the agreement to continue. However, if these terms are not met and the artist still wants to retain the manager, the artist can still bind the manager to the agreement. This might occur if the manager is the artist's only link to the big time record business.

It should be noted that similar to recording contracts, the term of many artist management agreements are based on a number of albums deal, such as three album cycle. This most often occurs with established artists rather than new ones.

24

3.   The geographic area in which the Manager's rights shall be exclusive is worldwide. *Some contracts are written to read the universe!*

4.   The Artist further warrants and represents as follows:

(a)   The Artist is free to enter into this agreement and to carry out its provisions and that there are no other obligations or agreements in conflict herewith, and that Artist will not incur any obligation or enter into any agreement that may conflict or interfere with the obligations and services hereby secured to the Manager and hereby granted to it.

This section further secures the manager as the exclusive representative of the artist, and confirms that the artist is not under contract with any other manager.

(b)   The artist will endeavor to do all things necessary and desirable to promote Artist's career and earnings.

Sometimes the artist insists that the words "within reason" appear in this section. Also, clauses that begin with "such as" are added.

(c)   The Artist will attend such locations as, when and where the Manager may require during the period of this agreement, in the performance of Artist's services hereunder, and will render such services to the best of Artist's skill and ability, punctually and willingly, in any manner as may be directed by the Manager or any persons, firms or corporations to whom Artist's services may be assigned, licensed or contracted for.

(d)   The Artist acknowledges that the Manager shall have the right after consultations with Artist to decide how it will present the Artist's personality to the public and determine Artist's conduct during the period of the agreement.

Both" c" and "d" are standard issues addressed in all artist/manager contracts.

(e)   The Artist will use best efforts and endeavors to maintain a good state of health and shall submit to any medical examination or treatment which the Manager may be advised is desirable by its doctor, or any insurer of the Artist, and the Artist will not during the period of this agreement (as same may be extended) take any unusual risk or activity which might affect or prevent the performance of Artist's services hereunder.

Although they refer to two completely different issues, it is interesting that, in this contract, the artist must use his or her "best" efforts and the manager need to use only "reasonable" efforts (see Number One).

(f)   The Artist will not incur any liability on behalf of the Manager, give any undertaking, authorize or enter into any negotiation, or make any agreement regarding the provision of Artist's services to a third party or the management or representation by any other manager or agent during the period of the agreement without the Manager's prior written consent, and in particular, without limiting the foregoing, will promptly refer to the Manager any offer or similar approach make to Artist by any third party proposing to use Artist's services or materials.

Section 4f again reinforces the manager as the artist's sole manager, and does not permit the artist to enter into any negotiations on his or her own behalf.

(g)   The Artist will not during the period of this agreement or at any time thereafter make any statement which Artist anticipates may be published in the Press or publicly repeated regarding the Manager or his services hereunder without the Manager's prior written consent, but Artist will provide to the Manager such information as it may require from time to time necessary to publicize the Artist and the services to be rendered by Artist hereunder, and in particular, Artist will throughout the period of this agreement permit the Manager to use Artist's name, likeness and biography in connection with the presentation of the Artist and any services, performances, materials or products involving the Artist, and to permit user of Artist's services to do so.

The first half of this section is not very common but the second half is. The manager continues to appear to be the boss.

(h)   The Artist will not enter into any agreement, in writing or otherwise, with respect to the exploitation of any material whether original or owned or controlled by Artist, musical or otherwise, without consulting with the manager and obtaining its consent.

(i)   The Artist will execute at the Manager's request whatever documents may be required by Manager to ensue that all proceeds resulting from performances, exploitation of copyrights, services, products or the like relating to the Artist will be paid directly to the Manager during the period of this agreement.

Normally, a business agent or accountant is selected by the artist and all funds collected are deposited directly into a trust account that he or she oversees. The artist however, is given the right to examine the books. This system deters any misappropriation and helps to guard against any false mistrusts.

Also, someone must be responsible for keeping accurate accounting records and the artist must be allowed to request an audit.

(j)   The Artist acknowledges that the Manager's services are not exclusive and that it is free to perform similar services to others. Moreover, the Artist acknowledges that the Manager is not a theatrical booking agency and that the Manager has neither offered nor promised to obtain employment for the Artist, nor will it be obliged to do so.

It is common for the manager not to be exclusive to a single artist. For the new artist, this may be beneficial, since it offers an opportunity to open the show for know acts under the same management.

Although the role of manager of local acts requires the manager to perform the duties of a booking agent, it is not in the job description of any big time managers. In fact, in California, it is against the law for a manager to be a licensed booking agent. However, excluded from this law is the procurement of a recording contract, and this is expected of a personal manager.

(k)   The Artist acknowledges that it will be necessary to obtain the services and assistance of a booking agency to obtain employment for the artist, and that the Manager alone is authorized to negotiate and enter into agency relationships and contracts in the name of the Artist.

The manager who works very closely with the booking agent and is usually chosen by the manager after consultation with the artist.

(l)   The Artist will not fail or refuse to honor or complete any engagement for the purpose of limiting Artist's income and recognizes that Artist may not thereby limit the Manager's compensation for any personal or business purposes.

(m)   The Artist agrees to indemnify the Manager against any and all claims, loss, damages and lawsuits, including the cost of defending against same, arising out of any acts or agreements authorized by this agreement, including without limitation, any loss, claims or suits resulting from the Artist's breach of any contract or commitment entered into by the Manager in the

27

Artist's behalf with a third party.

Section 4m states that the manager wants the artist to cover all legal costs against any suits that might occur and to indemnify the manager against any other claims. This appears to be a normal procedure except in the cases that are brought about because of the manager's irresponsibility. The artist would have to sue the manager unless this section included a statement regarding any losses or suits resulting from the manager's breach of any commitment.

(n)   The Artist acknowledges that his services and talents are unique and that, in addition to any and all other remedies at law available to the Manager, in the event of the Artist's breach, the Manager shall be entitled to any and all equitable relief, including injunctive remedies to prevent the Artist's breach of this agreement.

This section must be clearly defined. Although manager should be entitled to some protection in the event of an artist's breach, the manager should have only the contractual right to seek any and all equitable relief. What is an "equitable relief?" Should the artist be responsible for paying all court costs or should it be negotiable?

5.   The artist hereby grants the Manager the irrevocable right to renew and extend this agreement for ____ consecutive option period of ___ years following the expiration of the initial term upon all of the terms and conditions herein set forth. The Manager shall elect to exercise each such option by posting a notice by registered or certified mail, return receipt requested, to the Artist prior to the expiration of the current term. The address to which such notice shall be sent to the Artist shall be that which appears above, unless the Artist shall have furnished a notice of change of address in writing.

This section covers the option period of the contract. The total contract should extend for not more than five to seven years (in fact, in California, seven years in the limit on personal representation contracts). Sometimes, instead of granting the manager the "irrevocable" right to renewal, each option is connected to a gross earning figure, or an adjusted gross earning figure that takes into account specific expenses. This protects the artist from extensions of the contract that he or she may not want. Also, the time period in which the manager shall post notice to exercise each option should be defined. Thirty or sixty days prior to the expiration of the current term is a normal time period.

6.   The Manager agrees that all sums received by it by reason of the exploitation of the

Artist's services and materials and of any other rights or products relating thereto, shall be paid or applied promptly to the Artist's account except that said monies shall first be paid or applied to as follows:

(a)   Reimbursement to Manager of all direct expenses incurred in earning or recovering the sum received, including without limitation, all commissions to booking agencies and other (but excluding any payments or commissions earned and due to the Manager) and all travel and business expenses incurred by or on behalf of the Artist in connection with the engagement or disposition of materials from which such sum has been earned.

(b)   Reimbursement to Manager of all costs of photographs, publicity posters, publicists and publicity materials relating to the Artist and the Manager shall also reimburse itself for any advances or expenditures for wardrobe, instruments, equipment, long distance telephone, telegraph, Manager's travel in connection with the Artist's engagements, limousine, messenger, and similar charges other than normal office overhead expenses, which overhead shall be the responsibility of the Manager.

In this section, the manager seeks to be reimbursed for expenses before any monies are deposited into the account. Sometimes the reimbursement for travel is negotiated, especially if the manager chooses not to live in one of the centers of the recording industry. The key is to avoid the accumulation of a large debt, so many times a revolving credit arrangement is negotiated or a clause is inserted that allows the payments to be made on a monthly or periodic basis.

(c)   In addition to the foregoing the Manager shall deduct as and for its commission and compensation for all services rendered and to be rendered hereunder, a sum equivalent to _____ % of all gross compensation received directly or indirectly as result of the Artist's activities in all areas in which the Artist and Manager have contracted with each other hereunder; "gross compensation" for the purposes of this agreement shall include any money or monies worth or other thing of value earned, advanced, received or applied to the account of the Artist prior to any of the deductions or expenses set forth above, and shall include any such sums as shall be earned, advanced, received or applied to the account of any firm or corporation in which the Artist shall be a stockholder or principal. The Manager's compensation and commission shall continue to be payable to the Manager in the same percentage and manner as set forth above notwithstanding the expiration of this agreement, except that it shall be limited to any and all engagements, contracts and agreements entered into or negotiated during the term of the agreement and any and all direct or indirect renewals, extensions or substitutions therefore or amendments thereto, and with respect to any contracts or negotiations that were entered into during the term of the agreement and within a period of ninety (90) days past said term regardless of when the services are to be performed or products delivered.

Section 6c defines the commission and compensation schedule. Usually the manager's commission ranges from a low of 15% of gross to 25%. Most new artists want the commission to be based on net, however this is unrealistic. For example, while on the road, the artist may want a limo and stay in a four star hotel. If the manager is receiving a commission on net, he or she might be upset with the artist for these expenses. The manager should not have to share in the expenses of the artist's lifestyle. However, the manager should only be entitled to a commission on a performance fee after the agency takes its commission and other out of pocket expenses (such as stage production costs, transportation) and musician and road crew salaries have been deducted. The term for this is **net on net after agency commission.** *"*

This section also entitles the manager to a commission on agreements negotiated during the term of the contract, should the option period not be granted or extended, and/or the contract expires. It further states that the manager is due commission on any agreements signed up to ninety days past said term of the contract. This is always a difficult area to negotiate. Whether there is a buy out of the contract by a new manager or the contract expires, these are always highly negotiated points.

(d)   In the event Artist forms a corporation or becomes a stockholder of a corporation to provide, in part, professional services, as well as produce other acts, hire sidemen, and to engage in such other activities normally engaged in by an entertainment company, the Manager, specifically or his nominee, in such event will be equal stockholder and director of such corporation to direct the corporation's activities with respect to its operations and its services. This agreement will not be adversely affected by any such incorporation, except that any compensation received by Manager from such corporation shall be applied against Manager's compensation under this agreement.

This a standard clause that allows the manager to take part in any corporation that may be formed to enhance the business activities of the artist. It should be made very clear that this may pertain to matters in the entertainment field and not other business ventures the artist may engage in.

7.   Without intending to limit the Manager's rights here under, the Artist acknowledges that the Manager is irrevocably empowered during the term of this agreement to do any of the following:

The artist may want to negotiate down the use of the term "irrevocably empowered"
to simply "empowered."

(a)   Approve and permit any and all publicity and advertising.

(b)   Approve and permit the use of Artist's name, photographs, likeness, voice, sound effects, caricatures, literary, artistic and musical materials, for purposes of advertising, trade and publicity, and in the promotion and advertising of Artist and any and all products and services.

(c)   Execute for Artist and in Artist's name or on his behalf, any and all agreements, documents, and contracts for his services, as his attorney-in-fact and shall have the right to have all of Artist's contracts require payments to be made to and in the name of the Manager.

(d)   Execute for Artist or in his name and/or his behalf, any and all agreements, documents and contracts for his services, talents, and/or artistic, literary and musical materials, as his attorney-in-fact.

(e)   Collect and receive all Artist's compensation, and endorse his name upon, and cash any and all checks, payable to Artist for his services and literary and artistic materials and retain therefrom all sums owing to Manager.

(f)   Engage as well as discharge and/or direct, for Artist and in his name, theatrical agents and employment agencies as well as attorneys and accountants, if necessary, and other persons, firms or corporations who may be retained to render professional services or obtain contracts, engagements or employment for Artist.

Sections 7c through 7f refer to giving the manager power-of-attorney. Sections c and d refer to the execution of contracts. This includes the daily execution of personal appearance contracts and other routine contracts. However, this should not include any unusual, long term or extraordinary contracts such as a recording contract. A reputable manager would not take on that responsibility without the artist's approval. So the artist should request that a clause be added that allows the manager to execute any short term contracts of six months or less, but any contracts that last longer than six months should require artist approval.

Section 7e is similar to Section 4i. All funds should be deposited in the artist's account by the business agent or accountant.

The artist may want the phrase "with artist's approval" inserted in Section 7f.

8.   The Manager shall not be in breach or default of this agreement unless and until the Artist shall have first delivered to the Manager in writing by registered mail, return receipt requested, a description of the precise breach or default claimed and the Manager shall thereafter fail for a period of fortyfive (45) consecutive days to cure or correct the condition or circumstance complained of, or to commence said cure or corrective procedure.

In Section 5, the artist did not receive 45 days to correct any complaint before the manager had the right to pass on the option period, why does the manager have this right. Also in addition to including a time period to commence a corrective procedure, the artist should seek to add a deadline for the completion of the correction.

9.   All notices and accounts required to be delivered hereunder by either party to the other shall be certified or registered mail, return receipt requested, addressed to the party at their respective addresses appearing in this agreement, or at such other address as either party shall designate in writing hereafter.

Both parties should agree to have courtesy copies sent to the respective attorneys.

10.   The rights of the Manager hereunder may be exercised by another member of Manager's company if Manager is disabled, in whole or in part during the term of this agreement.

The term "disabled" should be clearly defined. Also, this contract should contain a clause covering the possibility that the artist becomes disabled.

11.   This agreement contains the entire understanding of the parties. No verbal or written agreement, representation, promise or offer shall survive the execution of this agreement, unless expressly incorporated herein. This agreement may not be amended or modified except in writing duly executed by each of the parties.

12.   In the event that any provision of this agreement is held to be void, the balance of the agreement shall survive and shall be construed as if the voided provision contained herein was omitted from the inception.

13.   In the event of any dispute under or relating to the terms of this agreement, or the breach, validity or legality thereof, it is agreed that the same shall be submitted to arbitration to the

American Arbitration Association in New York City and in accordance with the rules promulgated by the said association, and judgement upon the award rendered by the arbitrator(s) may be entered in any court having jurisdiction thereof. In the event of litigation or arbitration the prevailing party shall be entitled to recover any and all reasonable attorney's fees and other costs incurred in the enforcement of the terms of this agreement, or for the breach thereof. This arbitration provision shall remain in full force and effect notwithstanding the nature of any claim or defense hereunder.

The parties hereto have set their hands and seals on the day and year first   above written.

By:_____ ARTIST

SUMMARY

1. A written agreement between an artist and personal manager is employed in the industry for protection. It is signed by both parties so that each is protected from the other.

2. In order to attain success, a trusting relationship is needed between an artist and the personal manager. However, the artist is always the boss.

3. The manager acts in a fiduciary capacity for the artist. This means that the relationship is one involving a confidence or a trust. The manager should never act in his or her self-interest.

4. Contracts need not be in writing to be valid. However, a dispute involving a verbal contract must rely on testimony by a witness in order to be resolved.

5. The four parts to any legal contract are: mutual consent, consideration, capacity, and legality.

6. Neither the artist nor the manager should sign a binding contract between one another without counsel.

7. The American Federation of Musicians lists guidelines as to what areas advice and counsel should be offered by the manager.

8. The contents of an artist/personal manager agreement should be fully understood by both parties, and all clauses should be clearly defined.

PROJECTS

1. Role play a negotiating session between an artist and a personal manager.
2. Compose a fair agreement for both parties.
3. Locate (from local bands or attorneys) several artist/personal manager agreements and discuss their contents.
4. Survey local bands that claim to have managers and see if they have a written agreement.
5. Research Billboard Magazine for articles concerning artist/personal manager lawsuits and discuss the reported reasons for the suits.

CHAPTER THREE

LEGAL   ASPECTS

"How do you know when an attorney is lying?"
"His/Her lips are moving!"   (popular joke)

By the end of this chapter you should be able to:

1. Explain the legal basis by which you can claim rights to a name.
2. Complete a name search.
3. Define trademark and servicemark.
4. Explain how to register a trademark or servicemark.
5. Explain what rights you are granted when you file a federal registration.
6. Explain what determines secondary meaning.
7. Define and discuss how to set up the three forms of business entities in the music business.
8. Discuss the basic tools used in bookkeeping.
9. Discuss the issues that should be negotiated in case of a performing group's breakup.

SELECTING A NAME

Naming a group or choosing a stage name is one of the most important decisions an artist will make. The name should be memorable, and should not allow your artist to be confused with any other artist. It would not be a good idea to call the group the Beetles, even though the name is spelled differently by the famous group. This would obviously confuse the public, and besides, it is not a very original idea.

Since the 1950's, the names of rock groups have gone through many changes. There were the so called "bird" groups of the early 1950's --the "Cardinals," "Orioles," and "Ravens"-- that evolved from the rhythm and blues style of the 1930's and 40's. Then, in the mid-50's there were thousands of "Doo-Wop" groups. Their names were associated with things that were hip and topical at the time. Some examples are: "Cadillacs," "Teen Queens," "El Dorados," "Safaris," and "Shep and the Limelites." Some argue that there was a relationship between the name of the group and the style of music performed; however, with over 15,000 groups that cut at least one single at that time,[1] there were many exceptions. Imitators of famous groups were prevalent.

During the San Francisco era of the 1960's, group names took on a surrealistic tone. Names such as: "Ball Point Banana," "Blue Light District," "Dancing Food and Entertainment" and "Freudian Slips,"[2] were performing along side the more famous San Francisco bands. The "Disco" and the "Punk" styles of music in the 1970's spawned names that were easily associated with the sound of the styles (from the "Stylistics" to "Clash").

Today, the names of groups are used to associate the group with the style of music being performed. Many heavy metal groups use macho names ("Iron Maiden," "Metallica"), black and dance performers use slick names ("Expose," "Pebbles"), and groups that consider themselves performers of the next important style use names like "Pearl Jam," "Depeche Mode," "10,000 Maniacs," "Gene Loves Jezebel," and "Faster Pussycat"[3]. Whatever your reason for choosing a certain name, remember . . . originality is most important.

In terms of the legal aspects, using someone else's name without permission is an infringement. The basis of the law is what is termed "**priority of use.**"[4] It is not who owns the name or who has registered the name, but who has established first use of the name or has used the name continuously that matters.

TRADEMARK AND SERVICEMARK

A trademark is a brand name of a product. It can be used as the logo for a product or independently (ie: Coca-Cola). When it is used for a service, such as performing music, it is called a servicemark. In some instances, a servicemark acts like a trademark (on an artist's t-shirt), and there are some legal differences between the two.[5] However, for the purpose of this discussion, it is only necessary to understand that rights to either are based on **use.**

The law also permits you to use a brand name on a completely different product, such as using Remington[R] on something different than a shaver. However, if the use causes a high degree of confusion to the public, the courts may not permit you to continue its use.

If you are a singer and your real name is Frank Sinatra, would you be able to use it as your stage name? Unfortunately, the answer is no. The Frank Sinatra has "priority of use," and the use of your name would cause confusion.

There are two classes of federal trademark and servicemark registration. They are "Principal Registration" and "Supplemental Registration." A mark must be "distinctive" (as opposed to common) to qualify for the Principal Register[6]. For example, the group Chicago's logo is very unique and distinctive and therefore qualifies. Registration on this register gives constructive notice to the public, which means that it satisfies the legal requirements as to notification, and gives the holder exclusive rights to the name[7].

Registration on the Supplemental Register does not give the user exclusive rights to the name nor does it give constructive notice to the public. An example of a common name that would be included on the Supplemental Register is "The Blues Band." The name is not distinctive and does not clearly describe any uniqueness in the product[8].

COMPLETING A SEARCH

After a name is selected and <u>before</u> it is used, a search must be conducted to insure that no one is currently using it. The procedure for conducting a search is as follows:

1. Check with the local newspapers, "underground" papers, rock and music magazines, the local musician's union, and local talent agencies for use of the name.

2. Check all of the national music and entertainment trade publications and organizations for use of the name.

3. Investigate record company and talent agency rosters for its use.

4. Check with international music and entertainment directories for its use.

5. Search the web, specifically the U.S. Government agency site: **www.ustpo.gov**

6. Check all databases.

7. If needed, employ a professional searching bureau to ascertain if the name has been registered with the U.S. Patent and Trademark office of any state bureau.

Even if a thorough search has been conducted, you can never be 100% sure that the name isn't being used somewhere by someone.[9]

If the name does appear in the course of your search, you should return to square one and come up with another name. There is an illustrious history of small unknown acts, that have successfully sued larger acts based on priority of use. If you believe that you'll only be successful if you use a particular name, you might try to buy the rights to that name from the current user, if your convinced that they do, indeed, own the rights.

REGISTERING FOR A FEDERAL TRADEMARK OR SERVICEMARK

If you are interested in filing for a federal trademark or servicemark, and you have completed your search, you should begin by using the name across state lines. You will have to be

----

able to prove that you've done this. Proving it may be as simple as saving newspaper advertisements announcing the appearance in another state, or keeping actual contracts. Then you must file for federal registration with the Patent and Trademark Office in Washington D.C. According to Stan Soocher, in a <u>Musician</u> <u>Magazine</u> article, the procedure for filing is expensive for the following reasons:

1. A fee of $200 is required for each class in which a name is registered (ie. $200 for use on recordings, another $200 for use on t-shirts, etc.).

2. Attorneys charge up to $600 to complete the complicated federal filing procedure.

3. Companies that conduct searches for purposes of federal trademark registration charge about $200 per search.[10]

The procedure for filing a federal registration is as follows:

1. File an application with the U.S. Patent and Trademark office. In order to file, you must be able to prove that you used the name across state lines. Keep copies of advertisements or contracts to use as proof (the process takes about a year).

2. In order to have the rights to the name, you must continue to use the name. Two years of nonuse constitutes abandonment.

3. After the fifth anniversary of the registration you must file an affidavit stating that the name has been used continuously.

4. Renewal must occur every twenty years.[11]

Even though it is expensive, there are many benefits to obtaining a federal registration. Federal registration gives you the following rights:

1. You can sue someone for infringement in federal court.

2. It provides "constructive notice" so that any subsequent user cannot claim "no knowledge of your right."[12]

3. After the registration has been approved, you may use the symbol R to protect your name.

WHO OWNS THE RIGHT TO USE THE NAME

The basis of the law is "**priority of use**." If the name is registered on the Supplemental Register (as opposed to the Principal Register), the first person or group to use the name may not have the right to use it anywhere at anytime. They may need to establish "**secondary meaning.**" Secondary meaning is determined by four factors:[13]

1. The geographic region in which the user works.
2. The duration of the use of the name.
3. The drawing power of the user (or how big a star).
4. The extent of its use in advertising

Two artists may establish secondary meaning in two different geographic regions. If neither has the name federally registered, then both artists may use the name in their respective geographic regions.

Continued use is the key to obtaining legal rights to a name. However, there is such a thing as **residual use** of a name. Residual use usually means that the name is still associated with an artist after they have stopped performing, but their products continue to sell. Acts, such as the "Beatles," have a residual use right to the name, and it has been continuously used by EMI-Capitol Records. For further information concerning trademarks and servicemarks, contact the U.S. Office of Patents and Trademarks or consult an attorney. Worldwide use of a name is a far more complicated issue, and an attorney should again be consulted.

STARTING YOUR OWN BUSINESS

Bands usually begin performing and making money before they become an actual business. They play the gig and split up the money. Expenses are covered before anyone is paid. If each member owns his or her own equipment and there is no overhead, this method of conducting business may continue indefinitely. However, when a band decides to purchase something as a band (usually a sound reinforcement system), and wishes to pay it off in credit installations, it is forced to make some decisions about becoming a legitimate business. Either one member (or a member's parent) becomes responsible for paying off the loan, or the band becomes a legitimate business entity.

The three forms of business entities practiced in the music industry are: **proprietorship, partnership, and corporation.**

PROPRIETORSHIP

A proprietorship is the simplest and the easiest form of business to begin because, by definition, it is a business conducted by one self-employed person who is the owner. The procedure for setting up a proprietorship is as follows:

1.   File a "DBA" (Doing Business As) form with the county clerk in the county you'll be conducting business. If you intend to use your own name (John Smith as opposed to John Smith Productions) completing a DBA form is not necessary. Figure 3.1 is the form used in New Jersey.

2.   You may have to publish a legal notice in the local newspaper stating that you're doing business under the name. Check with you local county clerk's office.

3.   You should file Form SS-4 (See Figure 3.2) with the Internal Revenue Service to obtain an employer's tax I.D. number (even if you haven't any employees).

4.   If you intend to sell (retail) goods, you must obtain a resale tax permit from the state tax authority.

5.   Open a checking account in the company's name.

Contact your local county clerk for a free brochure explaining the specifics.

T 928—Business Name Certificate.

JULIUS BLUMBERG, INC.
PUBLISHER, NYC 10013

STATE OF NEW JERSEY, COUNTY OF ss.:

The undersigned hereby certifies that

conducting a business under the following name style, or designation, viz.:

at No. Street or Avenue, in the

of in the County of and State of New Jersey.

That the nature of the business is

and the true, real, or full name or names, post office address and residence of all persons interested or members of such firm, partnership or business is as follows, viz.:

Names	P.O. Address	Residence

WITNESS: hand this day of 19

....

....

Signed in the Presence of }

....

....

....

STATE OF NEW JERSEY, COUNTY OF ss.:

The undersigned being duly sworn according to law on oath depose and say that

person named in the foregoing certificate and that the statements contained therein are true.

....

Subscribed and sworn to this
day of 19
before me at }

....

....

....

....

JULIUS BLUMBERG, INC.
PUBLISHER, NYC 10013

Form SS-4 (Rev 5-76)
Department of the Treasury
Internal Revenue Service

Application for Employer Identification Number
(For use by employers and others as explained in the Instructions)

1 Name (True name as distinguished from trade name. If partnership, see Instructions on page 4)

2 Trade name, if any (Enter name under which business is operated, if different from item 1)

3 Social security number, if sole proprietor

4 Address of principal place of business (Number and street)

5 Ending month of accounting year

6 City and State

7 ZIP code

8 County of business location

9 Type of organization
☐ Individual
☐ Partnership
☐ Other (specify)
☐ Governmental (See instr. on page 4)
☐ Nonprofit organization (See instr. on page 4)
☐ Corporation

10 Date you acquired or started this business (Mo., day, year)

11 Reason for applying
☐ Started new business
☐ Purchased going business
☐ Other (specify)

12 First date you paid or will pay wages for this business (Mo., day, year)

13 Nature of business (See Instructions on page 4)

14 Do you operate more than one place of business? ☐ Yes ☐ No

15 Peak number of employees expected in next 12 months (If none, enter "0") ▶
Nonagricultural | Agricultural | Household

16 If nature of business is manufacturing, state principal product and raw material used

17 To whom do you sell most of your products or services?
☐ Business establishments
☐ General public
☐ Other (specify)

18 Have you ever applied for an identification number for this or any other business? ☐ Yes ☐ No

If "Yes," enter name and trade name (If any). ▶
Also enter the approximate date, city, and State where you first applied and previous number if known.

Date | Signature and title | Telephone number

Please leave blank ▶ | Geo. | Ind. | Class | Size | Reas. for appl. | Part 1

Figure 3.2

The advantage of a proprietorship is that you have complete control of any and all decisions made and make all the profit. However, you are personally libel for any accidents that might occur and also must absorb any losses. You are not protected from a creditor who places a lien on you personal property. There are many tax issues involved and an accountant should be consulted concerning the laws.

PARTNERSHIP

There are several types of partnerships: general partnerships, joint ventures, and limited partnerships.

1. General Partnership

A general partnership is an "association of two or more persons conducting business on a continuing basis as co-owners for profit"[14] Each partner contributes property, service, and/or money to the business. Partners may also loan property to the business.

Each partner owns a part or interest in the whole partnership ("assets in common") and acts on behalf of the partnership. The entire general partnership (not an individual partner) is responsible for any law suit except where bodily harm or injury has occurred.

Many bands form partnerships when they begin to purchase equipment that is used by the entire group or is too expensive for an individual to buy. It's actually a good idea for a partnership to acquire some assets because all of the partnership's assets must be liquidated before creditors have access to any individual partner's personal property. The procedure for setting up a general partnership is similar to setting up a proprietorship. However, an attorney should compose the actual terms of the agreement.

2. Joint Venture

On many occasions in this industry, a group and an entrepreneur join together to complete a project (such as writing a song, or producing a master recording, etc.). When the project is completed, there is no reason for the relationship to continue. In these situations, the two or more people are conducting business for one purpose, and are actually partners for the business transaction. This is a joint venture. One party is contributing service and one party is contributing service or money.

3. Limited Partnership

A limited partnership is a vehicle for funding a business project. A general partner takes on the normal business responsibilities, and the limited partner contributes capital but takes no part in the management of the business and has no liability beyond his or her capital contribution.[15] The limited partner acts as a backer to finance a project usually for a limited time period. Limited partnerships are governed by state and federal security laws, and an attorney should be consulted before agreements are made.

CORPORATION

Most recording artists form one or more corporations to handle their business affairs. All contractual obligations are made through the corporation, who in turn, make the artist available for fulfilling the responsibilities of the specific deals.

A corporation is a separate business entity from the persons who manage it. Ownership is obtained by buying shares of stock in the corporation. Personal assets of individuals are thereby protected from business creditors.

Corporations are governed by a board of directors who are elected by the shareholders. The business affairs are managed by a group of officers, who are employees of the corporation hired by the board of directors.[16] Or in other words:

Shareholders
ELECT
Board of Directors
WHO APPOINT
Officers
TO MANAGE
employees

There are two types of corporations: **private and public**. The stock of public corporations is traded publicly on one of the stock exchanges and anyone can buy shares in (and own a part of) the business. Excluding the major record and film companies, for many years, public corporations formed by artists, didn't exist in the entertainment business. Recently, however, many established entrepreneurs have used "going public" to raise capital. Examples have included Dick Clark and Donny Osmond.

Private corporations do not trade their stock on the open market. All the stock is held by shareholders who have some relationship to the business. The procedure for forming either type of a corporation is as follows:

1. A corporation charter, or a document that describes the business and the structure of the corporation must be filed in the state in which you plan to be incorporated.

2. By-laws for the corporation must be formed.

3. Several sets of taxes and fees must be paid.

When forming a corporation, an attorney should be retained. Usually a corporation immediately becomes an employer because it begins paying someone a salary, even if the only employee is the artist. Therefore, there are many legal obligations, such as tax laws and labor laws, that must be followed. An accountant should also be retained.

BOOKKEEPING

Today, computer programs are extremely helpful in maintaining accurate financial records of all business transactions. Many programs complete several accounting procedures automatically. The basic tools used in bookkeeping are as follows:

1.   Checkbook - It is essential to open a separate checking account under the company's name. All of the business accounts and cash disbursements should be accounted for by a check.

2.   Ledger (monthly)- The ledger is a book containing all accounts and transactions are
posted monthly.

3.   Cash disbursement record - This is usually designed in the form of a monthly chart that shows how any cash is spent. Items usually include parking, tolls, taxi, etc..

4.   Accounts receivable - This is a listing of all accounts from which the company receives money. It is usually posted monthly.

5.   Accounts payable - This is a listing of all accounts the company owes money to on account, and makes payments to. It is usually posted monthly.

6.   Receipt file - A place where receipts are kept.

7.   Balance sheet - The balance sheet is a monthly account of the financial condition of the company. The debits and credits for the month must balance (be equal).

8.   Calculator - "Don't leave home without it!"

If you cannot keep accurate records or hate to, hire someone who will!

GROUP BREAKUPS

There are several different degrees of group breakups in the music industry. If the group totally disbands, things are not quite as messy as when one of two members want to continue with new personnel, or when the remaining group members, and the group members who are leaving

47

----

both want to use the group's name. If the group is under contract with a major label, things will become more complicated, as all the major labels contractually protect themselves against not recouping any owed advance money (money they have advanced the artist for recording expenses). They do this by requiring the continuing group (provided the record company accepts the new members) to recoup any remaining advances before they may collect any royalties. This is an important point and must be negotiated carefully (see Chapter Six). In any case, the best time to plan for a breakup is at the formation of the group. The following areas should be covered in the group's partnership agreement before anyone says "I DO!"

1.   A clear procedure for changing, adding, or subtracting group members. This should include any "buy outs" or the division of any of the group's assets.

2.   Who owns the rights to the group's name.

3.   How to deal with the record company should any changes in the group's personnel occur. This should include the right of approval of new members, recouping advances, key man clauses (the most important group member), and any other matters.

4.   A clear procedure for the complete disbanding of the group and the dissolution of the partnership, its assets and liabilities.

SUMMARY

1. Choosing a group's name is one of the most important decisions a group makes.

2. Using someone else's name without permission may be an infringement. The basis of the law is "priority of use," or continued use, not who has registered the name.

3. A trademark is a brand name of a product. When it's used for a service it's a servicemark.

4. After a name is selected and <u>before</u> is used, a search must be conducted. If the name appears in the search, do NOT use it.

5. In order to file for a federal trademark or servicemark, you must first use the name across state lines.

6. Filing is expensive.

7. There are two classes of federal registration. Principal registration automatically gives constructive notice to the public, allows you to sue someone for infringement in federal court, and gives you the right to use the symbol R. Supplemental registration does not, and "secondary meaning" must be established.

8. When two or more people on the registered on the Supplemental Register are using the name, the person who establishes "secondary meaning" has the greatest rights to a name. Secondary meaning is determined by four factors: the geographic region in which the user works, the duration of the use of the name, the drawing power of the user, and the extent of the user's advertising.

9. The three forms of businesses practiced in the music industry are: proprietorship, partnership, and corporation.

10. A proprietorship is a business conducted by one self-employed person who is the owner. A general partnership is an association of two or more persons conducting business on a continuing basis as co-owners for profit. A corporation is a separate business entity from the persons managing it. An attorney should compose any partnership or corporation agreements.

11. The basic tools used in bookkeeping are: checkbook, ledger, cash disbursement record, accounts receivable, accounts payable, receipt file, balance sheet, and a calculator.

12. Groups breakups can be complicated issues. The best time to plan for a breakup is at the formation of the group.

PROJECTS

1.   Choose an original name and conduct a mini-search.

2.   Contact an established performing group in your area, and find out if they legally have a right to their name. What evidence do they have that assures them of the right? Did they establish secondary meaning?

3.   Contact an established performing group in your area and find out what business entity they are conducting business. Do they have any employees and are they receiving legal treatment under the labor laws?

4.   Contact an established performing group in your area and find out if they have made any provisions for changing members or totally disbanding.

5.   Read a recording contract and discuss the parts dealing with breakups and disbandments.

NOTES

1. Barry Hansen. "Doo-Wop." <u>The Rolling Stone Illustrated</u> <u>History of Rock and Roll</u>. Random House, New York. 1980. pg. 84.
2. Ralph J. Gleason. <u>The Jefferson Airplane and the San Francisco Sound</u>. Ballantine Books, New York. 1969. pg. 331-333.
3. Top Pop Albums Chart. <u>Billboard</u>. 12 March 1988. pg. 72 & 75.
4. Stephen Bigger. "Entertainment Group Name Selection and Protection." <u>The Musicians Manual: A Practical Guide</u>. Beverly Hills Bar Assn., Beverly Hills, CA. 1986 pg. 1.
5. Ibid. pg. 2.
6. Sidney Shemel & M. William Krasilovsky. <u>This Business of Music</u>. Billboard Publications Inc., New York. 1985, pg. 337.
7. Ibid.
8. Ibid.
9. Op. Cit. <u>The Musicians Manual: A Practical Guide</u>. pg. 3.
10. Stan Soocher. "Protecting Band Names: A Legal Survival Kit." <u>Musician</u>. September 1987. pg. 45.
11. Op. Cit. <u>The Musicians Manual: A Practical Guide.</u> pg. 7.
12. Ibid. pg. 6.
13. Op. Cit. <u>Musician</u>.
14. Edward R. Hearn. "Forms of Business Entities To Use In Starting Your Own Business." <u>The Musicians Manual: A Practical Guide</u>. Beverly Hills Bar Assn., Beverly Hills, CA. 1986 pg. 11.
15. Ibid. pg. 13.
16. Ibid.

CHAPTER FOUR

MARKETING THE ARTIST

"There is no such thing as too much publicity. There's only not enough." Diane
Rapaport. Publicity: There's Never Enough. In
<u>The Musician's Business and Legal Guide.</u>

By the end of this chapter you should be able to:

1. Discuss the role of rock 'n' roll music in the popular culture marketplace.
2. Discuss the scope of today's market, including the domestic and international scene for prerecorded and live music.
3. Describe the role of the artist.
4. Discuss how stardom is achieved.
5. Define positive deviance.
6. Define the process of de-labeling a star.
7. Describe the process of creating and managing an image.
8. List the contents of a press kit and describe their roles.
9. Define media mix.
10. Write a news alert and a news release.

The Marketplace

Since the 1960s, rock 'n'roll music has become a major player in the popular culture marketing mix. As the war babies became of age and began representing the largest segment of the population, their consumer behavior became of interest to every leisure time activity marketer in business. It was actually the first Woodstock Music and Art Festival in August 1969, that convinced retailers to take serious notice of the buying habits of these young adults. By merging the behavior of flower children with mainstream marketing techniques, the potential for making big money became a reality.

The record industry saw this potential as well. In fact, the potential was so great, that until around 1980, the record industry was considered inflationproof! According to R.I.A.A statistics, every year until 1979, sales as well as software unit shipments increased. Up until very recently, thanks to the soundtrack recordings of Saturday Night Fever and Grease, sales and units shipped figures of 1978 were considered one of the industry's crowning achievements.

As these war babies reached middle age in the early 1980s, it was originally thought that they would "grow up," leave rock 'n' roll behind, and turn to records by Sinatra, Steve and Edie, and various cover artists. Surprise! A new generation gap never really evolved. Their listening habits did not change. As it became hip to be square, Mick and Keith, Steven Tyler, Roger Waters, and Bruce continued to rock. Metallica's following increased (in number as well as average age level), and in her 50s, Tina Turner recorded a very sexy mainstream AC album. As the alternative scene developed, white kids had a increasingly difficult time using music as a tool for rebelling (and also discovering a music that their parents did not enjoy). This dilemma did not hurt the industry. By the mid-1980s, sales of recorded music software in the U. S. began to rise again. Helped by the new software configuration (always a sure booster of catalog sales), the CD, the industry has increased sales each year to date. For an industry that measures its achievements quantitatively, this all adds up to success.

What does all this mean to the artist? As a product, the artist retails his/herself through two formats: the recorded product and the performance ticket. Just as the retail record store sells records to the consumer, the concert promoter sells tickets to the fan. Both markets play significant roles in the success of the artist.

The Scope of Today's Market
The Domestic Scene
Prerecorded Music

According to R. I. A. A. statistics, industry domestic shipments of prerecorded product topped $12 billion for the fourth year in a row (at $12,237) in 1997. This represents a modest decrease of 2.4% from 1996, and a 6.5% net unit decrease. The configuration of choice is the CD, although down 3%, it represents 71 of every one hundred units of prerecorded music shipped to retail. The sales of the CD Single, up 54%, continue to represent the fastest growing configuration. This was the first year (1997) that sales of the CD Single out paced the cassette single. The music video, up another 10%, continues to be in strong demand as a sell-through item. There is considerable industry talk about the Digital Video Disk (DVD), however, at this writing, hardware is still scarce. Cassettes, although down another 23%, are still a viable format as manufacturers continue to produce and distribute every genre in this format.

The consumer profile of the 1996 American record buyer is as follows: Based on the number of units sold, fifteen to nineteen year old comprise 17.2% of the market, but more importantly, fifteen through twenty-nine years old make up almost 45% of the domestic buying power. Although about equal, males buy more than females, and about half the money used to purchase records is spent at a record store.[1] Finally, we are buying rock; almost as much as all other genres of music combined.

Live Performance

It has been proven that the headlining artist makes more money touring to sellout audiences than through selling records. Today's tours have several "legs" and last twelve, eighteen, sometimes twenty-four months (more about touring in Chapter Nine). According to a recent *Amusement Business Magazine,* the two top grossing domestic single concert shows by different artists were: The Rolling Stones, with Smashing Pumpkins, Dave Mathews Band, and Third Eye Blind, $3,680,635; and U2, $2,297,613 [2] It is estimated that the Rolling Stones' "Bridges to Babylon" tour will gross in the $200 million range in ticket sales alone. Even after expenses are deducted, it's easy to see that sellout stadium and arena touring is very lucrative.

The International Scene

Prerecorded Music

The international scene has expanded significantly. According to the International Federation of the Phonographic Industry (IFPI) 1996 statistics, the U. S. represents 31% of the sale of prerecorded music throughout the world. This is down considerably from the 1970s, when the U. S. represented almost one-half. The second and third biggest world markets, Japan and Germany, represent 25% of the world market. It is important to note that Japan, with 17%, and the U. S. total almost one half of the world market. However, different countries have different methods of calculating sales and many countries do not include every type of retail outlet or distribution point in the statistics they submit. Consequently, "real" sales can and do vary greatly from what is reported. For the purposes of this book, it should be noted that with over two-thirds of the records being sold outside the U. S., it is very important for artists to become international stars. Although royalty rates are lower and currency exchange rates are very volatile, there is still a great deal of money to made from international sales. For more information concerning international sales, e-mail: **info@ifpi.org**. [3]

Live Performance

In 1992, The Rolling Stones performed nine dates in Japan and grossed over $30 million (in U. S. currency)![4] Of course, The Stones only work for the most ethical promoters and in the most exclusive venues, however, there is a very lucrative concert scene outside of the U. S..

The Role of The Artist

American Pop Culture's need for heros and icons is filled by rock music artists. Being a successful rock musician is literally a 24 hour job. Fans expect their fantasy to be fulfilled whether they see their favorite hero on stage or off.   Today's artist is expected to hold his/her image even during off hours. Consequently, the artist's image must fit the lifestyle s/he leads.

For many reasons, being a rock star is a risky existence, especially before the perks associated with being a success are delivered. Pop musicians have been considered social deviants for many years.   Not necessarily negative deviants, but deviants none the less. In fact, sociologist George Lewis, used the term *positive deviant* to describe the musician. He defined one as having "behavior that deviates from the expected, but is not negatively valued."[5] Another sociologist, Howard Becker, used the terms legitimate occupations versus illegitimate careers.[6]

There are the characteristics of the musician's behavior that make him/her perceived as being a deviant. Firstly, there are the work habits.   A musician works when others (the fans) are off. A musician works at night, and sleeps during the day. A musician *plays* an instrument. Secondly, the social circle of a musician is very limited. Because s/he works nights, s/he is subjected to many occupational hazards. Most of his/her fans are either musicians or night people. Drugs and other abusively used substances seem to be more available after dark. Consequently, for some, the straight life is alien and unfriendly.   Lastly, conforming to the routines of day people are often difficult. Because musicians need sleep as much as anyone else, banking, shopping, and attending to medical needs are often a hassle.

Stardom

What is a star and who determines who becomes labeled as one? Lewis defines a star as "a person whose productions are so much in demand that, to some extent at least, he is able to use distributors as his adjuncts."[7] However, in demand by whom, and how do these productions become in demand? Lewis continues, "his success as a star depends upon his 'playing with the market.'[8] And the star label "is bestowed upon certain people by a specific audience which intentionally wishes to bestow such a quality."[9] Consequently, one becomes labeled as a star by a quantitative measure, and hence a positive deviant.

What happens when the star no longer lives up to the audience's expectations? Is there any procedure for de-labeling the musician as a star? Few artists are able to handle both their audience generated image and their personal identity with much success. Much of the problem is due to the amount of insulation from the real world that occurs. It compounds the situation. Not only can some not distinguish between on and off stage personas, but there is "no appropriate institution for "de-labeling" the star."[10]   The premature deterioration of Elvis is a good example of the worst case scenario. Unfortunately, Elvis did not surround himself with people who were sensitive to his needs as a star.

Creating The Image

What determines the image? It's obvious that the artist must feel comfortable with what is fabricated for him/her, but, isn't this determined by what the fans want or need? Shouldn't a good manager and PR team identify the market that is attracted to the music and develop the image accordingly? Capitalize on what the market needs to feel hip, and then exaggerate it and make it bigger than life.

For example, it isn't coincidental that every time Bruce Springsteen is photographed, he is wearing a faded pair of blue jeans. Or that Pearl Jam is in baggy shorts and flannel shirts. Or any number of rappers are in gold chains etc. It would be odd if it were any other way; as strange as if Keith Richards, while guest hosting The Tonight Show, came out in a three piece suit and sang "Spinning Wheel!"

What would be wrong with this picture? For one, the image would be totally inconsistent with Keith's image of the last twenty-five years. His fans trust him, buy his records, go to his concerts, and follow his career because he has been consistent over time. He has never "sold out" by conforming to society's middle of the road safeness. As a spokesperson for rock 'n' roll, he has gained the respect and loyalty of millions of people because of the consistency of his rebellious image.

Managing the Image

As mentioned earlier, stars are so much in demand (by fans) that insulation from them becomes, to many, a means of survival. This becomes a problem because the onstage image gets confused with the reality of life and some artists are not mature enough to keep the two separate. Also, fans are so demanding to see the artist as a larger than life fantasy, that they do not care to see the artist as a everyday human being. Therefore, by definition, it is impossible for the artist to live up to the expectation.

The artists that have control of the situation are the artists that do not allow themselves to be so insulated from the public that they lose sight of reality. They may be surrounded by bodyguards (ie. Madonna, Mick, Cher), however, they go about their lives in the environment of reality, compared to one constructed to fit their on stage persona (ie. Elvis).

The second problem is the difficult process of changing the image (if needed).

Some artists, such as David Bowie, Madonna, and Miles Davis have done this fairly easily. For many, the consequence outweighs the risk. The artist's audience may feel alienated if the change if too great, however, the artist may feel trapped without the freedom of artistic experimentation. One may think that his/her fans are a great group of long haired liberals, however, the need that a consistent image fills is actually very conservative.

De-labeling the Star

How can a manager and an artist create a positive image, manage the image through a prosperous career, and then successfully transform the artist back to a life of John Doe? There is no creative procedure. Getting in touch with his/her personal identity, not the fabricated identity, is the key.   Avoiding burnout, rather than drinking oneself into oblivion, is the mature process of transformation.

Unfortunately, the music industry has never taken this task seriously. It is only recently that some members of the industry (and NARAS) are taking action to develop health plans, detoxication centers, and old age residences for artists that either blew their "fortunes" from their careers, or never really made it.   For the time being, it is the responsibility of the manager and the artist to see that this transition (if needed) is completed successfully.

The Media Tools

The Press Kit

The press kit is still one of the artist's most useful marketing tools. It establishes credibility by presenting the artist's accomplishments in an organized professional presentation. The kit must reinforce the image that was created to fit the needs of the audience, and contain a publicity angle.

The publicity angle is a uniqueness about the artist. It must be newsworthy , fresh, informative and believable. For example, one of the band members has played with someone famous, or the band has been politically active in their hometown. The angle must grab the attention of the press and eventually the fan. It must be consistent with the image and complement the music. Try to avoid trite sayings that describe characteristics of the band, which hype the same characteristics as every other band.

Ingredients

Every press kit should contain a **biography** (bio) of the artist (or band). It must be exciting and capture the essence of the artist's musical style as well as the most interesting characteristic of the artist (or band members). In a few short typewritten pages, it should shape the image. Important quotes may be tailored to the image desired and incorporated into the story. The bio should have a beginning, middle and an end.

The **8 X 10 black and white glossy photo** is another basic part of the kit. It may be a headshot of the artist or a full body one. A good publicity photo is the most difficult piece of the kit to get right. Like the bio, it must represent the image of the artist, look natural, and make one want to hear the music. The photo should also reproduce well for printing in a newspaper, so a picture with small details, should not be considered. Most likely the photo will be cropped to fit in the available space in the newspaper. Therefore, the focal point of the photo must be kept in the center of the photo.

As many **newspaper clippings** as possible should also be part of the mix. They are important because they are generated by the media. They legitimize and support the artist's efforts. A good manager and PR person will concentrate on doing everything in his/her power to get the press interested in the artist and write or talk about the him/her and the music. Clippings are especially important for a new artist. If the artist has accumulated a number of good press clippings, the best ones may be pulled and included in a easy to read one page **quote sheet**.

Depending on the objective of the artist, other materials may be included. For example, a lyric sheet may be important. An audio recording of the artist's best material maybe requested by club owners, if the artist does not have a record contract. If the artist is particularly visual and his/her stage presence is a strong part of the act, a video may be important. A calendar showing how busy the artist is may be impressive to a prospective purchaser of talent. Flyers with space for the date, time and place of the engagement is also recommended.

The Webpage

In addition to being featured on record company webpages, many artists have their own webpage. It is too early to measure the value of the sites, however, statistics show that more and more people are purchasing products over the internet and surfing the net for information.

The obvious should be displayed on the page: calendar, tour itinerary, bio facts, fan club information, merchandise; however, it will also be useful to link the page other pages so that search engines, such as Yahoo, can display the page when someone isn't necessarily looking for the artist by name. An example of this is the following: Suppose an artist is a left handed guitar player. Linking the artist's webpage with the page on left handed guitar players (if one exists), then when someone clicks on the artist's name, their webpage will be displayed. This is a useful tool to introduce the artist to a new audience without any major expense. Now there is no need to learn the programming language for developing a website (html), a search on the net will reveal scores of professional webpage designers and maintenance companies who will create a site for a reasonable cost.

The Media Mix

Print, radio and television make up the medial mix. Compiling a media list is the job of the PR person working for the artist. A new artist must do the legwork his/herself. Today, media lists may be bought (either in hardcopy or on a disk), or are found in any number of industry sourcebooks and by surfing the net. However, names and addresses change often, and it is difficult to stay current. It's a jungle out there and compiling mailing labels and lists is very time consuming, so target the outlets carefully. Also do not forget the fan base. Keeping them informed is a well worth the effort.

The Campaign

Planning and managing a press campaign is a fulltime job. Being organized shortcuts wasting time. Staying focused on the objective of the campaign, and understanding what the media needs to do their job is essential. The key to getting any type of publicity is meeting deadlines. They are real.

There are several types of press releases employed. All releases must be on the artist's letterhead, typewritten and double spaced. A **news alert** is a short announcement describing who, what, where, when, and why. It is usually sent to calendar listings and is direct and to the point. Figure 4.1 is an example.

NEWS ALERT FORMAT

For Immediate Release	Contact Person: _____
Date: _____	Address: _____
	_____
	Phone: _____
	Fax: _____
Title of Release: **Performance**	
The Dumbbells will be performing at The **Weightlifter Club** on **Sunday April 1, 1999 at 9 PM. $9 admission**, tickets at the door.	

Figure 4.1

A **news release** is usually two or three paragraphs describing some newsworthy event that is accompanied by other materials, such as the press kit or a new recording. It offers the opportunity to expand on the artist's latest activities while focusing on the specific objective of the release. It should be written so that it anticipates questions the reader of the publication might ask and answers them (see Figure 4.2).

NEWS RELEASE FORMAT

For Immediate Release   Contact Person: _____

Date: _____   Address: _____

                                                                            _____

                                                                    Phone: _____

                                                                    Fax: _____

<u>Title of Release:</u> **Performance**

The Dumbbells will be performing at The **Weightlifter Club** on **Sunday April 1, 1999 at 9 PM. $9 admission**, tickets at the door.

The Dumbbells are a new alternative band. Musicians include: **Muscle Shoals on Guitar and Arm Strong on Drums.** Barbelly Magazine said **"power, sheer power!"** to describe their last gig.

Look for The Dumbbells **at Wimpy's and Celulite's on Easter weekend.**

Also, coming soon, The Dumbbells first CD: **Lifting for Love** on Heavyweight Records.

Figure 4.2

If a great shot of the artist doing something creative or unique (newsworthy), a catchy **photo caption release** detailing what's happening in the photo. Since the goal of the picture is to catch the reader's eye, the caption should complement it by filling in the blanks that are missing about the artist's story. [11]

It is very important to create and follow a campaign **timetable**. Just as media centers adhere to deadlines, the publicity campaign must follow a organized routine. If your campaign is concentrating on a performance, the work begins three to four weeks prior to the gig. Get out a news alert so that it will have plenty of time to be published in various calendar listings. About two weeks before the performance, send out a news release and begin hanging flyers where they will do the most good.

On the day of the show, make certain that those invited are on the guest list. Remember, one of the objectives is to generate press reviews, so reminder phone calls to the local reviewers is recommended. Immediately after the performance check all the local rags and other outlets and

---

save all the reviews, good or bad.   And don't ignore e mail or the web, a following can easily be developed by publishing a hip webpage linked to e mail address. This legwork is extremely tedious, but a required activity . . .persevere![12]

In Chapter Five (Figure 5.3) is a complete marketing campaign for an album that went multiplatinum. Study it and use it as a guide for creating your own campaign.

The Image Makers

The publicist must create a trust between s/he and his/her client. The artist puts his/her pubic image in the hands of the publicist and relies on the credibility of the publicist to do his/her work justice. What follows are a series of quotes by industry image makers. They are taken from an out of print book, <u>The Making of Superstars </u>by Robert Stephen Spitz.

Next to music, image is perhaps the most important aspect of recording artist's career. The way a particular artist looks and feels, thinks and reacts to situations plays heavily upon the way the public views that person and, many times, creates an appeal equally as important as the music. But unless the artist is so unique a talent or a personality before embarking on a recording career, it is up the publicist to create an image that will catch the public eye and lure them into giving this artist a chance to be heard.

Publicity is an art in itself, distinguished by those in the profession who have achieved credibility be creatively formulating image within the bounds of reality from those who merely "hype" false praise.   Robert Stephen Spitz.

My responsibility to my clients is to represent them accurately and to better translate their interesting points to the public. An artist does not know what makes him interesting to a magazine or to the public and that's what I'm there to tell him.

I think even the big acts need press all the time. A career should build. It's very hard for an artist to get a record company behind them when their record in five months old and they won't have another one coming out for three or four months.

Credibility is perhaps the most useful quality which a publicist can develop. I maintain my credibility by trying never to lie about the proportions of the act I'm publicizing.   C. J. Strauss

Breaking a new artist by press is extraordinarily difficult. There is a certain amount of luck involved. First of all, the music has to be there. You cannot hype anything for very long that is either not musically valid or entertaining. But we'll try, though.

When conferring with a new artist, we spend a lot of time discussing the strong character points of an artist and how to bring them out.

I always strive to have our publicity department "bunch" things. We try to get as many things going on a particular artist in the hope that they will all break around the same time. Concentration of that nature, I always find, inundates the public's awareness. If it's spread out over a year, publicity loses its effectiveness.
Bob Regehr

Basically, my job is to get my clients the best possible space in the best possible public showcases. I try to take the real part of my clients and build those aspects into publicity so that when they are in the public eye they don't fall short of the press which they received. I am careful not to overbuild an artist- especially a new artist- because people will become disappointed and turn off to them. Pat Costello

Direct to Consumer Marketing

More and more artists are gathering information about their fan base, and buyers of their music and merchandise, to create data bases to use in direct to consumer marketing. Independent music marketing firms are hired to create data bases and contact buyers of products, and make use of the demographic information to alert these buyers to other products s/he may be interested in, or to activities the artist may be involved with.

Some record companies, such as PGD are beginning to complete this task in- house, because it is a very effective tool for artists that are not very "radio friendly" but have a loyal fan base. As long as there is product in the marketplace, a marketing company can expand on the marketing tools.

SUMMARY

1. Since the 1960s, rock 'n' roll music has played a major role in the pop culture marketing mix.

2. Domestic shipments of prerecorded product topped $12 billion in 1994.

3. Many headlining artists gross $400,000 per arena show.

4. In 1994, the U.S. accounted for a bit less than 1/3 of the world sales of prerecorded music.

5. The artist's image must fit the lifestyle s/he leads.

6. Being a rock musician is a risky existence.

7. Musicians can be considered positive deviants because they exhibit behavior that deviates for the expected, but not in a negative way.

8. A star is a person whose productions are so much in demand that s/he is able to use distributors as his/her adjuncts.

9. The star label is bestowed upon an artist by his/her audience.

10. There is no appropriate institution for de-labeling a star.

11. The fans wants and needs determine the image that is created.

12. Many artist insulate themselves so much from their audience that they have trouble separate their stage image from real life.

13. It is a difficult process to change an image.

14. The press kit is still the main media tool in the industry.

15. A press kit should include a bio, glossy photo, newspaper clippings, and a quote sheet.

16. Two types of press releases are the news alert and the news release.

17. It is important to follow a press campaign a timetable to respect deadlines.

18. Direct to consumer marketing is very useful to some artists.

PROJECTS

1. Compile a press kit.

2. Locate an artist that is perfomring live, and write a news alert and a news release announcing the event.

3. Choose an artist on tour and track the gross receipts for a leg of the tour.

4. Discuss the images of three current stars and determine if they are fabricated.

5. Formulate a marketing campaign for local artist, including a timetable the media mix.

NOTES

1.   "Our Greatest Hits". The Annual Report of the Recording Industry Association of America. 1997.

2.   "Boxscore, Top 10 Concert Grosses." Amusement Business Magazine. As reported in Billboard Magazine. December 27, 1997.

3.   "World Record Sales". Popular Music (1998), Vol. 16/No. 3. Pg. 311-313.

4.   George Lewis. "Positive Deviance: A Labeling Approach To The Star Syndrome In Popular Music." Popular Music and Society. Fall, 1980. p. 74.

6.   Howard Becker. Outsiders. Free Press. Glencoe, Ill. 1963.

7.   Op, cit. Lewis.

8.   Ibid.

9.   Ibid, p. 75.

10.   Ibid.

11.   Veronique Berry. Guide To Independent Music Publicity. Audio & Video Labs, Inc. Philadelphia, PA. 1993.

12.   Diane Rapaport. "Publicity: There's Never Enough." The Musician's Business and Legal Guide. Badlands Press. Badlands, AR. 1992.

CHAPTER FIVE

THE MULTINATIONALS

The world is our audience (Time Warner). *Think globally* (Sony). *A truly global organization* (Thorn-EMI). *A European based global recording company* (Polygram). *Globalize local repertoire* (BMG).[1]

By the end of this chapter, you should be able to:

1. Describe a multinational company.
2. Discuss, with examples, how they have become so powerful.
3. Discuss the "big six" multinationals that control the music industry and give examples of their music related and non-music related businesses.

`The term multinational or transnational company is used to describe a company that conducts business on an international scale and who has a global presence. This megacompany may be headquartered on the other side of the globe, but is able to complete business transactions as if it lived right next store. It is truly international in its ability to look and behave as if its interest lie on the local level as well as all across the globe.

Globalization is the buzz word of its mission statement as exemplified in the slogans of several (see chapter title). Reading between the lines, the feeling that is generated is that the multinationals envision a world business community that is expanding as it's becoming smaller. That is, more countries are participating in the trading of merchandise (enlarging the community), but new delivery systems and distributions channels are shortening the time it takes for products to arrive at their destinations.

The ownerships of the multinationals that control the recording industry are also truly international. Two are located in Japan, one is in England, one in Germany, one in Holland, and ownership of one is still in the good old USA. This is a far cry from the pre-1980s, when all but two were owned by Americans.

Integration and Concentration

The six multinationals account for almost 90% of the world's record sales. They have become so powerful because they have created conglomerates that have expanded both horizontally and (or) vertically, and (or) because they have gained control of a specific segment of a business.

An example of **horizontal expansion** is when a record company buys another record company or merges with another company. Companies that once competed join forces to create an even larger company. An example of this is SONY's acquisition of CBS Records Group in the 1980s. SONY was and still is one of the largest electronics companies in the world. It had a label presence is its own country of Japan, but in order to take part in the profits of the worldwide sales of products that utilized its hardware, it needed to become a software company as well.

Sometimes two companies are bought by a parent company of one and continue to compete. The parent company increases in size and revenue, but the companies continue to fight for home run hitting artists. An example of this is Bertelsmann's purchase of the RCA and Arista Music Groups. Philips also used a similar tactic with Polygram.

An example of a **vertical merger** is when a record company buys a distribution or retail company. It increases in size and decreases its expenses by owning another piece of the product merchandising chain (ie; producing and manufacturing, or distributing and retailing). EMI owns HMV music shops and Virgin Records which brought with it the Virgin Megastores.

Concentrating on a specific segment of the entertainment industry and controlling every phase of that segment has also proven to be a profitable way of gaining market share. For example, if a company envisions itself as a media company, then its ownership will include: film, video, print, and record companies. It will share in all profits to the rights of the **video** of the **single** from the **soundtrack** of the **movie** of the **book,** as they are all part of its business. Time Warner is an example of this.

The Big Six

Table 5.1 illustrates the six multinationals that control the music business.

NAME	OWNERSHIP	COUNTRY	LABELS OWNED AND/OR DISTRIBUTED
BMG	Bertelsmann AG	Germany	Arista, BMG, Imago, Jive, La Face, Novus, RCA,Windham Hill
SONY	SONY	Japan	SONY, Columbia, Epic, 550
Polygram	Philips	Holland	A&M, Island, Megaforce, Mercury, Motown, Polydor, Nippon, Wing
EMI	EMI	England	Angel, Blue Note, EMI, Chrysalis, Capitol, Sparrow, Virgin, SBK,
MCA	Seagrams	Canada	DreamWorks, Geffen/DCG, Interscope, Narada, Universal
Time Warner	Time Pub./Warner Comm.	USA	Atco, Asylum, Atlantic, Eastwest, Electra, Maverick, Nonesuch, Paisley Park, Quest, Reprise, Rhino, Sire, Tommy Boy, Warner Bros.

Table 5.1

The entertainment business is clearly an internationally owned industry. In terms of corporate revenue, the ranking is as follows: SONY, EMI, Time Warner, Bertelsmann, Seagrams, and Polygram.

Table 5.2 illustrates many of the non-music businesses that each own.

BMG	Gruner + Jahr Magazines; Bantam, Brown, Doubleday, and Dell Publishers; BMG Retail
SONY	SONY Electronics which also owns Merv Griffin Ent. , And makes Sega and Nintendo Games; SONY Pictures
Polygram	Philips Electronics
EMI	EMI Electronics; HMV Group;
MCA	Universal Pictures; Universal Theme Parks; Universal Television; Seagrams Beverages; Cineplex Odeon Theatres; Tropicana
Time Warner	Warner Bros. Films and Cartoons; WB Television Network; HBO; Time Warner Cable; Turner Broadcasting which includes TBS and TNT Networks, New Line Cinema, Atlanta Braves

Table 5.2

It is obvious that the major players in the record industry are all tied to other businesses.

Lastly, Table 5.3 illustrates the role the music division plays in each conglomerate. It represents over a fifth of each of the sales of EMI, Time Warner, and Bertelsmann.

MUSIC SALES AS PERCENT OF TOTAL SALES: 1992[2]

CONGLOMERATE	MUSIC SALES
EMI	28
Time Warner	24
Bertelsmann	21
SONY	11
Philips	10
Matsushita*	8

*Owned MCA in 1992.

SUMMARY

1. The term multinational company is used to describe a company that conducts business on an international scale and who has global presence.

2. The ownership of the multinationals that control the recording industry are truly international.

3. The six multinationals account for almost 90% of the world's record sales.

4. They became so powerful because they expanded horizontally and vertically and also took control of a specific segment of the industry.

5. In terms of corporate revenue, the ranking of the conglomerates are: SONY, EMI, Time Warner, Bertelsmann, Seagrams, and Polygram.

6. All the multinational take part in non-music businesses.

PROJECTS

1. Investigate on the web or through publications who the CEOs, Board Members, and Presidents of the music division are in each of the big six.

2. Research the big six and find out what percentage of their sales, revenue, and expenses the music division is of each.

3. Investigate the structure of DreamWorks Inc. What artists have they signed, what and genre of music do they perform?

NOTES

1. Robert Burnett. The Global Jukebox. Routledge Press. London, U.K. 1996. p. 8.
2. Ibid. p. 58.

CHAPTER SIX

THE RECORD COMPANY

"Vice President/NYC

Manage & direct heavy metal, country, alternative & dance music sectors of international music recording & distributing company. Exercise final approval discretion on selection of talent. Identify promising artistic talent. Negotiate contract terms w. agents of artists, exercising final approval agreements. Coordinate with Company attorneys in foregoing task. Create broad plans & policies for achieving corporate financial & development goals established by management, including budget & sales forecasting. Conceive, supervise, coordinate & implement activities that create public awareness & demand for corporate products & artist, by way of advertising, sales campaigns, market analysis, & media exposure. Develop image strategies for recording artist, including supervision of artwork, photography, image consultants posters & packaging, editorial & label copy. Develop & exercise final discretion on methods to enhance career growth of Company artist, including finding & selecting material to be recorded & recordings to be released. Spvse & direct artists tour support, incl. market & venue selection, budgetary control & timing. Use all available mkt info to guide decision making. Hire & fire staff. Direct Company's outside recording studio activities, incl. studio selection, product & staff quality evalu. & cost oversight. Associate's degree, or foreign equiv. in Business Administration; 5 yrs. exp. in job. Exp. must be with internally distributed recorded media. At least 2 yrs. extensive exp. providing interntl. & domestic tour booking & supervision to groups playing 200 seat club to 15,000+ seat arena venues. Reqs. at 2 yrs. recording exp. as producer or exec. producer. 2 yrs. exp. in music publishing (finding & selecting material to be recorded). $200,000/yr.; 40 hr./wk. Resume in dupl. to CJ-112, Rm 501, One Main St., Brooklyn, NY 11201."

Classified ad. Billboard Oct. 19, 1991

By the end of this chapter, you should be able to:

1. Discuss the role of the record company in the life of the artist.
2. Discuss the three type of financial advances offered to an artist.
3. Discuss, with examples, the three types of record companies in the industry, and the advantages and disadvantages of each.
4. Discuss the structure of a record company and the functions of the various departments.
5. Describe the internal path of a product thorough the various departments.
6. Discuss, in detail, the various ingredients in a marketing campaign.
7. Describe, with examples, the costs of releasing a product and how to calculate royalties.
8. Calculate the artist's and the record company's share of royalty revenue.

This is it!

I've made it!

I'm one of the best!

These are the thoughts that run though the mind of an artist during his/her first visit to **his/her** record company as a royalty artist. After all, this is the stuff dreams are made of! It is truly one of the most exciting off stage appearances an artist makes. You feel like your a part of one big happy family, and not only does everyone get along with each other, but everyone can't wait to help you deliver a hit. You envision a long association with the label as you career develops. Feeling a bit guilty, you repeat to yourself, "Boy, what did I do to deserve this life."

Record companies are tuned into this feeling and create slogans that help convince people that music and careers are as important as the bottom line of product sales. Arista Records has used the slogan "where careers are launched." With this slogan, Arista announces that their interest and intention is in discovering new talent and developing solid foundations for long and prosperous careers, rather than releasing a bunch of records with the hopes that a few will make money and pay the bills.

Another example is CBS Records, now SONY. For years, CBS had the indignation to call itself "**THE** Music Company", The slogan positioned CBS as the knowledgeable company that recorded material that deserved to be recorded and classified as music, and the other labels didn't. Certainly CBS would have a hard time convincing most of us that everything they've released over the years should be considered great music. However, as a former artist with the company, this author recalls the feeling of being something special signed to CBS.

These assurances are very healthy for the artist and the manager. However, if all or even most of the above it true, why do two-thirds to three-quarters of the pop records released never recuperate their recording costs?[1] And fewer become hits? Why do so many managers say that they do not feel secure in leaving the record company alone to run the show? Why do so many artists fail to sell records and are eventually dropped from the label's roster? Why do so many good records get lost in the shuffle? How can companies continue to operate with what might be considered such a dismal track record? These questions will be addressed later in this chapter when we look at the typical route of a new recording as it travels through the many departments of the company.

THE ROLE OF THE RECORD COMPANY

Choosing a label is by far the most significant business decision the artist and his/her manager make together. The record company plays many roles in the life of the artist. Two aspects of this relationship are most important. One is obvious and the other subtle. The obvious role a company plays is to produce, manufacture, release, promote, and distribute the artist's recorded product. And, through sales, generate income for the artist. Although it is not an easy task, it is the company's main function in the industry and an artist should expect these tasks to be carried out effectively and efficiently.

The more subtle role is one of a financial backer. Through various types of financial "advances" which are charged against the artist's royalty account, the record company acts as a reservoir or bank for the artist to obtain funds.

ADVANCES

The term advance is used to describe the loaning of money to a royalty artist (normally with interest charged), with the understanding that the money will be paid back to the company before any royalty checks are delivered to the artist. As we will learn in Chapter Seven, The Record Contract, record companies will seek every conceivable way to generate the revenue to payback any of the expenses (including advances) that they have incurred. If permitted, they will "cross-collateralize" revenue generated into royalty accounts from past and future recordings, merchandising, endorsements, sponsorships, etc., to guarantee as many sources of revenue as possible. Therefore, the artist and manager should be careful not to over extend the debt to the company. Remember, because it is charged to the royalty account, it's the artist's money that is

---

[1]   *RIAA estimate. It is estimated that this is also true for ninety percent of the classical releases and the percentage is even greater for operatic recordings.

being spent. Three types of advances commonly given by the company are **personal, production, and inducement** advances.

Personal Advance

A personal advance is the lending of money to the artist for such needs as normal living and household expenses when there is insufficient revenue being generated by personal appearances. The artist is loaned money to pay the bills and even though s/he is not obligated to pay back any of it (should the sales of the recording never reach their expected level), every precaution should be taken to see that the artist does not accumulate unnecessary personal expenses prematurely. Personal advances are sometimes used to pay the salaries of employees. Again, the number of employees should be kept at a minimum until desperately needed.

Production Advance

A production advance is the lending of money by a company for the production of the recording. These expenses might include new instruments, or technical support items such as lighting, staging, or a rehearsal hall. Production advances are usually part of the all inclusive "recording fund" as are personal advances needed specifically during the recording process. This is discussed later in this chapter and in Chapter Seven.

Inducement or Bonus Advances

This type of advance is usually reserved for the established artist with a proven track record of successful sales. In some instances, in order to sign the artist, the record company becomes involved in a bidding war for the artist against another label, and the artist's manager seizes the opportunity to ask for a sum of money to be delivered upon signing. Although the adage "one in the hand is worth more than two in the bush" may be true, the artist and manager should be concerned with the longevity of the relationship with the company and what the company can accomplish to insure a successful career rather than the fast buck!

TYPES OF RECORD COMPANIES

The simplest way to distinguish between record companies is by size: large vs. small. However, other terms are used in the industry, ie: major, independent, specialty, or boutique. Efficient companies come in all sizes, and hit artists have become enormously successful regardless of the size of the label. For example, the group U2 has recorded multi-platinum records for Island Records, an independent label identified mostly with reggae music, and now is a subsidiary of Polygram. Whitney Houston has done the same for Arista Records.

MAJOR LABELS

Major labels with their subsidiaries and associated labels, dominate the business and account for approximately almost 90% of the records sold worldwide. Most major labels are owned by larger non-American multinational conglomerates whose businesses extend beyond the entertainment industry. As stated earlier, distinguishing a label as major does not relate only to size. A monster hit can launch an act into superstardom and increase the size and distinction or the label almost overnight.

A record label is considered a major label if it owns or controls the distribution of its releases and employs its own radio promotion force. Majors also distribute their subsidiary and associated labels, as well as other label's product. Using this definition of a major, there are six in the U.S. They are:

Record Company	Distribution Company
SONY Music Group	SONY Distribution
EMI Records	EMD Distribution
Polygram Music Group	PGD Distribution
Bertelsmann Music Group	BMG Distribution
Warners Music Group	WEA Distribution
Universal Music Group	UNVD Distribution

Major labels offer the following **advantages** to their artists:
1. an in-house distribution network
2. an in-house promotion department
3. prestige
4. large financial resources
5. stability

However, there are **disadvantages** and they are:
1. the risk of getting lost among a large roster of talent
2. the possible lack of individual attention
3. the administration of the company may not be in total control of the company and may have to answer to the parent company which

may have little involvement with the music and entertainment business

INDEPENDENT LABEL

Although total independence in record companies is a thing of the past, we tend to classify any label that is not owned by one of the majors as an independent. Consequently, a label is considered an independent if it **relies** on another label for one or more of the following services.

Distribution- An independent label will rely on either a major label's distributor or an independent record distributor for distribution of their product.

Promotion- Depending on the size of the record label, the services of the distributor may also include a promotion staff.

Merchandising/Sales- same as above

Financial Resources- It is common for someone (or company) to give start-up money to a new independent label and financially back it for a period of time.

The **advantages** of an independent label to an artist are:

1. the strong possibility of receiving individual attention in all of the record company's departments
2. the possibility of becoming a big fish in a smaller pond and generating more publicity than they would on a major.

However, the **disadvantages** to an artist are:

1. the possibility of limited available resources
2. inadequate distribution network
3. less prestige

SPECIALTY LABEL

Specialty labels usually release only one style of music. There are jazz, classical, folk, children, etc. specialty labels. The style of music need not be without financial success, as there are labels that move a great deal of rap, metal, dance, and new age music. Artist owned labels fall into this category as do many subsidiary labels of majors.

The **advantages** to an artist are:

1. the expertise of a company's staff in the genre
2. the ability to communicate easily with other artists in the same genre on the label.

The **disadvantages** might be:

1. a lack of financial resources
2. the inability to distribute to large chain record retailers

BOUTIQUE LABEL

Although it is not an "official" term, it is used to describe a midsize company that behaves like a major, but is more selective in its choice of artists. These companies usually have a higher percentage of hitmakers within a smaller roster of artists. A&M, Arista, and DreamWorks Records are examples of three of these so-called labels. The advantages to an artist are obvious and many. The downside is very minimal, although it does not allow the artist to make very many excuses for poor selling records!

THE STRUCTURE

Record companies are obviously in business to make money. Structurally there are two major divisions in any company. They are the creative division and the business/administrative division. Although the creative areas are concerned with making a profit, the tug or war between areas concerned primarily with the bottom line and areas concerned with the artistic merits of a release are common. In fact, in some a&r departments there is the distinction made between "pop product" that is released to rocket up the charts and disappear after one or two monster releases, and product with artistic quality that has the promise of longevity.

Figure 6.1 is a representation of the structure of a major record company. The departments or areas in italics represent the creative areas and the departments in plain text represent the business areas. At the top of the chart are the stockholders of the "parent company." They are the owners of the company and are the true "bosses." The company as a corporation may be a public company, with stockholders that invest capital through the purchase of shares on the open stockmarkets, or they may be private investors who purchase shares in return for financial support. As with any corporation, the board of directors is directly responsible to the stockholders and is represented by their chairperson. The board of directors receive their information concerning operations of the (parent) company from the president of the company. The operations of the record label is represented to all of the above by the label president. S/he is in the hot seat! If the entertainment business is newly acquired or only a small part of the central operations of the parent company, then the label president's ability to communicate the successes and failures of the label becomes crucial to its future.

Under the label president are the senior vice presidents and vice presidents of each department. Their job is to make the president look credible, responsible, and in control. The chart describes, in outline form, the functions of each department. What follows is a short synopsis each of the department's responsibilities.

STRUCTURE OF A RECORD COMPANY

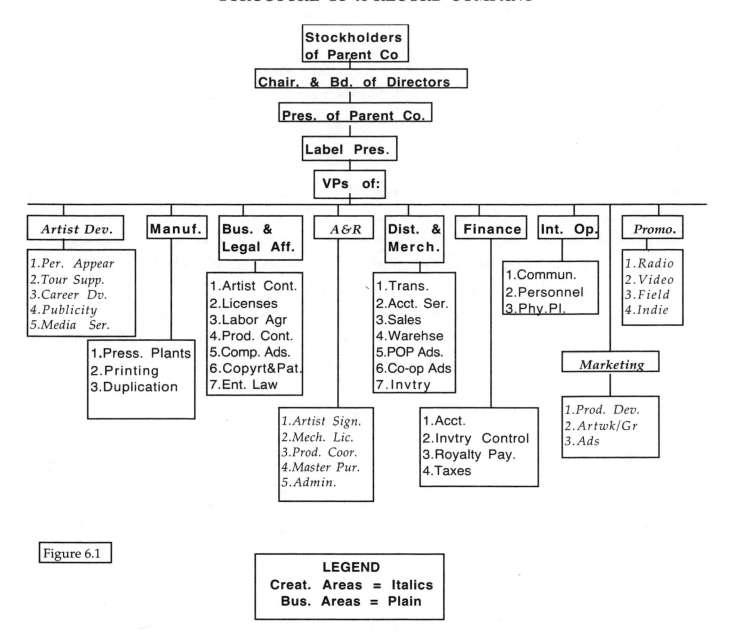

Figure 6.1

LEGEND
Creat. Areas = Italics
Bus. Areas = Plain

Artist Development

The activities of this department involve increasing the artist's (not necessarily his/her product) recognition in the marketplace, including short and long term career development, and publicity.

Artists and Repertoire

Until the mid 1960's, when the industry superstars began employing independent producers, the a&r department would discover the talent, pick the songs to be recorded, and produce the records. Everything was completed "in house" and the "head" of a&r was considered the most important person in the company. Mitch Miller, who was responsible for the careers of Doris Day, Tony Bennett, and others, was head of a&r at Columbia Records in the 1950's and considered the most influential person in the industry.

Presently, a&r still play a significant role in the musical direction of the company. They discover artists, locate material to be recorded, match artists with producers, and deem the recorded product acceptable for release. Although still considered to be the most creative department in the company, the actual production of the record is completed by an independent producer. Consequently they are not active in the actual recording or mixing of the recording. The administration of the department keeps track of the budget of each recording session.

Because the large umbrella category known as popular music is subdivided into narrowcasted "micro" formats (such as metal, urban, rap, dance, new age, etc.), each department usually employs a specialist to discover artists, and direct activities in his/her area of expertise. Although being a musician is not a qualification for the position, these are the few **MUSIC** people left in a company.

Business and Legal Affairs

Although separate departments in names, these two departments work closely in contracting various agreements that concern the revenue flow of the company. These include artist agreements, licensing agreements, labor agreements, and any regulatory agreements that involve income and expenditures. These departments employ the people that wear the suits (and/or high heels) to work and make the important but not glamorous bottom line decisions. Artists and managers tend to question the rationale of many of their decisions.

Distribution and Merchandising

These two departments also work closely in servicing the branch distributors, tracking inventory, and servicing point of purchase promotional vehicles for in-store display. Because

Billboard Magazine has introduced "Soundscan," a computerized sales tracking device for servicing their charts, retail sales have taken on greater industry significance.

Finance

Again an important but non-glamorous department that accounts for every penny that the company spends and receives. These people tend not to have decision making power outside of consulting with the administration and business affairs to offer the most cost effective options for the company.

Internal Operations

This department has the greatest variety of responsibilities, from paper clips to personnel to telephone and data processing systems to tropical plants to kosher meats for the kitchens. Their goal is the most cost effective efficient operation of the company.

Marketing and Promotion

The marketing department is an umbrella department with several areas that are responsible for the integrity of the recorded product once it has been delivered to the company by the producer, and the a&r department has pronounced it acceptable for release. They design a marketing campaign for the record that includes the visual concept for the cover artwork, print advertising, point of purchase displays, and any merchandise that will be sold in conjunction with the release.

A great number of companies separate the marketing and promotion departments with individual vice presidents for each. Promotion departments are also separated by radio formats, with National Directors leading the staff in each. Promotion departments live and die by airplay, and are responsible for completing the radio and video portions of the campaign.

The decision to employ free-lance or independent experts for any of the marketing plan's responsibilities is made by this department's vice president.

Manufacturing

The goal of this department is attaining the most cost effective efficient method of product duplication possible.

PRODUCT FLOW

The following describes the internal path a product takes from the time the master is delivered, and the a&r department decides to "sign off" on the recording as being "commercially acceptable," and all necessary forms and releases have been completed. In Figure 6.2, the diamonds represent decisions that must be addressed, and the rectangles represent actions. The diagram represents the linear flow of the product but does not represent simultaneous actions completed by separate departments.

PRODUCT FLOW CHART

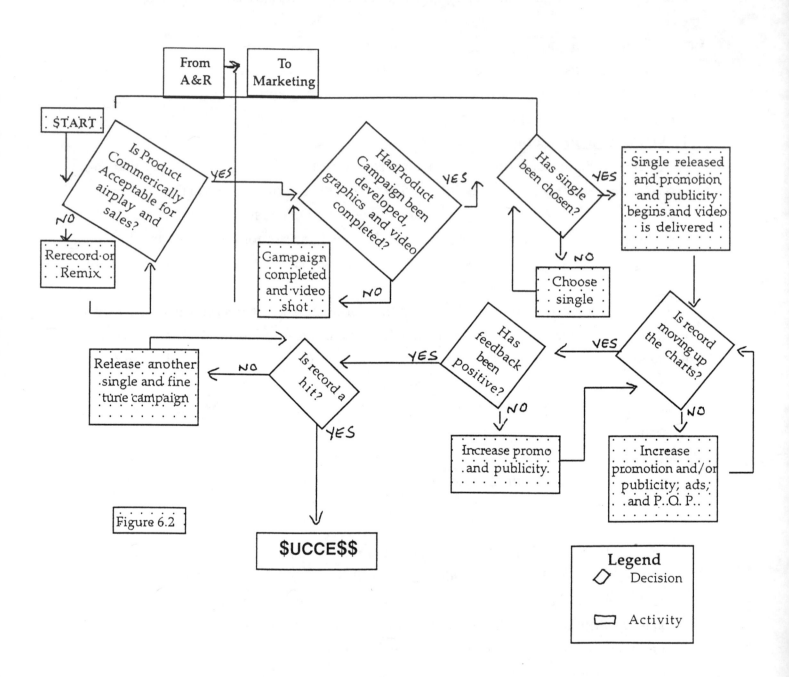

Figure 6.2

Is the Product Commercially Acceptable for airplay and sale, and the first single chosen?

This is the most important decision made and it's a&r's responsibility. The term **"commercially acceptable"** is the term used in the recording contract that allows the record company to make a release decision based on just the technical integrity of the recording. It allows the company to censor the recording. They may feel the lyrics may offend a certain segment of society and if aired, have a negative effect on sales, or they may deem the lyrics as obscene. The company may feel that the recording sounds too much like a previously copyrighted work and may be bordering on infringement. Whatever the "problem" with the recording, the term commercially acceptable allows the company the legal freedom to hold back a release for reasons beyond a recording's technical inefficiencies. Recently, several record companies have required the legal department to review (and sign off on) the lyrics on all material scheduled for release. As also stated in the recording contract chapter, artists are very skeptical about this term and should be. However, very few artists (if any) have the term substituted in the contract.

Choosing the first single to be released is also an a&r decision. It is the manager's responsibility to make certain that the right song is selected. Major battles are fought everyday over this decision, and a good manager persuades a&r to make the right choice. Sometimes the company's administration gets involved with the choice, and managers find themselves trying to persuade a president that the record s/he really wants as the single is the same record the manager and artist wants.

There is quite a bit of paperwork involved in delivering the master recording to a&r for release. The names and social security numbers of each performer on the record must be submitted and a host of other forms completed. For example, the federal government is very concerned that, in the workplace, citizens of the USA are not replaced by foreigners. Various labor union forms must also be completed. All expenses pertaining to the actual recording and other debits to the recording fund must be accounted for. The manager and artist's accountant and attorney should review all expense statements as well as other "official" documents.

Has product Campaign Been Developed, Graphics and Video Completed?

The actual marketing campaign has many facets that must be coordinated by the product manager responsible for the project. Figure 6.3 represents a summary of an actual campaign that successfully delivered a multi-platinum album. The ingredients include the media mix and p-o-p displays.

A&M Marketing Plan

Blues Traveler
<u>Live From the Fall</u>

Album Title:	<u>Live From the Fall</u>
Producers:	Dave Swanson, Richard Vink, & Blues Traveler
Configuration:	CS-Comm
	CD-Comm
Street Date:	July 2nd, 1996

Selections:

Love and Greed	Alone
Mulling It Over	Freedom
Closing Down the Park	Mountains Win Again
Regarding Steven	What's For Breakfast
New York Prophesie	Go Outside and Drive
100 Years	Low Rider
Crash Burn	Runaround
Gina	Sweet Talking Hippy
But Anyway	Imagine
Mountain Cry	

Management:	Dave Frey & Susan Bank--Silent Partner	(212)-582-0222
Agent:	Chip Hooper--Monterey Peninsula Artists	(408)-375-4889
A&R:	David Anderle	(213)-856-2756
Publicist:	Stacey Sanner	(212)-333-1339
Product Manager:	Bob Garcia	(213)-856-2657

"Blues Traveler dedicates this album in complete appreciation to everyone involved with our live show and related experience. Everyone who works at a venue, everyone who has driven a bus or a truck, or anyone who has helped in any way to make the circus happen. But most importantly, above all else, the infinitely patient, festive, and supportive audience who has grown with us for the better part of a decade, we pledge our love and loyalty to you who have collectively provided us with an outlet for our aspirations, and a way of life that would not otherwise be possible." ---- dedication from Live From the Fall.

In the six short years since their A&M debut, Blues Traveler has left an indelible mark on the modern music scene. From its modest beginnings in Princeton, NJ, Blues Traveler has become the "godfather" to the "road warrior" H.O.R.D.E. bands. By constant touring and word of mouth, the band plays over 150 sold out shows per year. Their previous four releases are closing in on seven million units.

Live From the Fall is a specially priced double compact disc and a "must have" for Blues Traveler fans everywhere. The album contains a generous sampling of Traveler tunes from the first four albums as well as unreleased tracks which have become standards in the Blues Traveler live show. Blues Traveler's previous studio album four has just be certified quintuple platinum. Their self titled debut has been certified gold and is well on its way to platinum.

Sales

The HORDE tour will offer the opportunity to market Live From the Fall as well as the entire Blues Traveler catalog. Sales incentives in addition to a focused cooperative advertising campaign will be used throughout the tour to capture the Blues Traveler fan. A special 4 cut CD sampler for Fall will also be available May 31st featuring "Regarding Steven", "Crash Burn", "Mulling It Over", and "Closing Down the Park". The Blues Traveler Fan Club mailing list now contains over 28,000 active subscribers. We will use this list to actively market Live From the Fall. Blues Traveler also has a usenet conference on the Internet (35,000 active subscribers) whose marketing potential will also be exploited. The band will also embark on several World Wide Web promotions on its just completed web site (www.bluestraveler.com) in support of Live From the Fall.

The album carries a 3% discount plus 30 days dating.

Initial forecast   200,000 units   180,000 CD (2GD) and 20,000 cassette (2ST)

Promotion

The 1996 tour will kick off over the Independence Day holiday with two sold out shows at Red Rocks. Media America will broadcast the 4th of July show live across America to celebrate the release of Live From the Fall. "But Anyway" (Studio) will be used in the movie "King Pin" in which Blues Traveler makes a cameo appearance. The movie will be released in mid-July on over 1500 screens. The "Kingpin" soundtrack will have a sticker highlighting <u>Live From the Fall</u>. We will service all formats with a CD Pro containing two studio edited versions of "But Anyway" as well as edited and full versions of the song live to set up the release of <u>Live From the Fall.</u>

Publicity

The set up for <u>Live From the Fall</u> will include major daily newspapers, entertainment news weeklies and monthlies for reviews. In addition, we will be targeting on camera interviews around the launch of the H.O.R.D.E. TOUR with MTV, VH1 and other entertainment based news programs, syndicated radio interviews with MJI, Westwood One and Premiere, and print interviews with USA Today, Reuters, Billboard and Hits. We will also look for a Letterman appearance early in the life of the project to promote the release of the album.

Touring

The fifth annual H.O.R.D.E. (Horizons of Rock Developing Everywhere) kicks off on July 5th in Minneapolis, Minnesota. Once again, Blues Traveler will be headlining the event along with Lenny Kravitz, Rusted Root, Dave Matthews, and other guests. H.O.R.D.E.'96 will hit 40 cities across America before it ends up in September on the East Coast. (See tour dates below)

Direct Advertising

Advertisements will run in the many consumer publications upon release of <u>Live From the Fall</u> including:

Rolling Stone	**Huh**
US	**Relix**
High Times	**Live**

In addition, a street posting campaign will be mounted in the opening markets of the movie "Kingpin" to announce the Media America broadcast of the Blues Traveler performance at Red Rocks and the release of <u>Live From the Fall</u>.

MGM is also planning to spend over 12 million dollars in advertising to open "Kingpin". There will be advertising bought on the NBA Finals, Stanley Cup Playoffs, and a half a million dollar MTV buy. MGM will spend a good deal of their advertising dollars in radio spot buys. All of this will most likely feature music from the film including Blues Traveler's "But Anyway".

Video

We will produce a video for "But Anyway" that will be serviced to MTV and VH-1 in early June to set up the release of <u>Live From the Fall.</u> The video will feature live performance footage of the band mixed with scenes from the "Kingpin" movie.

Materials Available: Advance Sampler CD's, Posters, Ad mats, Minis, Video

Also Available:

Blues Traveler
Traveler's and Thieves
Save His Soul
Four
All Access: The H.O.R.D.E. CD Rom

Preliminary Timeline

May 21	Bulk single ship date
May 23	Sales categories single ship date
May 30	Categories single ship date
May 31	Live sampler bulk date
June 3	Solicitation begins
	Deliver "But Anyway" video to MTV, VH-1, and other video outlets
June 5	CHR/Alternative/AOR work date for "But Anyway"
June 11	Media blitz begins for "Kingpin" movie at TV and radio
June 21	Bulk album ship date
June 25	Category album ship date
July 2	<u>Live From the Fall</u> release date
July 3-4	Red Rocks performance
July 4	Media America live broadcast of Red Rocks performance
July 5	Kickoff H.O.R.D.E. tour (see below)
July 12	"Kingpin" movie opens nationwide
Sept.-Oct.	Fall tour dates TBA

H.O.R.D.E. Tour 1996

July 5-6	Minneapolis	August 4	Seattle
July 9	Cleveland	August 8	Kansas City
July 10	Columbus	August 9	St. Louis
July 12	Indianapolis	August 10	Nashville
July 13	Chicago	August 11	Cincinnati
July 14-15	Detroit	August 13	Pittsburgh
July 17	Birmingham	August 15	Boston

July 18	Memphis	August 16-17	New York
July 19	Dallas	August 18	Saratoga
July 20	Austin	August 20	Buffalo
July 21	Houston	August 21	Hartford
July 23	Las Cruces	August 23	Burlington
July 24	Phoenix	August 24	Philadelphia
July 26-27	Los Angeles	August 25	Washington DC
July 28	San Francisco	August 27	Raleigh
July 29	Concord	August 28	Atlanta
July 30	Sacramento	August 29	Charlotte
August 1	Salt Lake City	August 30	Virginia Beach
August 3	Portland	September 1	West Palm Beach

Equally important to the ingredients of the marketing campaign is the timetable. The timetable for releases must create and maintain a momentum for airplay and product sales. The timetable for the introduction of the items in the marketing campaign must keep the public aware of the product. Carefully, **study** the mix and the timetable for the introduction of the items in the marketing campaign in Figures 6.3 and 6.4. The prerelease campaign for the product in Figure 6.4 had a hefty $500,000 pricetag attached to it. Capitol Records decided that it was not going to leave the fate of this record to chance.

MC HAMMER *"TOO LEGIT TOO QUIT"* CAMPAIGN

Promotional video clips for 12 of the album's 17 songs

Two long form videos

Second TV Blitz December 15-22

Paramount film "The Addams Family" November 22 release will feature four Hammer tunes, including "Addams Groove" which will be the film's prerelease in-theater, radio, and TV ad campaigns

"Hammerman" cartoon show continues to get support

Mattel introduced two Hammer dolls into Barbie's celebrity friend line

HBO special "Influences: James Brown & Hammer"

Saturday Night Live and The Arsenio Hall show appearances

New Pepsi commercial with Hammer and Too Legit Too Quit in background

World tour planned

from Billboard Magazine October 26, 1991 Pg. 1

Figure 6.4

Videos are considered integral part of the marketing campaign. In fact, according Denisoff in his book "Tarnished Gold," in 1984, 68% of survey respondents indicated that they purchased the record after viewing it on MTV, and only 63% of respondents indicated that they purchased the record after listening to it on the radio. MTV claimed that it was the number one vehicle for record recognition among buyers, surpassing radio. However, this is no longer true. Recent studies show that overwhelmingly, radio is the first contact that buyers have to new product. In fact, it was reported in Billboard Magazine in August, 1997 that according to Strategic Record Research,

80% of record buyers said that radio influenced them to buy the record. Seeing the video only influenced 43% of the record buyers.

MTV has literally cornered the market on video presentation. The station was launched nationally on August 1, 1981 and used a very narrow format. It was heavily criticized for not airing black music videos, but has since become a leading outlet for rap artists. John Sykes, the first Vice President of Programming, said that MTV was like an art gallery. The station aired videos in the same manner as a gallery hangs paintings, and the station does not take responsibility for a video's content. Concentrating on rap and heavy metal artists, it saw the need for an outlet for adult contemporary artists. A second channel was launched, VH-1, specifically as an outlet for softer artists. Presently, there is an all latino channel as well.

By the mid 1980s, MTV was offering the major record company's money and advertising spots, for the rights of first refusal on a percent of the company's video releases. The station was willing to pay for exclusivity, and the record company's jumped at the chance to generate income to help defray some of the cost of video production. It was a bold move on MTV's part because radio has never been willing to or have ever paid a dime for records. It was a brilliant decision and they were the only outlet at the time that could afford to make the offer. It secured the station's position as number one and killed the competition.

Although music video sell-through is growing, videos are still essentially a promotional vehicle for a record, and acceptance for airing by MTV, VH-1, or the M2 Channel is crucial. If a video is not accepted by the MTV networks for airplay, its potential viewing audience is dramatically reduced. MTV is so powerful that it is estimated that all the other outlets for airing videos combined, does not equal the strength of a regular rotation airing on MTV.

Has A Single Been Chosen?

Choosing of the first single to be released off of a record is not a scientific process. Companies usually have a weekly meeting to decide what is to be released and when. Obviously, the a & r department play the biggest role in the decision, but company administrators also like to get their egos in on the decision. In fact, Clive Davis, President of Arista Records, has been involved in choosing singles and editing down album cuts for single release since his reign as President of Columbia Records over twenty years ago. Release meetings may also include personnel from the marketing and merchandising departments.

A fierce battle can occur if the artist's manager and the a & r department do not agree on the release schedule of the singles. It is the manager's responsibility to convince the a & r department that the single s/he and the artist want to be released, is the same single that they have chosen. If the manager muscles the company and wins the battle but the project loses priority status, the artist may lose the war as the company's interest in the project may be jeopardized. Consequently, the strength of the manager's persuasive skills may be of extreme importance.

Is The Record Moving Up The Charts?

The record industry measures success quantitatively. How high up the charts did it go? How much airplay did it receive? And ultimately, how many records did it sell. Therefore the goal of any marketing campaign is to sell records. The bottom line of project is for a salesclerk to answer "yes" when asks by a customer if the record is in the store.

Record companies believe that airplay is the key to exposure. Many industry studies have shown a strong correlation between heavy radio listeners and buyers. Airplay is the job of the promotion department.

Record promotion is handled either in-house by the company's staff field promotion people, or by an independent record promotion person hired by the company or the artist's manager. Independent promotion people are hired when either the record has a specific sound or style to it they may need exposure on specific radio stations before other stations will air it, or the record receives a heavy priority within the company and the "indies" are called in to increase its success potential.

Independent promotion people claim to have an above average success rate for airplay on stations that play the particular style of music that they claim is their expertise. They claim to deliver hits, and if successful, can charge a very high fee to "work" a record. It has been reported that some indies make a million dollars a year.

So what happens if the record isn't "growing legs" with the marketing plan's tactics? Does the manager scream at the record company to get "on" the record? Does the promotion department hire a few "indies" to work the record? If the promotion department doesn't do enough to increase the record's airplay, does the manager hire an indie? Does the artist increase his/her publicity activities? Does the manager start calling radio stations to try to increase airplay? Does someone hound MTV for more exposure? Do the company's field merchandising staff push for in-store airplay? The answer is one or all of the above, plus anything else that can be thought of. Few singles have ever received a second chance to become a success. Fewer artists have ever been given priority status in a company after recording a "dog."

Has Feedback Been Positive?

The old adage, "Any publicity is better than no publicity" is still true. However, lukewarm feedback does a record little good. Although it has been reported that less than eight percent of

----

record buyers are influenced by record reviews, the industry still enjoys positive responses. Because the company has relatively little control of the media, the marketing campaign spends a great deal of the artist's money giving free publicity paraphernalia to whom it considers influential people. Their stamp of approval gives the record and the artist credibility, and once they publically announce their approval of artist's work, they are usually hounded by the record company to give additional positive responses. If

feedback has not been positive, the record company should alter the promotional and publicity activities to induce the kind of feedback that will help the record gain respect. This usually requires additional financial commitments by the company, which of course is the ultimately the artist's money.

Is The Record A Hit?

This is really the third time the same question has been voiced in the chart, and doing all that can be done to make the record a success can not be emphasized too strongly. If the record has not grown its own legs by this time, it is probably time to release another single and fine tune the campaign. If the artist's manager was very insistent on getting his/her own way regarding the choice of the first single and it was a dog, no matter what the reason was (choice of single or lack of promotion), his/her power has been diminished and a & r will have the upper hand in choosing this one. Hopefully all this new activity will generate action on the chart.

The flow chart has illustrated the path of the product through the marketing department, including the responsibilities of the publicity and artist development departments. The product manager monitors the record through the sales, merchandising, and distribution departments to make certain that all facets of the marketing campaign are completed.

WHERE THE MONEY GOES

Keeping track of the recording budget during the recording is the responsibility of the a & r administration department. Record companies use a *Recording Authorization Form* to keep track of the expense. Each line item is estimated at the time the recording proposal is submitted. When the budget is approved by the Vice President of A & R, the artist and manager or producer must seek to have budget reapproved if additional funds are needed. Therefore, estimates should be made as accurately as possible. Some of the typical expense categories found in most *Recording Authorization Form* S are listed below. They are:

- producer fee
- artist advance
- AFM payment
- AFTRA payment
- travel/hotel
- per diem
- Studio time
- mixdown time
- engineer fee
- tape
- rental instruments
- misc.
- unforeseen expenses

For example, let's assume the studio time for an initial recording of a rock group is estimated as requiring 200 hours of studio time (24 track) @$250 per hour including mixdown and engineer. Tape costs are additional, and 200 hours might use 15 rolls of two inch wide tape. This would bring the entire studio bill to $50,000. AFM and AFTRA payments to the four member group might be $5000 plus additional studio musicians and instrument rental is another $2000. The producer might have a fee of $40,000 plus accommodations for everyone is another $7500, and miscellaneous expenses could equal $5000. The bottom line of the Recording Authorization form could read $100,000 without any waste. Additional money might also have been spent on recording one or several videos totally $200,000, plus additional advance incentive money of $75,000. Therefore it would not be outrageous for a new artist to be in debt to the record company for approximately $300,000 on the day the record is released.

Remember these expenses are all charge-backs recoupable out of the artist's royalty account and paid back or credited to the record company out of record sales before the artist realizes any royalty checks. Consequently, the artist and his/her manager should be very interested in the number of records (units) that must be sold in order to bring the artist's royalty account out of the red and back to zero. Or, in other words, what is the break-even sales point.

To understand this, let's use the example that the artist's royalty rate is 12% of the retail list price (superstars may demand a 15 to 22 % rate). Let's use a retail list price of $16.98 and

----

multiply this figure by 12%. The answer is $2.04. $2.04 will be credited to the artist's royalty account for every record sold. To find the break-even point we need to calculate how many $2.04 (or albums sold) will equal $300,000. So by dividing $300,000 by $2.04 we arrive at 147,059 albums (units) must be sold in order for the artist's royalty account to break-even.

$$\$16.98 \text{ (retail list price)}$$
$$\underline{\text{x} .12} \text{ (royalty rate)}$$
$$\$2.04$$

$$\$300,000 \text{ divided by } 2.04 = 147,059 \text{ units}$$

Although this is an incredible number of records to sell before the artist sees any royalties, the calculations are a bit more complex than this, and the number of records that need to be sold is even greater. We need to calculate various account allowances and adjustments.

Packaging Allowances are deducted from the royalty base as a percentage. The record company may seek a package or container allowance as high as 25%. A long standing pet argument of this author's has been the packaging allowance. Isn't normal packaging just part of the cost of manufacturing records? If an artist doesn't ask for anything out of the ordinary, why must a packaging allowance be debited to the royalty account? Wouldn't a similar example be if you were charged extra for the standard tires on a new car? If the artist is going to be charged, shouldn't the record company give the artist the right to shop for packaging by an independent company? However, attorneys say that packaging allowances are nonnegotiable.

Record Companies also charge a **CD Reduction rate** of 20% through a CD Reduction Clause in the contract. However, for this example, let's assume a 25% packaging allowance, and not calculate the CD reduction rate.

The **Free Goods Allowance** is usually 15%. Stated another way: "of every 100 albums shipped, 15 will be royalty fee." Some companies add a clause that states that they will pay on 85% of the records shipped (SONY and EMI). Some companies use 90% (A&M and Atlantic). When attorneys approach this clause with the argument that it replaces the free goods allowance clause, some companies deny it. Executing both clauses would allow the record company to pay 85% of 85%, before the packaging allowance! For this example let's assume 15%.

The industry is not standardized on its use of several contractual terms. For example, some companies do not use the term wholesale price, but choose to use the term "normal retail channels." **Royalty base** is another confusing term. For our purposes, we'll define it as **the percentage of the retail list price that remains after all allowances and deductions, which the royalty rate is based on**.

We can now calculate the artist's royalty amount more accurately by using the royalty base and the royalty rate figures. If we subtract 25% for packaging and 15% for free goods from a royalty base retail list price of $16.98, the answer is $10.18. The artist's royalty rate is 12% of the retail list price, however, to calculate, we must multiply 12% by the adjusted list price of $10.18. The artist's royalty rate is really $1.22 on every record sold. Now if we divide $300,000 by $1.22 we arrive at **245,902 albums (units)** must be sold in order for the artist's royalty account to break-even.

The calculation is as follows:

retail list price x (royalty base or 100% - allowances) = adjusted retail list price

adjusted retail list price x artist royalty rate = royalty per unit

royalty account debit / royalty per unit = break-even number

Although we will not go into other scenarios here, there could be further allowances deducted from the original royalty base. For instance, a breakage allowance, a CD reduction rate, and/or a "Special Marketing Discount" is common, or the producer's cut in an "all in deal."

THE RECORD COMPANY'S SHARE

Using a wholesale price of $10.70 and subtracting the $1.22 royalty to the artist per unit, there remains $9.48 that the record company receives. Out the remaining $9.48 manufacturing costs, distribution costs, mechanical royalties, and union benefits must be paid.

Let's use as an example a ten-song recording, and the record company will pay a 25%

_____

percent reduction from the statutory rate, currently at $.0695 per song, on negotiated mechanical licenses, which equals $0.53. Add to this a manufacturing cost of $2.25 (or less). Subtract the $2.78 from $9.48 and the company is left with $6.70.

By law, record companies must contribute to two American Federation of Musicians (AFM) funds. They must contribute about $.05 to the Special Payments Fund, and about $.03 to the Music Performance Trust Fund. The record company may also have to contribute a lump sum to the vocalists' union, the American Federation of Television and Radio Artists (AFTRA). For our example let's assume that it doesn't. If we subtract $.08 from the remaining $6.70, we are left with $6.62.

If we multiply $6.62 x 245,902 (the number of units that must be sold for the artist to break-even) we get $1,627,871.24 as the amount the record company receives. However, this is not all profit for the company. Promotion and advertising expenses must be subtracted from this, as well as a portion of the general overhead and operating costs. In fact, some estimate that the record company's break-even unit number is approximately **twice** that of the artist.

Figure 6.6 illustrates where the money goes from the sale of a recording ($16.98 list price was used). With about three quarters of the records released never regaining their recording costs, superstars have a big job in the record business, they must deliver the multi-platinum sellers that pay the bills for all the "stiffs." Remember, record companies are in the business for one reason, **to sell records!**

(Please note that all calculations were simplified for illustration purposes.)

FINANCIAL CUTS ON A RECORDING
($16.98 RETAIL LIST PRICE)*

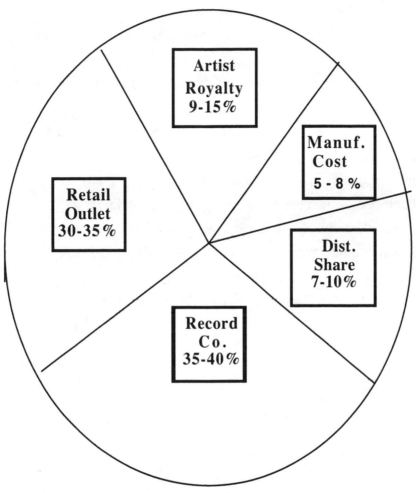

* (All figures are approximations)

Figure 6.6. Adapted From Country Music Assn. March 1981.

SUMMARY

1. The relationship of the artist and his/her record company is a business relationship and an emotional one.

2. The record company manufactures, releases, promotes, and distributes the artist's works, but also acts as a financial backer.

3. The three types of advances given to an artist under contract are: personal advance, production advance, and bonus advance.

4. The types of record companies include: major, independent, specialty, and boutique.

5. The major record companies own their own distribution networks.

6. A record company has a creative division and a business/administrative division.

7. Record companies demand master tapes that are "commercially acceptable".

8. A product flows through the record departments in an organized manner.

9. The artist's royalty account is credited after all record company expenses are met.

PROJECTS

1. Set up a record company in class and ask individual students to list the responsibilities of each department.

2. Create a listening party in class. Have students listen to a new release and as they represent various departments of the company, formulate a marketing plan.

BIBLIOGRAPHY

Brabec, J. & Brabec, T. Music, Money, and Success. Schirmer Books. New York, 1994.

Denisoff, R. Serge. Tarnished Gold. Transaction Books, Inc. New Brunswick, 1987.

Wadhams, Wayne. Sound Advice. Schirmer Books. New York, 1990.

CHAPTER SEVEN

THE RECORDING CONTRACT

"Astute artist attorneys recognize that having key record company executives excited by an artist's music and committed to breaking the artist in the marketplace is far more important than specific contractual guarantees, particularly if the guarantees being requested are of dubious practical value." Michael J. Pollack, V.P. and General Counsel, Arista Records. Billboard Magazine. July 23, 1988.

By the end of this chapter, you should be able to:

1. Intelligently discuss every clause of the example agreement in this chapter.
2. When given a different example contract, transfer what you have studied in this chapter to the corresponding clauses of the new contract, and discuss its content.
3. Discuss the current royalty and mechanical rates negotiated in new artist recording contracts.

The brass ring.

The major leagues.

Big time.

The beginning.

All these words describe what securing a long term royalty artist recording contract from a nationally distributed label means to an artist. It also means that the artist is no longer just a local or regional phenomenon. In fact it is the most important goal of any new artist, and the payoff to years of practicing, rehearsing, and also performing in the endless number of beerjoints and at nondescript fraternity parties. It is a payoff. A payoff that, by percentages, very few musicians ever receive.

However, it is also the beginning. It's the beginning of a career. The chance to be idolized by the hometown musicians. The chance for the artist to receive respect from his or her parents and relatives when revealing his or her occupation. But most importantly, the chance for the artist to perform original material in his or her own unique style and not be required to work another job to pay the bills!

Then why do so many artist's blow their chance? Industry estimates are that from two-thirds to three-quarters of the pop recordings released never regain their recording costs.

Consequently, many artists are dropped by labels after only one release, and play out their "careers" performing their "hit" in hotel cocktail lounges. Actually a "stiff" is not always the artist's fault. However, the consequence is the same.

When offering a long term royalty contract to an artist, what does a company look for? What is the selection criteria used by a company's a&r staff? How does an a&r rep. judge the value of the artist in the marketplace six to nine months (the minimum amount of time needed to negotiate a contract with a major label and complete the recording of an album) after he or she is convinced that the artist is worthy of a deal?

These are some of the usual answers. "Intuition!" "It's just a feeling I have about the artist and the songs." "You can feel the electricity in the air when he or she performs." "He or she is a unique talent." None of this offers any insight for the unsigned musician. However, some helpful criteria might be:

1. charisma -- The magnetic quality of a person's personality.

2. stage-presence -- The artist's command of an audience.

3. uniqueness -- Is the artist new or different?

4. worth in the marketplace -- Is the artist and his or her music a saleable commodity? And for how long?

There are basically three ways a new artist may attempt to secure a recording contract. They are:

1. The artist makes a demo recording and the manager or an attorney tries to secure a deal (shops the demo).

2. The artist locates a producer and makes a demo recording and the producer (or the production company) shops the demo.

3. The artist, with or without a producer, makes a master recording and shops the master.

When securing a recording contract, it is generally not a good idea for an artist to be tied to the producer as a third party. The producer will insist on final control over who produces the recording, and any attempt by the artist to nurture a relationship with the company may be hindered.

The following is an actual first draft recording contract submitted to a new artist by a major recording company. Included are our editorial comments. Although it is not written to be grossly unfair to either side, upon examination, any competent attorney would not allow his or her client to sign it without serious negotiations.

This deal differs from the contract that would generally be offered by an independent label. If an independent label agreed to sign the artist, the contract would most likely be a per recording commitment which is also known as a "step deal." The step deal could encompass either a single to single contract based on sales, or a single to album commitment. However, it would probably not include much, if any, advance money.

Many new artists believe the recording contract is an agreement "written in stone" and demand that every word be negotiated. Obviously both sides must feel comfortable with the language, not only for the financial aspects, but more importantly, because the contract should be the basis for a long-term relationship. Although it provides the guidelines for this relationship, one cannot contractualize the strong company commitment that is necessary for the artist to succeed. Consequently, everything is negotiable.

EXCLUSIVE RECORDING AGREEMENT

Agreement made as of (today's date), between John Doe (hereinafter "you") and "Major" Records, 000 Zero Street, Anywhere, USA (hereinafter "Major").

Many attorneys suggest that the definitions section of the contract, in this case Section 14, be read and understood before trying to understand the rest of the agreement.

1. <u>TERM</u>

1.01.   (a)   The term of this agreement will begin today.

        (b)   The first Contract Period of the term will end nine (9) months after the earlier of the dates referred to in sections (1) and (2) below:

        (1)   the date of completion of the lacquer, copper, or equivalent masters to be used in manufacturing the disc Phonograph Record units to be derived from the last Master Recordings made in fulfillment of your Recording Commitment for that contract period under paragraph 3.01 below; or

        (2)   the date 30 days after you give Major notice that you have completed the Delivery of those Master Recordings; but will not end earlier than one year after the date of its commencement.

Clause 1.01 describes the contract period of the term of the agreement, which in this case _reads nine months. However, the beginning of the term occurs on either of the two dates describe in (1) or (2). (1) reads that the term begins at the completion of the master which is to be used in manufacturing the recording and, (2) says it will begin 30 days after you notify the company that you have delivered the master._

The last sentence that begins with "but will not ..." may be struck from the contract. It suggests that the artist cannot complete his/her obligation in less than a year, and may be negotiated for a shorter period of time.

1.02. You grant Major three (3) separate options to extend that term for additional Contract Periods ("Option Periods") on the same terms and conditions. Major may exercise each of those options by sending you a notice not later than the expiration date of the Contract Period which is then in effect (the "current Contract Period"). If Major exercises such an option, the Option Period concerned will begin immediately after the end of the current Contract Period.

Record companies negotiate from the position that, the more option periods to extend the contract, the better. It gives them an easy way to move to the option periods. However, if the artist is unsuccessful, a longer contract will not force the record company to allow the artist to record, or release any product.

In the fourth line of 1.02 after "sending you a notice," the phrase 90 days, or 60 days, or at least 30 days prior to the expiration date may be inserted. The artist should have the right to know whether the record company is going to exercise the option period before it expires, in order to have time to shop for another deal. Usually, record companies are not willing to change this clause.

2. <u>SERVICES</u>

2.01. During the term of this agreement you will render your services as a performing artist for the purpose of making Master Recordings for Major, you will cause those Recordings to be produced, and you will Deliver the Recordings to Major, as provided in this agreement. (You are sometimes called "the Artist" below; all references in this agreement to "you and the Artist," and the like, will be understood to refer to you alone.)

2.02. (a) Your obligations will include furnishing the services of the producers of those Master Recordings, and you will be solely responsible for engaging and paying them. (Producers whom you engage are sometimes referred to in this agreement by the capitalized term "Producers.")

This agreement is known as an "all in royalty" deal, meaning that the artist will supply the producer for the recordings and is responsible for paying him or her. Therefore the royalty rate reflects this.

(b) If Major, instead, engages producers for any of those Master Recordings, or if the producers of any such Recordings are regularly employed on Major's staff or render their services under contract with Major, the following terms will apply:

Should this provision apply, the artist should still be able to consent to the engagement of a specific producer.

(1)   Your royalty account and the production budget for the recording project concerned will be charged with a Recording Cost item of fifteen thousand dollars ($15,000) (or one thousand five hundred dollars ($1,500) per Side for a project for the recording of less than an Album). If Major is obligated to pay those producers a higher fixed amount attributable to that project, the charge under this section will be that amount instead.

(2)   Your royalty on Phonograph Records made from those Recordings under Article 9 will be reduced by the amount of a royalty of seven and six one-hundredths percent (7.06%) on Albums under section 9.01(a)(1), adjusted in proportion to the other royalty rates and royalty adjustments provided for in the other provisions of Articles 9 and 10. (If a higher royalty is payable to the producers, the reduction under this section will be the amount of that royalty instead.)

If (b) becomes a reality, provisions (1) and (2) go into effect. The recording fund is reduced by the amounts described in (1), and your royalty account is reduced accordingly as stated in (2). The best negotiation position on this point is simply to not allow this to occur.

3. RECORDING COMMITMENT

3.01. During each Contract Period you will perform for the recording of Master Recordings sufficient to constitute one Album, cause those Master Recordings to be produced, and Deliver them to Major (the "Minimum Recording commitment").

3.02. You will fulfill the Minimum Recording Commitment for each Contract Period within the first three (3) months of the Period.

It would better serve the artist if the three month period was longer, and extended to, for example, to at least five months.

3.03.   (a) During each Contract Period Major will have the option to increase the Recording Commitment for that Period by Master Recordings constituting one additional Album ("Overcall Recordings"). Major may exercise that option by sending you a notice at any time before the end of the Contract Period concerned.

If the artist is successful, the record company will exercise its option to increase the number of albums due. As it reads they may ask for the "Overcall Recording" at any time. The artist may want at least thirty days notice, should the artist need time to complete another project.

(b) Each time Major exercises such an option:

(1)   you will Deliver the Overcall Recordings to major within three (3) months; and

(2)   the current Contract Period will continue for nine (9) months after whichever of the following dates in the earlier:

In (1), three months should be increased to at least five months, so that the artist has a bit more time to deliver a product. In (2) it is in the artist's best interest to negotiate the opposite, therefore the nine months should be changed to less.

(i)   The date of completion of the lacquer, copper, or equivalent masters to be used in manufacturing the disc Phonograph Record units of the Album comprising the Overcall Recordings; or

(ii)   The date thirty (30) days after you give Major notice that you have completed the Delivery of the Overcall Recordings.

3.04. Each Album (or other group of Master Recordings) Delivered to Major in fulfillment of your Recording Commitment will consist entirely of Master Recordings made in the course of the same Album (or other) recording project, unless Major consents otherwise. Major may withhold that consent in its unrestricted discretion.

Only new material will fulfill the commitment. Material in "the can" from previous recording commitments will not be permitted. This allows the record company to afford material for big multi-disc sets, should the artist become a superstar.

4. RECORDING PROCEDURE

4.01. You will follow the procedure set forth below in connection with Master Recordings made hereunder:

(a)   Except as expressly noted otherwise in this agreement, prior to the commencement of recording in each instance you shall obtain the approval of Major of each of the following, in order, before proceeding further:

(1)   Selection of Producer.

The artist may want to construct a formula based on the sales of the first album, that when reached, would automatically approve the producer for the "Overcall Recording" as well. For example, if the first album sells more than 500,000 units (a gold record), the producer will be considered deemed approved for the "Overcall Recording." This places an objective contingency on the clause rather than leaving it to the subjective approval of the record company.

(2)   Selection of material, including the number of Compositions to be recorded. Major shall not be deemed to be unreasonable in rejecting any request to record an Album consisting of more than one twelve inch 33 1/3 rpm Record. You shall advise Major of the content of each medley before it is recorded.

For a new artist, this is not a negotiated point. The record company has the sole authority to reject any request and no rejection shall be deemed unreasonable. For a super star artist its another story.

(3)   Selection of dates of recording and studios where recording is to take place, including the cost of recording there. Major will not be deemed to be unreasonable in rejecting any request to begin recording any Album which is a part of the Recording commitment within three (3) months after the acceptance of a prior Album under this agreement. The scheduling and booking of all studio time will be done by Major. Major's facilities and the services of its engineers will be used to the extent required by Major's union agreements.

The artist should insist that language be inserted that states that only a first class studio will be deemed acceptable.

(4)   A proposed budget (which you will submit to Major sufficiently in advance of the planned commencement of recording to give Major a reasonable time to review and approve or disapprove it at least fourteen (14) days before the planned commencement of recording). A budget not exceeding the amount of the minimum Recording fund fixed in paragraph 6.02 will be deemed approved.

(b)   You shall notify the appropriate Local of American Federation of Musicians in advance of each recording session.

(c)   You will comply with the following procedures in connection with the requirements of the U. S. Immigration Law:

(1)   Before each recording session:

(i)   You will require each background instrumentalist, background vocalist, and other person to be employed in connection with the session to complete and sign the EMPLOYEE INFORMATION AND VERIFICATION ("employee") section of a

U.S. Immigration and Naturalization Service Employment Eligibility Certificate (Form I-9), unless you have already obtained such a Certificate from the person concerned within the past three years;

(ii)   You will complete and sign the EMPLOYER REVIEW AND VERIFICATION ("employer") section of each such Certificate; and

(iii)   You will attach copies of the documents establishing identity and employment eligibility which you examine in accordance with the instructions in the employer section. If any such person is engaged during a session you will comply with subsections (i) through (iii) above, with respect to that person, before he renders any services.

(2)   You will not permit any such person who fails to complete the employee section, or to furnish you with the required documentation, to render any services in connection with Recordings to be made under this agreement.

(3)   You will deliver those Certificates and documents to Major promptly, and in no event later than the Delivery of the Recordings concerned.

(4)   You will comply with any revised or additional verification and documentation requirements of which Major advises you in the future.

(d)   As and when required by Major, you shall allow Major's representatives to attend any or all recording sessions hereunder.

This is a vehicle for the record company to maintain its copyright claim as the artist is employed on a "work for hire" basis. The artist should require that some notice be given ahead of time as to when they are coming and how many representatives.

(e)   You shall timely supply Major with all of the information it needs in order: (1) to make payments due in connection with such Recordings; (2) to comply with any other obligations Major may have in connection with the making of such Master Recordings; and (3) to prepare to release Phonograph Records derived from such Master Recordings. Without limiting the generality of clause (2) of the preceding sentence:

(1)   You shall furnish Major with all information it requires to comply with its obligations under its union agreements, including, without limitation, the following:

(i)   If a session is held to record new tracks intended to be mixed with existing tracks (and if such information is requested by the American Federation of Musicians), the dates and places of the prior sessions at which such existing tracks were made, and the AFM Phonograph Recording Contract (Form "B") number(s) covering such sessions;

(ii)   Each change of title of any composition listed in an AFM Phonograph Recording Contract (Form "B"); and

(iii)   A listing of all the musical selections contained in Recordings Delivered to Major hereunder; and

    (2)   You will furnish Major with all of the immigration control documentation required by subparagraph 4.01(c) above, at the same time as the AFM or AFTRA session reports, tax withholding forms, and other documentation required by Major in order to make the payments to the session musicians and other employees concerned, if any.

(f)   You shall Deliver to Major's A&R Administration Department fully mixed, edited, and unequalized and equalized Master Recordings (including but not limited to a final two-track equalized tape copy), commercially satisfactory to major for its manufacture and sale of Phonograph Records, and all original and duplicate Master Recordings of the material recorded, together with all necessary licenses and permissions, and all materials required to be furnished by you to Major for use in the packaging and marketing of the Records. Each Master Recording will be clearly marked to identify the Artist and the recording artist, and to show the title(s) of the composition(s) and recording date(s).

Every artist would love to change the phrase commercially satisfactory to technically satisfactory. The issue is creative control and the record company will not give it up. However, superstars may be able to negotiate this, thereby giving the record company only the right to make certain that it is acceptable for airing on radio, but a new artist would not stand a chance.

4.02. No Composition previously recorded by the Artist will be recorded under this agreement. No "live" Recording, Joint Recording, or Recording not made in full compliance with this agreement will apply in fulfillment of your Recording commitment, nor will Major be required to make any payments in connection with any such Recording except any royalties which may become due under this agreement if the Recording is released by Major. No Recordings shall be made by unauthorized dubbing.

The record company will not accept a recording of a live performance, or any joint recording as fulfilling the recording commitment. Only composition recorded specifically for the commitment will be considered.

In line six, before royalties, the artist may want to insert "advances or" as advance money will be needed for production costs should the recording and release occur.

4.03. Nothing in this agreement shall obligate Major to continue or permit the continuation of any recording session or project, even if previously approved hereunder, if Major reasonably anticipates that the Recording Costs will exceed those specified in the approved budget or that the Recordings being produced will not be satisfactory.

This clause allows the record company to pull the plug if the recording budget is exceeded or the company anticipates that the budget will be exceeded. However, the question is exceeded by how much? One dollar? One thousand dollars? Obviously the record company wants the project finished and will allow the master to be delivered over budget. But cost overruns have caused problems.

4.04. The Artist will not be required to perform together with any other royalty artist without the Artist's consent. Major shall not be deemed to be unreasonable in rejecting any request for the Artist to record with another royalty artist.

5. RECOUPABLE AND REIMBURSABLE COSTS

5.01. Major will pay all union scale payments required to be made to Artist in connection with recordings made hereunder, all costs of instrumental, vocal and other amounts required to be paid by Major pursuant to any applicable law or any collective bargaining agreement between Major and any union representing Persons who render services in connection with such Master Recordings.

5.01 conveys that the artist will receive AFM union scale for recording his or her own record. At the rate or approximately $200 per three hour session per musician, substantial money can accumulate fairly quickly.

5.02. (a) All Recording Costs will constitute Advances. Any Recording Costs in excess of the Recording Fund fixed in paragraph 6.02 or other amount approved by Major, and all special Packaging Costs, will be your sole responsibility and will be paid by you promptly (or reimbursed by you if paid by Major). Those amounts will also be recoupable from all moneys becoming payable to you by Major under this agreement or otherwise to the extent to which they have not actually been paid or reimbursed as provided in the preceding sentence. All costs incurred by Major in connection with the production of motion pictures containing the Artist's performances (audiovisual or otherwise) or the acquisition of rights in such motion pictures, and all direct expenses paid or incurred by Major in connection with independent promotion of recordings of the Artist's performances (i.e., promotion by persons other than regular employees of Major), will constitute Advances.

All recording costs are advances and recoupable out of royalties. So that any expenses, including the union scale paid to the artist is recoupable out of royalties.

In line five, the word "promptly" should be struck because the demands on the artist are much more severe than on the record company throughout the agreement.

In order to remain consistent, in line eleven, the words "motion pictures" should be struck and replaced by "covered videos."

In line fourteen, the words "in connection with independent promotion of recordings" may be negotiated out of the clause. Independent promotion should be considered a business expense and not an expense that can be controlled by the artist.

(b) The amounts applicable to any Joint Recording which are payable by you or chargeable against you royalties under this paragraph 5.02 will be computed by apportionment as provided in paragraph 10.01.

(c) The costs of metal parts other than lacquer, copper or equivalent masters, and payments to the AFM Special Payments Fund and the Music Performance Trust Fund based upon record sales (so-called "per-record royalties"), will not be recoupable from your royalties or reimbursable by you.

The phrase "normal engineering charges that would be incurred for realtime mastering" should also be included in this clause. No matter where the mastering for the record occurs, the artist should not be responsible for the expense.

6. ADDITIONAL ADVANCES; MINIMUM ANNUAL COMPENSATION

6.01. All monies paid to or on behalf of you or Artist during the Term of this agreement, other than royalties paid pursuant to Articles 9 and 12, shall constitute Advances unless otherwise expressly agreed in writing by an authorized officer of Major.

6.02. (a) Promptly after your Delivery to Major of the Master Recordings constituting an Album recorded pursuant to your Recording Commitment, Major will pay you an advance in the amount by which the applicable sum indicated below ("Recording Fund") exceeds the Recording Costs for the Album.

This clause outlines the company's obligation to pay an advance with the recording of every album. However, the artist may negotiate to use the term "promptly after your delivery" as the point at which the total advance will be received. At least a two-tiered structure should be negotiated here. For example, one-half of the advance will be received upon commencement of the recording and one-half will be _received upon delivery._

(1)   The amount of the Recording Fund for the first Album Delivered during the initial Contract Period will be $150,000.

Obviously, all dollar amounts are negotiable.

(2)   The amount of the Recording Fund for each Album other than the first Album Delivered during the initial Contract Period will be two-thirds (2/3) of whichever of the following amounts is less (subject to section 6.02(a)(3) below):

This is within the normal language currently being employed.

(i)   the amount of the royalties credited to your account on Net Sales Through Normal Retail Channels in the United States of the more recent of the two "Preceding Albums" (defined below), as shown by the last semiannual accounting statement rendered to you by Major before the date on which the Album concerned is Delivered or required to be Delivered under Article 3 (whichever date is earlier);

or

The last semiannual accounting period may not represent an accurate depiction of how much money the record has made for the company. Most record companies keep a record of how much money the sale of the record has **accumulated** (some companies call it the "monthly trial balance"). This figure should be examined on the day the album concerned is delivered, and two-thirds of that amount should comprise the recording fund.

(ii)   The average of the amounts of such royalties on both of the Preceding Albums.

"The Preceding Albums" means the two Albums, made under this agreement, released most recently before the Delivery of the Album concerned (or, if only one such Album has then been released, that Album).

(3)   No such Recording Fund will be more than the applicable maximum or less than the applicable minimum prescribed below:

	Minimum	**Maximum**

(i)   The Overcall Album Delivered during the initial Contract Period:
$175,000 $350,000

(ii)   Albums Delivered during the first Option Period:
$200,000 $400,000

(iii)   Albums Delivered during the second Option Period:
$225,000 $450,000

(iv)   Albums Delivered during the third Option Period:
$250,000 $500,000

These are reasonable minimum and maximum amounts, however, every amount is negotiable.

(b)   Each such Advance will be reduced by the amount of any anticipated costs of mastering, remastering or remixing; any such anticipated costs which are deducted but not incurred will be remitted to you. All royalties paid to you during the term of this agreement will apply in reduction of such Advances which may thereafter become payable under this paragraph. If any Album other than the first Album recorded during the first Contract Period is not Delivered within the time prescribed in Article 3, the Recording Fund for that Album will be $140,000.

This is the penalty provision concerning unanticipated costs. After the word "within" in line eight, a reasonable amount of time may be inserted to give the artist reasonable time to complete the album.
$140,000 should also be deleted and as a compromise add "reduced on a month-to-month basis " each month the album is late not to exceed, in this case, a total of $140,000.

6.03. The aggregate amount of the compensation paid to you under this agreement will not be less than Six Thousand ($6000) per Fiscal Year. "Fiscal Year", in this paragraph, means the annual period beginning on the date of commencement of the term of this agreement, and each subsequent annual period during the continuance of that term beginning on the anniversary of that commencement date. If you have not received compensation of at least $6000 under this agreement for a Fiscal Year, Major will pay you the amount of the deficiency before the end of that Fiscal Year; at least forty (40) days before the end of each Fiscal Year you will notify Major if you have not received compensation of at least $6000 under this agreement for that year, and of the amount of the deficiency. Each such payment will constitute an Advance and will be applied in reduction of any and all monies subsequently becoming due to you under this agreement. Major may not withhold or require you to repay any such payment under any other provision of this agreement. If the term of this agreement referred to in the first and third sentences of this paragraph will be reduced proportionately for the purpose of computing the payment to be made under this paragraph for that Fiscal Year. You acknowledge that this paragraph is included to avoid compromise of Major's rights (including its entitlement of injunctive relief) by reason of a finding of applicability of California law, but does not constitute a concession by Major that California law is actually applicable.

Under California law, this clause binds the artist to the record company, provided the company advances the artist at least $6000 per year. According to line eleven, the artist must remind the record company to pay him or her.

7. RIGHTS IN RECORDINGS

7.01. Each Master Recording made or furnished to Major by you or the Artist under this agreement or during its term, from the Inception of Recording, will be considered a work made for hire for Major; if any such Master Recording is determined not to be a work made for hire it will be deemed transferred to Master by this agreement, together with all rights in it. All Master Recordings made or furnished to major by you or the Artist under this agreement or during its term, from the Inception of Recording, and all Matrices and Phonograph Records manufactured from them, together with the performances embodied on them, shall be the sole property of Major, free from any claims by you or any other Person; and Major shall have the exclusive right to copyright those Master Recordings in its name as the author and owner of them and to secure any and all renewals and extensions of such copyright throughout the world. You will execute and deliver to Major such instruments of transfer and other documents regarding the rights of Major in the Master Recordings subject to this agreement as Major may reasonably request to carry out the purposes of this agreement, and Major may sign such documents in your name or the name of the Artist and make appropriate disposition of them.

By designating the recordings as work for hire, the record company becomes their sole owner. However, the language in the next to the last line gives the record company power of attorney to sign documents in the artist's name. A clause should be inserted that at least requires the record company to give the artist notice to review the documents before they are signed.

7.02. Without limiting the generality of the foregoing, Major and any Person authorized by Major shall have the unlimited, exclusive rights, throughout the world: (a) to manufacture hereafter known, derived from the Master Recordings made under this agreement or during its term; (b) to sell, transfer or otherwise deal in the same under any trademarks, trade names and labels, or to refrain from such manufacture,sale and dealing; and (c) to reproduce, adapt, and otherwise use those Master Recordings in any medium and in any manner, including but not limited to use in audiovisual works, without payment of any compensation to you or the Artist except the royalties, if any, which may be expressly prescribed for the use concerned under Article 9.

This clause give the record company unlimited exclusive rights to derive income from the artist and his or her work. The last lines of 7.02 allow the record company to make money regardless of the use of the work, without giving the artist any compensation in addition to royalties. "(New and different uses not discussed in the contract will be negotiated)" may be added to the end of the entire clause.

8. NAMES AND LIKENESSES; PUBLICITY

8.01. Major and its Licensees shall have the rights and may grant to others the rights to use your name, the names, portraits, pictures and likenesses of the Artist and Producer(s) and all other persons performing services in connection with Master Recordings made under this agreement (including, without limitation, all professional, group, and other assumed or fictitious names used by them), and biographical material concerning them, as news or information, for the purposes of trade, or for advertising purposes, in any manner and in any medium. Major and its Licensees shall have the exclusive rights and may grant others the rights to reproduce the Artist's names, portraits, pictures and likenesses (including, without limitation, professional, group, or other assumed or fictitious names used by the Artist) on merchandise of any kind, without payment of additional compensation to you, the Artist, or any other Person. During the term of this agreement neither you nor Artist shall authorize any Person other than Major to use the name or likeness of Artist or any professional, group, or other assumed or fictitious name used by Artist, in connection with the advertising or sale of:

(a)   Phonograph Records; or

(b)   Blank recording tape or tape recording equipment.

The artist may not want to guarantee that he or she will be able to secure this information. The phrase "with artist's approval" should be added to the entire 8.01.
Also, any language that deals with merchandising, should be deleted. Merchandising should be dealt with as a third party contract or an outside deal. Although some record companies own merchandising companies, artists should ask

119

----

them to submit a deal as good as, and in the same form, as the best deal the artist is able to receive from an outside vendor, or in other words, the record company should have the right of first refusal on the merchandising of the artist's name and likeness.

8.02. You and the Artist will cooperate with Major, as it reasonably requests, in making photographs and preparing other materials for use in promoting and publicizing the Artist and the Recordings made under this agreement.

Several provisions normally found in this clause are not addressed and must be added. They are:

1.   The artist should specify exactly which "top line" label the record will be released on.

2.   "Coupling" (placing two different artists on the same album) restrictions should be addressed.

3.   Release commitments, both domestic (guaranteed releases within a certain time period) and foreign (with guarantees to release if domestic sales reach a certain amount), must be addressed.

4.   "Cutout" restrictions should be stated.

5.   Consultation on album cover artwork may also be negotiated.

9. ROYALTIES

9.01. Major will pay you a royalty computed at the applicable percentage, indicted below, of the applicable Royalty Base Price in respect of Net Sales of Phonograph Records (other than audiovisual Records) consisting entirely of Master Recordings recorded under this agreement and sold by Major or its Licensees Through Normal Retail Channels ("NRC Net Sales"):

"NRC Net Sales" in layman's terms is approximately the wholesale price.

(a)   <u>ON ALBUMS SOLD FOR DISTRIBUTION IN THE UNITED STATES</u>: 24%

The royalty rate pursuant to this subparagraph 9.01(a) will apply to the first 250,000 units of NRC Net Sales in the United States ("USNRC Net Sales") of each Album consisting of Master Recordings Delivered under this agreement. The royalty rate will be:

(1)   25%, rather than 24%, on the next 250,000 units of USNRC Net Sales of any such Album, and

(2)   26% on USNRC Net Sales of any such album in excess of 500,000 units.

(b)   <u>ON ALBUMS SOLD FOR DISTRIBUTION OUTSIDE THE UNITED STATES</u>:

(1)   18% on Albums sold for distribution in Canada and the United Kingdom;

(2)   16% on Albums sold for distribution in France, West Germany, Norway, Sweden, Denmark, Belgium, the Netherlands or Luxembourg; and

      (3)   12% on Albums sold for distribution elsewhere.

(c)   <u>ON SINGLES SOLD FOR DISTRIBUTION IN THE UNITED STATES</u>: 18%.

(d)   <u>ON SINGLES SOLD FOR DISTRIBUTION OUTSIDE THE UNITED STATES</u>:

      (1)   13.5% on Singles sold for distribution in Canada and the United Kingdom;

      (2)   12% on singles sold for distribution in France, West Germany. Norway, Sweden, Denmark, Belgium, the Netherlands or Luxembourg; and

      (3)   9% on Singles sold for distribution elsewhere.

9.01(a)&(b) state the royalty rate on albums sold. 9.01(c)&(d) state the royalty rate on singles. There is no provision for 12" singles, EP records., or for that matter CD singles. A provision should be added.

Noting that all numerical figures are negotiable, the rate of 24% may be negotiated to 26 or 27%.

Thirdly, raises in the rate are only tied to the number of units sold. Additional escalations should also be tied to the contract and option periods, so that when a new option period begins, it initiates a higher rate as well.

The royalty increase provisions of sections 9.01(a)(1) and (2) will not apply to any Recording not Delivered within the time prescribed for its Delivery in Article 3. Royalties on Records sold for distribution outside the United States will be computed on the basis or ninety percent (90%) of Net Sales.

The last sentence should be deleted and language should be inserted that allows negotiations to begin at a minimum level of 90%.

9.02. The royalty rate under paragraph 9.01 on Phonograph Records (other than audiovisual Records) sold through any Club Operation shall be seven percent (7%) and such royalties shall be computed on the basis of ninety percent (90%) of Net Sales of such Records. No royalty shall be payable with respect to (a) Phonograph Records received by members of any such club Operation in an introductory offer in connection with joining it or upon recommending that another join it or as a result of the purchase of a required number of Records including, without limitation, Records distributed as "bonus" or "free" Records, or (b) Phonograph Records for which such club Operation is not paid.

The 7% rate may be negotiated to a higher rate.

Secondly, a provision may be inserted that allows a percentage of "bonus" and "free" records to be accounted as records sold. There is the possibility that a hot album becomes one of the free introductory albums to hundreds of thousands of club members. The artist shouldn't be totally penalized for this.

9.03. The royalty rate on any Record described in clause (a), (b), or (c) of this sentence will be one-half (1/2) of the royalty rate that would apply if the Record concerned were sold through Normal Retail Channels: (a) any catalog Phonograph Record sold by Major's special products operations (hereafter, "CSP") to educational institutions or libraries, or to other CSP clients for their promotion or sales incentive purposes (but not for sale to the general public through normal retail channels); (b) any Record sold outside the United States by Major or its principal Licensee in the country concerned in conjunction with a television advertising campaign, during the calendar semiannual period in which that campaign begins or either of the next two (2) such periods; and (c) any non-catalog Phonograph Record created on a custom basis for computing royalties on any Records described in the preceding sentence. The royalty on any Record described in clause (c) will be computed on the basis of CSP's actual sales price less all taxes and Container Charges. In respect of any Master Recording leased by Major to others for their distribution of Phonograph Records in the United States, Major will pay you fifty percent (50%) of Major's net receipts form its Licensee. ("Net receipts", in the preceding sentence, means receipts as computed after deduction of all copyright, AFM and other applicable third party payments.) If another artist, a producer, or any other Person is entitled to royalties on sales of such Records, that payment will be divided among you in the same ratio as that among your respective basic royalty percentage rates.

This clause establishes the rate on special products to special customers.

9.04. (a) The royalty rate on any Budget Record, any Record bearing a Reissue label, any Multiple Record Set, any Record sold for distribution through military exchange channels, or any "picture disc" (i.e., a disc phonorecord with artwork reproduced on the surface of the Record itself) will be one-half (1/2) of the applicable royalty rate prescribed in paragraph 9.01. The royalty rate on any Record which is not an Album or a Single (for example , a twelve inch "dance single") will be one half (1/2) of the applicable Album royalty rate prescribed in paragraph 9.01. The royalty rate on any Audiophile Record other than a digital "compact disc" as that term is generally understood in the recording industry ("CD") will be one-half (1/2) of the rate which would otherwise be applicable under this agreement. Sections 9.01(a)(1) and (2) will not apply in computing royalties on any Records described in this subparagraph.

Language pertaining to multiple record sets, twelve inch dance singles should be pulled out and negotiated separately as two different items.

(b)   For any Album delivered during the initial Contract Period or the First Option Period, the royalty on any CD will be the amount of money equal to the royalty applicable in the territory concerned to:

(1)   A Standard disc unit of the same Record release; or

(2)   a standard tape unit of the same Record release, if no Standard disc version of it is in the active catalog of Major (or its principal Licensee in that territory).

For any Album delivered during the Second Option Period or thereafter, the royalty rate on any CD will be sixty-five percent (65%) of the applicable Album royalty rate prescribed in paragraph 9.01. Sections 9.01(a)(1) and (2) will not apply in computing royalties on any Records described in this subparagraph.

9.04(b) deals with CD product. It states that royalties form the sale of CDs during the second option period will be at 65% of the _album_ rate. This is absurd and because the CD is THE format of choice. Many record companies are now considering CD sales based on CD wholesale price not album retail price. At the very least, the 65% should be negotiated higher.

(c)   Notwithstanding anything to the contrary contained in this agreement, the royalty rate for each country in respect of net sales through normal retail channels of copies of any record in any New Medium shall be seventy percent (70%) of the royalty rate applicable to the first net sale of such record through normal retail channels in the applicable country pursuant to this agreement.

In this clause the company is protecting itself from being omitted from an new "way" to receive product. The 70% can be negotiated.

(d)   With respect to records in any form, configuration, format or technology not herein described, which is now known but not widely distributed or which hereafter becomes known ("New Technology Configurations"), the royalty rate payable shall be seventy-five (75%) percent of the applicable rates therefore mentioned in this agreement. At ARTIST's request, at any time during the TERM but subsequent to the date three (3) years form the date of COMPANY's initial commercial release in the United States of records embodying masters recorded and delivered hereunder in a particular New Technology Configuration, COMPANY shall review the royalty computation applicable to future sales of records in such particular New Technology

Configuration, which review will be in the light of then-current industry practices and COMPANY'S then current policies regarding the computation of royalties payable in respect of such particular New Technology Configuration.

With respect to the cost of manufacturing new configurations, the company is again creating a cushion for itself. The 75% rate is the protection. If the artist wants the rate to be recalculated s/he must notify *the company of his/her desire, and can only do this after an initial three year period.*

9.05. In respect of Phonograph Records derived from Master Recordings leased or otherwise furnished by Major's Licensees to others for their manufacture and distribution of Records outside the United States, Major will pay you one-half (1/2) of the amount which would be payable to you if Major or its Licensees manufactured and distributed such Records.

Change "one-half (1/2) of the amount which would be payable to you if Major or its Licensees manufactured and distributed such Records" to "50% of the net receipts derived from the transaction." There is no reason why the royalty must be linked to an amount if the record company or its affiliate manufactured and distributed the product.

9.06. Major will pay you royalties as follows in connection with the following uses of Covered Videos:

(a)   Major will pay you a royalty computed and adjusted in accordance with this Article 9, but at the following percentage rates instead of those specified in paragraphs 9.01 and 9.02, on Net Sales of audiovisual Phonograph Records which contain Covered Videos and are manufactured and distributed by Major Records in the United States or by components of Major Records International ("MRI", below) elsewhere.

9.06 is the section that discusses the use of video in sync with recorded music. Major will pay a royalty based on "net sales" in the U.S., or by components of Major outside the U.S.

(1)   <u>ON UNITS DISTRIBUTED IN THE UNITED STATES THROUGH CHANNELS OTHER THAN CLUB OPERATIONS</u>: ten percent (10%) on videodisc units and seven and one-half (7.5%) on videocassettes and all other audiovisual Records.

The artist may want to try to raise both rates to 15% or higher.

(2)   <u>ON UNITS DISTRIBUTED OUTSIDE THE UNITED STATES THROUGH CHANNELS OTHER THAN CLUB OPERATIONS</u>: seven and one-half percent (7.5%) on videodisc units and five percent (5%) on videocassettes and all other audiovisual Records.

The artist may want to try to raise both of these rates to 10% or higher.

(3)   <u>ON UNITS DISTRIBUTED THROUGH CLUB OPERATIONS</u>: The lower of: (i) fifty percent (50%) of the applicable rate prescribed in section 9.06(a)(1) or section 9.06(a)(2); <u>or</u> (ii) ten percent (10%) of the Club Operation's selling price.

For the purposes of this paragraph: (A) Audiovisual records manufactured by Major Records or components or MRI include only Records which are manufactured for the account of Major Records or the component concerned; they do not include Records which are manufactured for the account of anyone else, even though they may be manufactured under rights derived from Major Records or a component of MRI or distributed by Major Records or a component of MRI; and (B) a "Component" or MRI means a subsidiary of Major Inc. which engages in the Phonograph Record business outside the United States, or an affiliate of Major Inc. (including a joint venture in which it or any of its subsidiaries participates) which is its principal licensee for the distribution of Phonograph Records, other than audiovisual Records, in a particular territory. (For example: audiovisual Records manufactured for the account of The Major/Bingo Company are not Records manufactured by Major Records or a component of MRI, and are not subject to this subparagraph 9.06(a), even though they may be manufactured under rights derived by The Major/Bingo Company from Major Records or distributed by Major Records or a component of MRI under arrangement with The Major/Bingo company. Audiovisual Records manufactured for the account of Major/Minor Inc. and distributed by it are subject to this subparagraph 9.06(a).

(b)   (1)   (i)   Major will pay you a royalty as provided in this subparagraph 9.06(b) (the "Net Receipts Royalty", below) on all uses of a Covered Video which produce revenues directly for Major Records, except the uses described in subparagraph 9.06(a).

(ii)   The Net Receipts Royalty will be the amount equal to the same percentage of Major's Net Receipts (defined below) as the percentage rate used to calculate your royalty on Albums sold for distribution in the country concerned under section 9.01(a)(1) or section 9.01(b)(1). Sections 9.01(a)(1) and (2) will not apply in computing the Net Receipts Royalty under this subsection 9.06(b)(1)(ii).

Many artist attorneys negotiate to strike this entire section and replace it with the following: "The Net Receipts Royalty will be the amount equal to 50% of Major's Net Receipts which are defined below."

(iii)   The uses on which the Net Receipts Royalty will be payable include, without limitation, uses on audiovisual Records manufactured for distribution by divisions and components of Major Inc. or ventures in which Major Inc. participates, other than those specified in the first sentence of subparagraph 9.06(a). Uses of a Covered Records (for example, telecasting for promotional purposes without payment of a license fee to Major Records) will not be deemed revenue-producing uses for which royalties will be payable to you, even though those uses may result in indirect financial benefit to Major Records or generate direct revenues for the users (including other components of Major Inc.)

(2)   "Gross Receipts", in this subparagraph 9.06(b), means all moneys actually earned and received by Major Records directly from the exploitation of Covered Videos described in subsection 9.06(b)(1)(i). "Net Receipts" means Gross Receipts, after deduction and recoupment by Major of all expenses, taxes, and adjustments incurred in connection with the production of Covered Videos or the acquisition of rights in them, the exploitation of covered Videos described in subsection 9.06(b)(1)(i), or the collection and receipt of those Gross Receipts in the United States, and a distribution fee equal to thirty percent (30%) of those Gross Receipts. Any item of expenses which is actually recouped from Gross Receipts under this section will not be chargeable against royalties under paragraph 5.02. If any item of revenue or expenses is attributable to a Covered Video and to other audiovisual works, the amount of that item includable in Gross Receipts or deductible in computing Net Receipts will be determined by apportionment.

The artist may want to insert a statement that tells the record company that any money credited by a third party should have no bearing on the artist's financial arrangement in the event that the company has a deal with one of the artists. The artist may want negotiate to lower the distribution fee from the stated 30%.

(3)   If a use of a Covered Video on which a Net Receipts Royalty is payable under section 9.06(b)(1) is made by another division or component of Major Inc. or by a Major joint venture, Major Records' discretion in negotiating the amount of the compensation (if any) to be paid or credited to Major Records for that use and included in Gross Receipts will be conclusive, provided that amount is fair and reasonable under the circumstances. (The preceding sentence will apply whether or not the user derives revenues form the use, and the user's revenues will not be deemed Gross Receipts.) Any such amount will be deemed fair and reasonable if it is comparable to compensation then being negotiated by Major for comparable uses, or if Major notifies you that it proposes to agree to the amount concerned and you do not notify Major of your objection with five (5) business days. If you make any such objection you will also notify Major of your reasons for it and will negotiate with Major in good faith to resolve the difference if Major requests.

The artist may want to extend his or her opportunity to object to a time period longer than five (5) days.

(c)   The following amounts will be charged in reduction of all royalties payable or becoming payable to you in connection with Covered Videos under this paragraph 9.06:

(1)   All royalties and other compensation which may become payable to any Person, notwithstanding paragraphs 12.02 and 12.03, for the right to make any uses of copyrighted musical compositions in Covered Videos; and

There should be a provision added that covers the use of arrangements of public domain material. The artist may want to negotiate to capture 50% of the normal rate if indeed a Performing Rights Organization recognizes the material.

(2)   All Payments to record producers or other Persons which are measured by uses of Covered Videos or proceeds from those uses, whether such payments are to be computed as royalties on sales, as participation in

revenues, or in any other manner. (The amounts chargeable under the preceding sentence will not include non-contingent advances, but will include payments -- including payments in fixed amounts -- which accrue by reason that such sales, revenues, or other bases for computation attain particular levels.)

The artist may want to split this clause into two sections and add a sentence immediately before the parentheses. The new sentence may say "Fifty percent of all such payments which are attributable to the production of covered videos. Thus the artist and record share all costs on a 50-50 basis.

10. MISCELLANEOUS ROYALTY PROVISIONS

Notwithstanding anything to the contrary contained in Article 9:

10.01. In respect of Joint Recordings, the royalty rate to be used in determining the royalties payable to you shall be computed by multiplying the royalty rate otherwise applicable thereto by a fraction, the numerator of which shall be one and the denominator of which shall be the total number of royalty artists whose performances are embodied on a Joint Recording

10.02. The royalty rate on a Phonograph Record embodying Master Recordings made hereunder together with other Master Recordings will be computed by multiplying the royalty rate otherwise applicable by a fraction, the numerator of which is the number of Sides embodying Master Recordings made hereunder and the denominator or which is the total number of Sides contained on such Record. The royalty rate on an audiovisual Record containing a Covered Video and other audiovisual works will be determined by apportionment based on actual playing time of the Record concerned.

These two clauses that explain the specifics for joint recordings and coupling are standard and new artists usually accept the terms.

10.03. No royalties shall be payable to you in respect of Phonograph Records sold or distributed by Major or its Licensees for promotional purposes, as cutouts after the listing of such Records has been deleted from the catalog of Major or the particular Licensee, as "free," "no charge" or "bonus" Records (whether or not intended for resale), to Major employees and their relatives, or to radio stations. No royalties will be payable to you on "sampler" Records intended for free distribution to automobile purchasers and containing Recordings of not more than two (2) compositions made under this agreement.

11. ROYALTY ACCOUNTINGS

11.01. Major will compute your royalties as of each June 30th and December 31st for the prior six (6) months, in respect of each such six-month period in which there are sales or returns of Records, or Net Receipts derived from the exploitation of Covered Videos, on which royalties are payable to you. On the next September 30th or March 31st Major will send you a statement covering those royalties and will pay you any royalties which are due after deducting unrecouped Advances. Major will not act unreasonably in maintaining royalty reserves against anticipated returns and credits or anticipated payments referred to in subparagraph 9.06(c). If Major makes any overpayment to you, you will reimburse Major for it; Major may also deduct it from any payments due or becoming due to you. If Major pays you any royalties on Records which are returned later, those royalties will be considered overpayments.

This clause sets out the accounting periods of the royalty statements, in this case, semiannual periods. The royalty reserves are generally 50% and the artist should try to negotiate for reserves of under 50%, however, this could be difficult.
Language should be inserted that asks that reserves during one particular period be liquidated over the next four semiannual periods.

11.02. Sales of Records for distribution outside the United States are called "foreign sales" below. Major will compute your royalties for any foreign sale in the same national currency in which Major's Licensee pays Major for that sale, and Major will credit those royalties to your account at the same rate of exchange at which the Licensee pays Major. For purposes of accounting to you, Major will treat any foreign sale as a sale made during the same six-month period in which Major receives its Licensee's accounting and payment for that sale. If any Major Licensee deducts any taxes from its payments to Major, Major may deduct a proportionate amount of those taxes from your royalties. If any law, any government ruling, or any other restriction affects the amount of the payments which a Major Licensee can remit to Major, Major may deduct from your royalties an amount proportionate to the reduction in the Licensee's remittances to Major. If Major cannot collect payment for a foreign sale in the United States in U.S. dollars it will not be required to account to you for that sale.

Language should be inserted that asks that a foreign account be maintained in case payments are blocked by the government or for any reason.

11.03. Major will maintain books and records which report the sales of Phonograph Records, and the calculation of Net Receipts derived form the exploitation of Covered Videos, on which royalties are payable to you. You may, at you own expense, examine those books and records, as provided in this paragraph only. You may make those examinations only for the purpose of verifying the accuracy of the statements sent to you under paragraph 11.01. You may make such an examination for particular statement only once, and only within one year after the date when Major is required to send you that statement under 11.01. You may make those examinations only during Major's usual business hours, and at the place where it keeps the books and records to be examined. If you wish to make an examination you will be required to notify Major at least thirty (30) days before the date when you plan to begin it. Major may postpone the commencement of your examination by notices given to you not later than five (5) days before the commencement date specified in you notice; if it does so, the running of the time within which the examination may be made will be suspended during the postponement. If your examination has not been completed within one month from the time you begin it, Major may require you to terminate it on seven (7) days notice to you at any time; Major will not be required to permit you to continue the examination after the end of that seven-day period. You will not be entitled to examine any manufacturing records or any other records that do not specifically report sales or other distributions of Phonograph Records, or calculations of Net Receipts, on which royalties are payable to you. You may appoint a certified public accountant to make such an examination for you, but not if he or his firm has begun an examination of Major's books and records for any Person except you unless the examination has been concluded and any applicable audit issues have been resolved.

Several clauses may be inserted in 11.03. Language should be included that allows an accountant to postpone the examination of the artist's statements until he or she completes the present audit, should one be in progress.
The artist should negotiate for more time before the audit must begin, and less time to give notice.

11.04. If you have any objections to a royalty statement, you will give major specific notice of that objection and your reasons for it within one year after the date when Major is required to send you that statement under paragraph 11.01. Each royalty statement will become conclusively binding on you at the end of that one year period, and you will no longer have any right to make any other objections to it. You will not have the right to sue Major in connection with any royalty accounting, or to sue Major for royalties on Records sold or Net Receipts derived by Major during the period a royalty accounting covers, unless you commence the suit within that one year period. If you commence suit on any controversy or claim concerning royalty accountings rendered to you under this agreement, the scope of the proceeding will be limited to determination of the amount of the royalties due for the accounting periods concerned, and the court will have no authority to consider any other issues or award any relief except recovery of any royalties found owing. Your recovery of any such royalties will be the sole remedy available to you or the Artist by reason of any claim related to Major's royalty accountings. Without limiting the generality of the preceding sentence, neither you nor the Artist will have any right to seek termination of this agreement or avoid the performance of your obligations under it by reason of any such claim.

Negotiate to extend the time to voice an objection and bring suit. Also it should be made clear that the terms of this clause are as stated unless there is fraud (which means there was intent to deceive), then a legal suit would be filed that introduce other remedies.

12. LICENSES FOR MUSICAL COMPOSITIONS

12.01. (a)   (1)   You grant to Major an irrevocable license, under copyright, to reproduce each Controlled Composition on Phonograph Records other than audiovisual Records, and to distribute them in the United States and Canada.

(2)   For that license, Major will pay Mechanical royalties, on the basis of Net Sales, at the following rates:

(i)   <u>On Records manufactured for distribution in the United States:</u> The rate equal to seventy-five percent (75%) of the minimum compulsory license rate applicable to the use of musical compositions on phonorecords under the United States copyright law on whichever of the following dates is the earlier:

12.01(a)(2)(i) discusses the minimum compulsory license rate that will be used to compute the mechanical royalty for a controlled composition (see definitions section). Actually there are two rates. One is based on a flat rate and the other is based on the length of the song. Therefore, the artist should urge the company to replace the word minimum with the word applicable. Also, unless there are at least two companies competing to sign the artist, the 75% will be nonnegotiable.

(A)   The date of commencement of recording of the Album project (or other recording project) concerned; or

The word commencement should be replaced with the word delivery. This allows an updated mechanical royalty rate (set periodically by the Copyright tribunal) to take effect.

        (B)   The date of expiration of the time within which the Recording concerned is required to be Delivered under Article 3.

(That minimum statutory rate is currently 6.95c per Composition.)

        (ii)   <u>On Records manufactured for distribution in Canada</u>: Two cents (2c) per composition.

The Mechanical Royalty on any Record described in paragraph 9.04 or sold through a club operation will be three-fourths (3/4) of the amount fixed above. If the Composition is an arranged version of a public domain work, the Mechanical Royalty on it will be half of the amount fixed in clause (i) or clause (ii) above. No Mechanical Royalties will be payable for any Records described in paragraph 10.03.

Language may be inserted that states that the rate will be 75% of the applicable Canadian rate, but not less than 2c. Also, if the composition is an arranged version of a public domain work and ASCAP,BMI, or SESAC credits the arrangement with a performance credit, then a mechanical royalty should also be credited.

(b)   The total Mechanical Royalty for all Compositions on any Album, including Controlled Compositions, will be limited to ten (10) times the amount which would be payable on it under section 12.01(a)(2) if it contained only one Controlled Composition. The total Mechanical Royalty on any Single will be limited to twice that amount. The total Mechanical Royalty on any Record which is not an Album or a single will be limited to three (3) times that amount.

Language must be inserted that deals with extended play records (EPs). The total mechanical royalty should be limited to five (5) times that amount.

(c)   Major will compute Mechanical Royalties on controlled compositions as of the end of each calendar quarter-annual period in which there are sales or returns of Records on which Mechanical Royalties are payable to you. On the next May 15th , August 15th, November 15th, or February 15th, Major will send a statement covering those royalties and will pay any net royalties which are due. Mechanical

Royalty reserves maintained by Major against anticipated returns and credits will not be held for an unreasonable period of time; retention of a reserve for two (2) years after it is established will not be considered unreasonable in any case. If Major makes any overpayment of Mechanical Royalties to any Person you will reimburse Major for it; Major may also recoup it from any payments due or becoming due to you. If Major pays any Mechanical Royalties on Records which are returned later, those royalties will be considered overpayments. If the total amount of the Mechanical Royalties which Major plays on any Record consisting of Master Recordings made under this agreement (including Mechanical Royalties for compositions which are not Controlled Compositions) is higher than the limit fixed for that Record under subparagraph 12.01(b), that excess amount will be considered any overpayment also. Paragraphs 11.03 and 11.04 will apply to Mechanical Royalty accountings.

Retention of a reserve may be replaced with an established rate no less favorable than one established with the Harry Fox Agency." This would be a compromise.
Also, a phrase should be added that asks the record company to pay mechanical royalties on 50% of records distributed as free records. Obviously, this would be difficult to negotiate for a new artist.

12.02. You also grant to Major an irrevocable license under copyright to reproduce each controlled composition in motion pictures and other audiovisual works ("pictures"), to reproduce those pictures, distribute them, and perform them in any manner (including, without limitation, publicly and for profit) to manufacture and distribute audiovisual Records and other copies of them, and to exploit them otherwise, by any method and in any form known now or in the future, throughout the world, and to authorize others to do so. Major will not be required to make any payment in connection with those uses, and that license will apply whether or not Major receives any payment in connection with any use of any picture.

The terms of the entire section should be limited to Covered Videos only.

12.03. (a)   If any Recordings made under this agreement contain copyrighted Compositions which are not Controlled Compositions, you will obtain licenses covering those compositions for Major's benefit on the same terms as those which apply to Controlled Compositions under this Article 12, if Major so requests.

An artist may temper this by inserting "you will use your best efforts to obtain licenses."

(b)   You will cause the issuance of effective licenses, under copyright and otherwise, to reproduce each Controlled Composition on Phonograph Records and distribute those Records outside the United States and Canada, on terms not less favorable to Major or its Licensees than the terms most general basis in the country concerned with respect to the use of musical compositions on Standard Records.

12.04. You warrant and represent that the "Schedule of Publishers" appended to this agreement is a complete list of the music publishers in which you or the Artist has a direct or indirect interest. Your will notify Major promptly of each additional music publisher in which you or the Artist acquire any such interest and of every other change required to keep the list currently accurate.

12.05. Neither you nor the Artist, nor any person deriving rights from you or the Artist, will authorize the use of any Controlled Composition in a radio or television commercial or any other advertising or promotional matter without Major's prior written consent, which it may withhold in its sole discretion. If you or the Artist, or any Person deriving rights from either you or the Artist, shall determine to grant any rights in any Controlled Composition to any music publisher or any other Person or to authorize the use of any music or lyrics written by you or the Artist in a Composition together with material written by anyone else, or if you or the Artist shall determine to collaborate with any other Person in the authorship of any Composition, you will first require the other Parties to the transaction or collaboration concerned to enter into a written agreement, for Major's benefit, requiring compliance with this paragraph. You will furnish Major with a copy of each such agreement.

This clause sets out the use of any Controlled Composition in a commercial. There has been trouble recently with the use of "sound-alike" artists being mistaken by the public as the actual artist, so the record company does not want the compositions licensed to any publishers and a "sound-alike" versions is then made. The remainder of the clause is standard for a new artist.

13. <u>WARRANTIES; REPRESENTATIONS; RESTRICTIONS; INDEMNITIES</u>

13.01. You warrant and represent:

(a)   You have the right and power to enter into and fully perform this agreement.

(b)   Major shall not be required to make any payments of any nature for, or in connection with, the acquisition, exercise or exploitation of rights by Major pursuant to this agreement except as specifically provided in this agreement.

(c)   The Artist is or will become and will remain, to the extent necessary to enable the performance of this agreement, a member in good standing of all labor unions or guilds, membership in which may be lawfully required for the performance of Artist's services hereunder.

(d)   No Materials, as hereinafter defined, or any use thereof, will violate any law or infringe upon or violate the rights of any Person. "Materials," as used in this Article, means:

(1)   all Controlled Compositions,

(2)   each name used by the Artist, individually or as a group, in connection with Recordings made hereunder, and (3) all other musical, dramatic, artistic and literary materials, ideas, and other intellectual properties, furnished or selected by you, the Artist or any Producer and contained in or used in connection with any Recordings made hereunder or the packaging, sale, distribution, advertising, publicizing or other exploitation.

(e)   No Person other than Major has any right to use any existing Master Recordings of the Artist's performances for making, promoting, or marketing Phonograph Records.

Add the sentence "Except those listed below:" and then list all prior recordings made for other record companies, as the artist may have recorded for another label.

13.02. (a)   During the term of this agreement:

(1)   Neither you nor the Artist will enter into any agreement which would interfere with the full and prompt performance of your obligations hereunder, and you will fully and promptly perform your obligations to the Artist;

Change the word "would" in sentence two to "will". The word would implies "might" and the word will implies the present.

(2)   No Person other than Major will be authorized to use any existing Master Recordings of the Artist's performances for making, promoting, or marketing Phonograph Records; and

Insert a sentence that allows any previous record companies to use the recording they own.

(3)   The Artist will not perform or render any services, as performing artist, a producer, or otherwise, for the purpose of making, promoting, or marketing Master Recordings or Phonograph Records for any Person except Major.

The purpose of this clause is to prevent the artist from being a featured artist on a record that is not his or her own. However it also prevents the artist from acting as a sideman or a producer and should be negotiated out of the contract.

(b)   (1)   A "restricted Composition", for the purposes of this paragraph, is a Composition which shall have been recorded by the artist for a Master Recording made or delivered to Major under this agreement or any other agreement with Major.

The last six words of this clause should be negotiated out of the contract entirely.

(2)   Neither you nor the Artist will authorize or knowingly permit the Artist's performance of any restricted Composition or any adaptation of a restricted Composition to be recorded for any Person except Major for the purpose of making Master Recordings or Phonograph Records, or for any other purpose (including, without limitation , radio or television commercials), at any time before the later of the following dates: (i) the date five (5) years after the date of Delivery to Major of all the Master Recordings made in the course of the same Album (or other) recording project as the Recording of the restricted composition concerned, or (ii) the date two (2) years after the expiration of the term of this agreement.

(c)   Neither you nor the Artist shall authorize or knowingly permit the Artist's performances to be recorded for any purpose without an express written agreement with the Person for whom the recording is to be made, for Major's benefit, prohibiting the use of such recording for making, promoting, or marketing Master Recordings or Phonograph Records in violation of the restrictions prescribed in subparagraphs 13.02(a) and 13.02(b). You will furnish Major with a fully executed counterpart of each such agreement promptly after its execution.

13.03. If you or Artist become aware of any unauthorized recording, manufacture, distribution, sale, or other activity by any third party contrary to the restrictions in this agreement, you and Artist will notify Major of it and will cooperate with Major in any action or proceeding Major commences against such third party.

13.04. (a)   During the term of this agreement the Artist will not render any musical performance (audiovisual or otherwise) for the purpose of making any motion picture or other audiovisual work ("picture", below) for any Person other than Major, and no Person other than Major will be authorized to produce, distribute, exhibit, or otherwise exploit any picture which contains any musical performance (audiovisual or otherwise) by the Artist, without an express written agreement providing that:

(1)   the picture concerned will not contain performances by the Artist of more than two (2) musical compositions, in whole or in part; and

(2)   not more than one-half (1/2) of any version of the picture may consist of featured musical performances (defined below) by the Artist or anyone else.

(b)   "Featured musical performance", in this paragraph, means:

(1)   any visual performance of a musical composition; and

(2)   Any background performance of a musical composition which is intended as a focus of audience attention, whether or not the visual matter is related dramatically to the lyrics or concept of the musical composition.

13.05. There is no paragraph 13.05.

13.06. The services of the Artist are unique and extraordinary, and the loss therefore cannot be adequately compensated in damages, and Major shall be entitled to injunctive relief to enforce the provisions of this agreement.

In this clause, insert the word "seek," before "injunctive relief ..."

13.07. You will at all times indemnify and hold harmless Major and any Licensee of Major from and against any and all claims, damages, liabilities, costs and expenses, including legal expenses and reasonable counsel fees, arising out of any breach or alleged breach by you of any warranty or representation made by you in this agreement. Pending the resolution of any claim in respect of which Major is entitled to be indemnified, Major will not withhold monies which would otherwise be payable to you under this agreement in an amount exceeding your potential liability to Major under this paragraph.

Insert language that states to the record company that only if the claim becomes an action should a reasonable amount of money be withheld.
Also, in line five, negotiate the words "or alleged breach" out of the clause.

----

14. DEFINITIONS

14.01. "Master Recording" - every recording of sound, whether or not coupled with a visual image, by any method and on any substance or material, whether now or hereafter known, which is used or useful in the recording, production and/or manufacture of Phonograph Records.

14.02. "Inception of Recording" - the first recording of performances or other sounds with a view to the eventual fixation of a Master Recording. "Master Recordings from the Inception of Recording" include, without limitation, all rehearsal recordings, "outtakes", and other preliminary or alternate versions of sound recordings which are created during the production of Master Recordings made under this agreement.

14.03. "Matrix" - any device now or hereafter used, directly or indirectly, in the manufacture of Phonograph Records and which is derived from a Master Recording.

14.04. "Person" and "Party" - any individual , corporation, partnership, association or other organized group of persons or legal successors or representatives of the foregoing.

14.05. "Records" and "Phonograph Records" - all forms of reproductions, now or hereafter known, manufactured or distributed primarily for home use, school use, jukebox use, or use in means of transportation, including Records of sound alone and audiovisual Records.

14.06. "Royalty Base Price" - the amount specified below ("Gross Royalty Base") applicable to the Phonograph Records concerned, less all taxes and less the applicable Container Charge. The Royalty Base Price for Records sold through any Club Operation will be the same as that for the identical Records Sold Through Normal Retail Channels in the territory concerned.

    (a)   WITH RESPECT TO RECORDS (INCLUDING AUDIOVISUAL RECORDS) SOLD FOR DISTRIBUTION IN THE UNITED STATES OR CANADA: The Gross Royalty Base is Major's published subdistributor price applicable to the price series of the unit concerned at the commencement of the accounting period in which the sale occurs, less ten percent (10%). Royalties will abdicated separately with respect to each price series in which units of a particular Record release are sold during the accounting period concerned.

    (b)   WITH RESPECT TO RECORDS (INCLUDING AUDIOVISUAL RECORDS) SOLD FOR DISTRIBUTION OUTSIDE OF THE UNITED STATES AND CANADA: The Gross Royalty base is the applicable amount specified in sections (1) through (3) below, in the country of sale (or section (4) below if it applies), at the commencement of the accounting period concerned, plus taxes:

(1) If a base intended as an equivalent of or substitute for an actual or hypothetical retail price ("Retail-related Base") is used for computing Mechanical Royalties on the Records concerned by agreement between Record manufacturers and a licensing organization, such as BIEM, the Gross Royalty Base will be one-half (1/2) of that base.

(2) If a majority of the major record companies in the country concerned use a different base for computing Mechanical Royalties (for example, a manufacturer's published price to dealers (p.p.d.")) adjusted by an "uplift" or other factor intended to convert it to a Retail-related Base and calculated on the basis of a industry-wide market survey, the Gross Royalty Base will be one-half (1/2) of Major's p.p.d. for the Records concerned, adjusted by the same conversion factor.

(3) If neither section (1) nor section (2) applies, the Gross Royalty Base will be one-half (1/2) of the base generally used by Major's principal Licensee in the country concerned to calculate the royalties it pays to recording artists.

(4) The Gross Royalty Base for a Record sold for distribution through military exchange channels is the amount prescribed in subparagraph 14.06(a).

14.07. "Container Charge" - The applicable percentage, specified below, of the Gross Royalty Base applicable to the Records concerned:

(a) Audiovisual Records - fifteen percent (15%).

(b) Audiophile Records - twenty-five percent (25%).

(c) Other Records - ten percent (10%) on disc Records and twenty percent (20%) on Records in non-disc configurations.

In this agreement, CD packaging would fall under (b) Audiophile Records.

14.08. "Net Sales" - eighty-five percent (85%) of gross sales, less returns, credits, and reserves against anticipated returns and credits.

14.09. "Club Operation" - any direct sales to consumers conducted by mail-order or on a membership basis (for example, sales through any record club in the United States or in Europe).

14.10. "Contract Period" - the initial period, or any option period, of the term hereof (as such periods may be suspended or extended as provided herein).

14.11. "Advance" - a prepayment of royalties, Major may recoup Advances from royalties to be paid to or on behalf of you or Artist pursuant to this or any other agreement, and from mechanical

_____

copyright royalties payable for the use of Controlled Compositions on Phonograph Records distributed by Major, subject to the next sentence. Not more than fifty percent (50%) of the aggregate amount of the motion picture production and acquisition costs referred to in subparagraph 5.02(a) may be recouped from your royalties on sales of Records which do not reproduce visual images ("audio royalties").

If the artist is acting as a producer of another act, this clause could be a problem. Strike the words "or any other agreement" from this clause. Should the producer perform on another artist's recording, the company could recoup advances.
Advances should not be recouped from mechanical royalties. You should try to negotiate this from the clause.

14.12. "Composition" - a single musical composition, irrespective of length, including all spoken words and bridging passages and including a medley,. Recordings of more than one arrangement or version of the same Composition, reproduced on the same Record will be considered, collectively, a recording of one Composition for all purposes under this agreement.

14.13. "Controlled Composition" - a Composition wholly or partly written, owned or controlled by you, the Artist, a Producer, or any Person in which you, the Artist, or a Producer has a direct or indirect interest.

14.14. (a) "Album" - one or more twelve inch 33 1/3 rpm Records, or the equivalent, at least thirty-five (35) minutes in playing time, sold in a single package. (b) "Single" - a disc Record not more than seven (7) inches in diameter, or the equivalent in a non-disc configuration. (Audiovisual Records are not Albums or singles.)

The definitions for a 12 inch single and an EP recording should be added to this clause.

14.15. "Side" - A Master Recording of a continuous performance of a particular arrangement or version of a composition, not less than two and one quarter (2 1/4) minutes in playing time. If any Album or other group of Master Recordings) Delivered to Major in fulfillment of a Recording Commitment expressed as a number of Sides includes Master Recordings of more than one arrangement or version of any Composition, all those Recordings will be deemed to constitute one Side.

14.16. "Joint Recording" -any Master Recording embodying the Artist's performance and any performance by another artist with respect to which Major is obligated to pay royalties.

14.17. "Sales Through Normal Retail Channels" - sales other than as described in paragraphs

9.02, 9.03, 9.05, 9.06, and 10.03.

14.18. "Licensees" - includes, without limitation, subsidiaries, wholly or partly owned, and other divisions of Major Inc.

14.19. "Delivery", when used with respect to Master Recordings - means the actual receipt by Major's A&R Administration Department of the Master Recordings concerned and all documents and other materials required to be furnished to major in connection with them. Without limiting the generality of the preceding sentence, no Master Recordings will be deemed Delivered until Major has received all of the related documentation required under subparagraphs 4.01(c) and 4.01(e) and all other material referred to in paragraph 4.01(f).

14.20. "Reissue Label" - A label, used primarily for reissues of recordings released previously.

14.21. "Budget Record" - A Record, whether or not previously released, bearing a Gross Royalty Base at least one dollar ($1.00) lower (if it is manufactured for distribution in the United States or Canada), or twenty percent (20%) lower (if it is manufactured for distribution elsewhere), than the Gross Royalty Base applicable to the Top Line Records in the same configuration (e.g., long-playing album, two-disc long-playing album, twelve inch single, tape cassette, compact disc, etc.) released by Major or its Licensees in the territory concerned. A "Top Line" Record release is one bearing the same Gross Royalty Base as the majority (or Plurality) of the Record Releases (other than classical releases) in the same configuration then in initial release in Major's active catalog. (For the purposes of the preceding sentence, a Record release will not be deemed in its initial release if it bears a Gross Royalty Base lower than that which applied to it when it was first released by Major.)

14.22. "Multiple Record Set" - An Album containing two (2) or more 12inch 33 1/3rpm Records packaged as a single unit, or the equivalent.

14.23. "Mechanical Royalties" - royalties payable to any Person for the right to reproduce and distribute copyrighted musical compositions on Phonograph Records other than audiovisual Records.

14.24. "Recording Costs" - all amounts representing direct expenses paid or incurred by Major in connection with the production of finished Master Recordings under this agreement. Recording Costs include, without limitation, the amounts referred to in paragraph 5.01, travel, rehearsal, and equipment rental expenses, advances to producers, studio and engineering charges in connection with Major's facilities and personnel or otherwise, all costs of mastering, remastering, and remixing, and the costs of lacquer, copper, and other equivalent masters.

14.25. "Special Packaging Costs" - include, without limitation, all costs incurred by Major in creating and producing Album covers, sleeves, and other packaging elements prepared from material furnished by you or the Artist or used at your request, in excess of the following amounts: (a) two thousand five hundred dollars ($2,500) per Album for design of artwork (including expenses for reproduction rights); (b) one thousand six hundred dollars ($1,600) per Album for engraving; (c) packaging manufacturing costs of twenty-one cents (21c) per long-playing disc Album unit, twenty-two cents (22c) per tape cassette Album unit (including the cost of the "C-O" cassette housing), and sixty-six cents (66c) per compact disc Album unit, for Albums manufactured for distribution in the United States or Canada; and (d) for Albums in those configurations manufacturing costs incurred by Major or the Major Licensee concerned for Albums; manufactured in the same territory as the Album units concerned.

These costs should be tied into cost changes in another industry. Insert here that all these prices will fluctuate with a manufacturing producer price index or some objective price index.

14.26. (a) "<u>Audiophile</u>" Records, units, etc. - Records (other than audiovisual Records) marketed in specially priced catalog series by reason of their superior sound quality or other distinctive technical or artistic characteristics. (All Records made for digital Playback are Audiophile Records.)

(b) "<u>Standard</u>" Records, units, etc. - Records other than Audiophile Records and audiovisual Records.

14.27. "<u>Covered Video</u>" - An audiovisual work owned or controlled by Major and containing a Master Recording made under this agreement.

15. <u>REMEDIES</u>

15.01. If you do not fulfill any portion of your Recording commitment within the time prescribed in Article 3, Major will have the following options:

In line two, insert an actual prescribed and agreed upon time period.

(a)   to suspend Major's obligations to make payments to you under this agreement until you have cured the default;

(b)   to terminate the term of this agreement at any time, whether or not you have commenced curing the default before such termination occurs; and

(c)   to require you to repay to Major the amount, not then recouped, of any Advance previously paid to you by Major and not specifically attributable under Article 6 to an Album which has actually been fully Delivered.

Major may exercise each of those options by sending you the appropriate notice, If Major terminates the term under clause 15.01(b) all Parties will be deemed to have fulfilled all of their obligations under this agreement except those obligations which survive the end of the term (such as indemnification obligations, re-recording restrictions, and your obligations under clause 15.01(c).) No exercise of an option under this paragraph will limit Major's rights to recover damages by reason of your default, its rights to exercise any other option under this paragraph, or any of its other rights.

15.02. If Major refuses without cause to allow you to fulfill your Recording commitment for any contract Period and if, not later than sixty (60) days after that refusal takes place, you notify Major of your desire to fulfill such Recording Commitment, then Major shall permit you to fulfill said Recording commitment by notice to you to such effect within sixty (60) days of Major's receipt of your notice, Should Major fail to give such notice, you shall have the option to terminate the term of this agreement by notice given to Major within thirty (30) days after the expiration of the latter sixty-day period; on receipt by Major of such notice the term of this agreement shall terminate and all parties will be deemed to have fulfilled all of their obligations hereunder except those obligations which survive the end of the term (e.g., warranties, re-recording restrictions and obligation to pay royalties), at which time Major shall pay you at the applicable minimum union scale rate in full settlement of its obligation in connection therewith, which payment shall constitute an Advance. In the event you fail to give Major either notice within the period specified therefore, Major shall be under no obligation to you for failing to permit you to fulfill such Recording Commitment.

15.03. If because of: act of God; inevitable accident; fire; lockout, strike or other labor dispute; riot or civil commotion; act of public enemy; enactment, rule, order or act of any government or governmental instrumentality (whether federal, state, local or foreign); failure of technical facilities, failure or delay of transportation facilities; illness or incapacity of any performer or producer; or other cause of a similar or different nature not reasonably within Major's control; Major is materially hampered in the recording, manufacture, distribution or sale of records, then, without limiting Major's rights, Major shall have the option by giving you notice to suspend the running of the then current Contract Period for the duration of any such contingency plus such additional time as is necessary so that Major shall have no less than thirty (30) days after the cessation of such contingency in which to exercise its option, if any, to extend the term of this agreement for the next following Option Period.

16. AGREEMENTS, APPROVAL & CONSENT

16.01. As to all matters treated herein to be determined by mutual agreement, or as to which any approval or consent is required, such agreement, approval or consent will not be unreasonably withheld.

16.02. Your agreement, approval or consent, or that of the Artist, whenever, required, shall be deemed to have been given unless you notify Major otherwise within ten (10) days following the date of Major's written request to you therefore.

17. NOTICES

17.01. Except as otherwise specifically provided herein, all notices hereunder shall be in writing and shall be given by personal delivery, registered or certified mail or telegraph (prepaid), at the addresses shown above, or such other address or addresses as may be designated by either Party. Notices shall be deemed given when mailed or when transmitted by telegraph, except that notice of change of address shall be effective only from the date of its receipt. Each notice sent to Major shall be directed to its Senior Vice-President, Business Affairs & Administration, and a copy of each such notice shall be sent simultaneously to Major Law Department, 000 Zero Street, Anywhere, USA, Attention: Associate General Counsel, Records Section.

> *Insert in 17.01 that a courtesy copy of all notices by sent directly to the artist's attorney. Also, in line eight, extend the time for mailing.*

18. EVENTS OF DEFAULT

18.01. In the event of your dissolution or the liquidation of your assets, or the filing by or against you of a petition for liquidation or reorganization under Title 11 of the United States Code as now or hereafter in effect or under any similar statute relating to insolvency, bankruptcy, liquidation or reorganization, or in the event of the appointment of a trustee, receiver or custodian for you or for any property, or in the event that you shall make an assignment for the benefit of creditors or commit any act for or in bankruptcy or become insolvent, or in the event you shall fail to fulfill any of any such event, in addition to any other remedies which any be available, Major shall have the option by notice to require that the Artist render his personal services directly to it for the remaining balance of the term of this agreement, including any extensions, for the purpose of making Master Recordings, upon the same terms and conditions, including, without limitation, Articles 3 and 9.

You will notify Major promptly of the occurrence of any event described in the paragraph the Artist shall be deemed substituted for you as a Party to this agreement as of the date of Major's option exercise, and, in respect of Master Recordings of the Artist's performances recorded subsequently, the royalties and any Advances payable hereunder shall be reduced to two-thirds (2/3) of the amounts prescribed in this agreement and, as so adjusted, will be payable to the Artist, subject to recoupment of all Advances.

On line ten, delete the word "your" as material obligations should be met.

19.02. Major will have the right, throughout the term of this agreement, to obtain or increase insurance on the life of the Artist in such amounts as Major determines, in Major's name and for its sole benefit or otherwise, in its discretion. The Artist will cooperate in such physical examination, supply such information, and sign such documents, and otherwise will cooperate fully with Major, as Major may request in connection with any such insurance, You and the Artist warrant and represent that, to your best knowledge, the Artist is in good health and does not suffer from any medical condition which might interfere with the timely performance of your obligations under this agreement.

19.03. (a) This agreement contains the entire understanding of the Parties relating to its subject matter. No change or termination of this agreement will be binding upon Major unless it is made by an instrument signed by an officer of Major. A waiver by either Party of any provision of this agreement in any instance shall not be deemed to waive it for the future. All remedies, right, undertakings, and obligations contained in this agreement are included for convenience only and will not affect the interpretation of any provision.

(b) No change of a budget prescribed in this agreement or established under it will be effective unless the change is approved in writing by Major's Senior Vice President, Business Affairs & Administration.

19.04. Those provisions of any applicable collective bargaining agreement between Major and any labor organization which are required, by the terms of such agreement, to be included in this agreement shall be deemed incorporated herein.

19.05. Major may assign its rights under this agreement in whole or in part.

Try to negotiate "with artist's approval" into this clause.
Also, add to this sentence "only to their affiliates or anyone who might buy the company."

19.06. Each option and election granted to Major in this agreement including, without limitation, to suspend the running of one or more periods of time, to terminate the term, to acquire the direct and individual services of leaving member (if a group artist is involved), or otherwise, is separate and distinct, and the exercise of any such option or election shall not operate as a waiver of any other option or election unless specifically so stated by Major in its notice of exercise of such option or election.

19.07. You shall not be entitled to recover damages or to terminate the term of this agreement by reason of any breach by Major of its material obligations hereunder, unless Major has failed to remedy such breach within a reasonable time following receipt of your notice thereof.

The words "within a reasonable time" should be modified with a clause that indicates that the record company will have a stated cure period of 30, 60, of 90 days, whichever is consistent with the rest of the contract.

19.08. This agreement has been entered into in the State of New York, and the validity, interpretation and legal effect of this agreement shall be governed by the laws of the State of New York applicable to contracts entered into and performed entirely within the State of New York. The New York courts (state and federal), only, will have jurisdiction of any controversies regarding this agreement; any action or other proceeding which involves such a controversy will be brought in those courts, in New York County, and not elsewhere. Any process in any such action or proceeding may, among other methods, be served upon you by delivering it or mailing it, by registered or certified mail, directed to the address first above written or such other address as you may designate pursuant to Article 17. Any such process, may among other methods, be served upon the Artist or any other Person who approves, ratifies, or assents to this agreement to induce Major to enter into it, by delivering the process or mailing it, by registered or certified mail, directed to the address first above written or such other address as the Artist or the other Person concerned may designate in the manner prescribed in Article 17. Any such delivery or mail service shall be deemed to have the same force and effect as personal service within the State of New York.

19.09. In entering into this agreement, and in providing services pursuant hereto, you and the Artist have and shall have the status of independent contractors and nothing herein contained shall contemplate or constitute you or the Artist as Major's agents or employees.

19.10. Monies to be paid to you under this agreement will not be assignable by you without Major's written consent, which Major may withhold in its unrestricted discretion.

19.11. This agreement shall not become effective until executed by all proposed parties hereto

19.12. Any and all riders annexed hereto together with this basic document shall be taken together to constitute the agreement between you and Major.

MAJOR RECORDS

By _____   My taxpayer

identification number (social security number or employer identification number) is_____ .
Under the penalties of perjury, I certify that this information is true, correct, and complete.

SCHEDULE OF PUBLISHERS
(appended in accordance with Article 12)

SUMMARY

1. A good artist-record company relationship is one of the most important business arrangements needed for success.

2. The record contract is one of the most important and complicated agreements in the industry.

3. An artist should not be expected to understand every clause of the contract.

4. The record contract must be negotiated for the artist by a competent music attorney.

5. Every item in a record contract should be considered negotiable, especially royalty rates.

6. Most new artists must settle for a contract less favorable to them than an established superstar.

7. In negotiations, a good rule-of-thumb to follow is, "if you don't ask for it, you won't get it."

PROJECTS

1.   Team up and perform mock negotiations.

2.   Find out if any bands you know have record contracts (even with small independent labels):

(A)   ask the band if they understood the terms when they signed

(B)   find out what they don't and do like about the contract

(C)   ask them what they would like to renegotiate if they were given the chance

(D)   ask to see the contract and compare the terms with the example in this chapter

(E)   renegotiate the contract for them explaining what you would insert or strike

3.   Research other agreements and compare their terms to the example in this chapter.

CHAPTER EIGHT

CARE AND FEEDING OF THE CREATIVE

BROWN'S "CONFUSIONAL MODEL OF CREATIVITY"

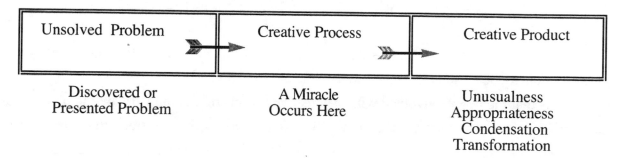

(Brown, Robert. "Confusional Model of Creativity". from Handbook of Creativity. Edited by Glover, Ronning, & Reynolds. Plenum Press, New York. 1989. pg. 30)

By the end of this chapter you should be able to:
1.   Discuss the characteristics of the creative process.
2.   List the traits of the creative person and the creative product.
3.   Discuss the factors that accompany age change that bring about a reduction in creativity.
4.   Describe some methods to evaluate creativity.
5.   Discuss the art and craft of songwriting.
6.   List the characteristics of a potentially successful song.
7.   Discuss how songwriters make money.
8.   When given a songwriter/publisher agreement, discuss the important clauses.
9.   Discuss the publisher's role in song exploitation.
10. List the six basic song uses that are revenue producing.
11. List the RIAA criteria for Gold and Platinum Video Awards.
12. Describe the first music videos and how they were presented.
13. Discuss the nonlinear concept of story evolution.
14. When given a recording contract, discuss the important issues of the video production clauses.
15. Discuss the differences among the live vs. audio vs. video media.
16. Discuss the role industry management should play in guiding creative talent.

THE CREATIVE PROCESS

Creativity itself is a quicksilver thing: an intangible, subjectively evaluated property, often purchased in commercial circles by the slightest whim or fancy." (Buxton, Edward. Creative People At Work. Executive Communications, Inc. N.Y. 1975 pg ix.)

How does it happen? Why do some people have it and others don't? What is the mystique about it? Can you learn to be creative? What's the big deal anyway?

The truth is that the people involved with the creative aspects of this industry are the highest paid. And one of the reasons they are the highest paid is because of the mystique that surrounds the creative process. Non-creative people find it magical that someone can be creative, a feat that is so superhuman that many will pay any price to be a part of the process.

Our creative thought is the function of the right hemisphere of the brain. The further to the "right" someone feels comfortable existing in, the more creative (but not necessarily useful), their output is. Accountants and scientists make daily use of the brain's left hemisphere. Because society has made laws and rules to govern its people, one must make use of the left side of the brain in order to survive. Supposedly, the more "centered" your are, the easier it is to cope with life's daily activities and the happier you are. Many creative people, (those who are rightsided), are uncomfortable making business decisions. They find it tedious and boring to constantly use the left side of their brain. Besides, it not as much fun. (This may be why so many entertainment attorneys are frustrated producers, songwriters, and musicians.)

This chapter explores the creativity as it pertains to this industry. It is divided into two sections, the creative process and the creative product. The areas investigated include: the creative personality; measuring creativity; and guiding the creative talent, followed by a detailed description of the industry's creative products.

Creative Traits

JACKSON AND MESSICK: FOUR CHARACTERISTICS OF CREATIVITY

Traits of the Person		Traits of the Product		
Intellectual Traits	Personal Traits	Product Properties	Standards	Reflective Reaction
1.Tolerance of Incongruity	Original	Unusualness	Norms	Surprise
2. Analysis and Intuition	Sensitive	Appropriateness	Context	Satisfaction
3. Open-mindedness	Flexible	Transformation	Constraint	Stimulation
4. Reflection & Spontaneity	Poetic	Condensation	Summary Power	Savoring

Source: Jackson and Messick. Copyright 1965 Duke University

Figure 8.1 John S. Dacey. Fundamentals of Creative Thinking. Lexington Books. Lexington, MA. 1989 pg. 7.

Figure 8.1, Jackson and Messick's "Four Characteristics of Creativity" illustrates attributes of creative people and their products. It is divided into two areas: "Traits of the Creative Person" and "Traits of the Creative Product." Intellectual traits of the creative person include being fearless of the unknown; being intuitive, open-minded, and spontaneous. Other personal traits of the creative personality include originality, sensitivity, and flexibility.

Accordingly, properties of the creative product are its unusualness, appropriateness, newness, and compactness. Jackson and Messick also say that our reaction to a truly creative product is one of surprise, satisfaction, and stimulation.[1]

In the music business, truly creative people are few in number. But many of the artists are truly creative, are sensitive, fearless, and willing to take risks. And if their products sell, they must satisfy a need.

Then what does the creative process entail? Well not only is it different for different people, but it is different for the same individual at different times. And there is never a guarantee that the result will be creative. In fact, the literature explains methods to help the creative process occur, but fails to agree on the contents of the process itself. Management must always be conscious of creating an environments that allows for the artist's own creative process to occur. (Further discussion appears later in this chapter).

The Creative Personality

"The creative person is commonly regarded as being filled with new ideas and projects; he views life from surprising perspectives, formulates problems contrary to what he has been told by parents and teachers, turns traditional and seemingly self-evident conceptions topsy-turvy, and wants to retest the validity of accepted truths."[2]

When creative people are described in the music business, such phrases as self-centered and ego driven are used. "According to psychologists, the general view is that creative people have a stronger, more pronounced sense of self. Call it ego, pride of authorship, or a larger-than-normal need for praise and approval."[3] One only needs to watch the annual telecast of the Grammy Awards presentation to agree.

Researchers have found the following characteristics (in one or more studies) to differentiate highly creative persons from less creative ones. Obviously with a list so long, one or several of these traits can be found in every entertainment artist. So the characteristics noted in **Bold** are frequently attributed to creative people in the music business.

1. **Accepts disorder**
2. **Adventurous**
3. **Strong affection**
4. Altruistic
5. Awareness of others
6. Always baffled by something
7. **Attracted to disorder**
8. **Attracted to mysterious**
9. Attempts difficult jobs
10. **Bashful outwardly**
11. Constructive in criticism
12. Courageous
13. Deep and conscientious   conventions
14. Defies conventions of courtesy
15. **Defies conventions of health**
16. Desires to excel
17. Determination
18. Differentiated value-hierarchy
19. Discontented
20. Disturbs organization
21. Dominant
22. **Emotional**
23. **Emotionally sensitive**
24. Energetic
25. A fault-finder
26. **Doesn't fear being thought as different**
27. **Feels whole parade is out of step**
28. Full of curiosity
29. Appears haughty and self-satisfied at times
30. **Likes solitude**
31. Independence in judgment
32. Independent in thinking
33. **Individualistic**
34. Intuitive
35. Industrious
36. Introversive
37. **Keeps unusual hours**
38. **Lack business ability**
39. Makes mistakes
40. Never bored
41. Nonconforming
42. Not hostile or negativistic
43. Not popular
44. **Oddities of habit**
45. Persistent
46. Becomes preoccupied with problem
47. Preference for complex ideas

48. Questioning
49. **Radical**
50. Receptive to external stimuli
51. Receptive to ideas of others
52. **Regresses occasionally**
53. Rejection of suppression as a mechanism of impulse control
54. Rejection of repression
55. Reserved
56. Resolute
57. Self-assertive
58. Self-aware
59. Self-starter
60. Self-confident
61. Self-sufficient
62. Sense of destiny
63. **Sense of humor**
64. Sensitive to beauty
65. Shuns power
66. Sincere
67. Not interested in small details
68. Speculative
69. Spirited in disagreement
70. Strives for distant goals
71. **Stubborn**
72. **Temperamental**
73. **Tenacious**
74. **Tender emotions**
75. Timid
76. Thorough
77. Unconcerned about power
78. Somewhat uncultured, primitive
79. Unsophisticated, naive
80. Unwilling to accept anything on mere say-so
81. Visionary
82. **Versatile**
83. **Willing to take risks**
84. **Somewhat withdrawn**

Figure 8.2. Paul E. Torrance. Guiding Creative Talent. Prentice-Hall Inc. Englewood Cliffs, NJ, 1962. Pg. 66-67.

Also, creative people think of themselves as special. Therefore, when there is a lack of recognition outside of their own community of peers, it leads many to frustration. People often say that creative people are very difficult to work with, and some creative people feel they are prisoners of the whims of their audience. Emotions run on high in this business and managers must deal with each artist accordingly.

Once You Have It, Do You Have It Forever

"Creativity is a cognitive, attitudinal, personal trait that every person has to some degree (unless in a coma or of very low intelligence)." [4]

The peripherals of music industry are filled with people who were "one hit wonders." Why can't the successes be easily repeated? Obviously there is no one answer. However there have been studies concerning, among other things, age and creative productivity. Lehman (1953) found that the greatest contributions to their field were made by musicians between the ages of thirty and forty. Lehman (1956) also pointed out that not age itself, but the factors that accompany **age change** bring about reduction in creative production.[5] Some of the general factors he found are listed in Figure 8.3.

1. A decline in physical vigor energy, and resistance to fatigue occur before the age of forty.
2. Sensory capacity and motor precision decline with age.
3. Serious illness and bodily infirmities have more negative effects on older than younger persons.
4. Creativity curves may be related to glandular changes.
5. Marital difficulties and sexual problems increase with age and may have a negative effect on creativity.
6. Indifference toward creativity may develop more frequently among older people because of the death of a loved one.
7. Older persons are more likely to be preoccupied with the practical demands of life.
8. Success, promotion, increased prestige, and responsibility may lead to less favorable conditions for concentrated work.
9. Having achieved these goals, those who desire prestige and recognition, rather than the creation of something new, strive less for achievement.
10. Easily won and early fame may lead to contentment with what has been done before accomplishing what could be the most creative work.
11. Nonrecognition and destructive criticism may lead to apathy of older workers.
12. Negative transfer, resulting in inflexibility, may be more of a handicap among older workers.
13. Older workers may become less motivated because of these factors.
14. Younger people may be better educated and have lived in more stimulating environments.
15. Psychoses, which occur more frequently in later life, may have clouded what was previously a brilliant mind.
16. Alcohol, narcotics, and such may have sapped an individual's productive power.

Figure 8.3. Paul E. Torrance. Guiding Creative Talent. Prentice-Hall Inc. Englewood Cliffs, NJ, 1962. Pg. 101-102.

So can you have it forever? Individuals are individuals and a general rule doesn't exist. However, as a word of caution, throughout history there have been few successful revolutionists over age forty.

Can It Be Taught?

"I think that talented, creative people are going to be successful anyway. I don't think a training program has anything to do with it."[6]

Unfortunately in areas that do not require a great deal of technique or prerequisite skills, the above quote is usually true. The craft of any creative endeavor (such as songwriting) can be learned, but learning the craft does not necessarily make someone successful. What can be taught is how to recognize creative uses of a craft, and exercises can be designed to practice those uses.

However, this is refining the craft not the art. Composers study the Mozart Symphonies to learn the mechanics of composing in the classical style, and to acknowledge the genius in Mozart's artistic use of the tools. Students then imitate the Mozart classical style to explore his techniques. With practice they improve, and the techniques of the style are learned. The craft is refined. Although there are rules that govern the use of certain notes, the artistry lies in the choice of notes. The notes are chosen from what the composer hears, and what is heard is an individual's choice. And that is where the creativity lies!

Evaluating Creativity

Can creativity be measured without measuring the creative product? How can the evaluation criterion derived? Are there critical factors? Who is qualified to do the measuring?

The literature does not agree on a method for evaluating creativity. Although most would agree that a quantitative measure alone, such as record sales, would do an injustice to a large amount of quality work, should a quantitative statistic play a role in the decision.

One method of measurement might be to identify creative people who are innovators by the number of representatives they spawn. For example, if someone decides to drive a car in reverse looking over his or her shoulder instead of in forward and no one chooses to pick up on the idea (the innovation) and drive like that (as a representative of the innovation), the original person who started driving in reverse would not be considered an innovator, but probably crazy! However, if several people liked the idea and started to drive in reverse, and then millions of people did, the innovator would be considered a genius. If the driving fad lasted two weeks and then someone began driving sideways, driving backwards would be considered part of the evolution of modern driving and a creative step in reaching the current state of driving practices. Because millions became users or representatives of the innovation, the innovator became recognized as highly creative. Therefore, using this logic, record sales as a quantitative measure, can be a valid part of the test for measuring creativity.

As a second example, if a composer composed a composition (an innovation) and no one ever performed it, it would not be considered a good work. However, if it received hundreds of performances (as representations) it would be.

A final definition of creativity, this one by Morris I. Stein reads, "Creativity is a process that results in a novel work that is accepted as useful, tenable, or satisfying by a significant group of people at some point in time."[7] Here Stein is including a quantitative measurement, by using the acceptance by a significant group of people, ie: record buyers or listeners.

THE CREATIVE PRODUCT

<u>Songwriting</u>

*"At the dawn of the century Chas K. Harris published a little red book of rules and
secrets called <u>How To Write A Popular Song</u>. To his readers he advised:
Look at newspapers for your story-line.
Acquaint yourself with the style in vogue.
Avoid slang.
Know the copyright laws."*[8]

Is it an art or a craft? Most debates settle with the compromise, "well it's both." This seems to be true as songwriting methods teach the mechanics of the craft but do not guarantee artistic or commercial acceptance. Some songs, such as Paul McCartney's "Yesterday", have great lyrics and a great melody, and others are successful because they fit the style that's in at the time (remember the big hit of the late 1970's "Shake Your Booty"). Concerning the craft, Harris gave very good advice. Most of what he said is still useful today.

In the Music Business Handbook, Baskerville suggests that if a song exhibits the following characteristics, it has very strong potential for making it in the marketplace:

1.   is memorable; it sticks in the mind. This is accomplished particularly by use of a "hook"

2.   has immediate appeal

3.   uses some kind of special imagery

4.   is well-crafted

5.   everything lyrical and musical holds to a central theme

6.   has an element of mystery[9]

Songwriting "how to" texts agree with Baskerville. There is a method to learning the craft, but creating hits cannot be guaranteed. Baskerville adds that the transformation of an artistic achievement into a commercial success may occur if the following takes place:

1.   The song gets an appealing initial performance.

2.   The record company promotes strong airplay.

3.   The song and the record suit the taste of the current market.

4.   the record is effectively distributed and is made readily available nationally.[10]

These events fall beyond the scope of the creative process, and are the personal manager's responsibility to see that they occur.

Making Money At It

The key to receiving revenue from the efforts of songwriting is through the **use** of the song. In the business this is referred to as "exploiting the copyright" and is the main function of the song's publisher. Revenue producing uses include:

1. recording sales (all configurations) through the issuing of mechanical licenses which generate mechanical royalties.

2. jukebox play

3. sheet music sales

4. special use licenses (i.e.. use in advertising jingles)

5. synchronization license (using the music in conjunction with visuals)

6. home taping tax (fee levied on digital audio tape recorders and blank tape)

7. broadcast performances (including network and local TV and radio, public and college broadcasts, cable and satellite)

8. non-broadcast performances (including concert and club performances, and other uses such as "Muzak", airline, and health club play)

9. dramatic performances, also known as "Grand" rights performances, which make use of live play acting.

Because revenue collection for the songwriter relies so heavily on the function of the song's publisher, the Songwriters Guild of America publishes a **Popular Songwriter Contract.** This songwriter/publisher agreement includes basic descriptions of all the revenue producing areas that are handled by the publisher for the songwriter. Although some major publishers feel that the contract is weighted in favor of the songwriter, and therefore insist on their own contracts, it is a good resource to use only as a guide and an outline when beginning negotiations on one's own deal. Pay particular attention to all parts of clauses numbered 4, 6, 9, and 18, and the instructions in the margins and included in parenthesis. Since the terms of the contract are based on the strength of the songwriters track record, the percentages noted in each subclause vary greatly. What follows is a reprint of those specific clauses with comments and advice. However, this is another agreement that **should not** be signed without legal representation.

4. In consideration of this contract, the Publisher agrees to pay the Writer as follows:

(a) $.....as an advance against royalties, receipt of which is hereby acknowledged, which sum shall remain the property of the Writer and shall be deductible only form payments hereafter becoming due the Writer under their contract.

*In 4a, the advance money conditions are stated. The money is advanced free and clear, and will be paid back to the publisher **before** any royalties are distributed. This contract does not include a clause forbidding "cross-collateralization", which means that monies advanced against one song under the guise of this contract, may be collected against the royalties on another song. As a songwriter, you may not be in favor of this, it is a standard clause in the industry, and unproven songwriters must accept it.*

(b) In respect of regular piano copies sold and paid for in he United States and Canada, the following royalties per copy:...% (in no case, however, less than 10%) of the wholesale selling price of the first 200,00 copies or less; plus ...% (in no case less than 12%) of the wholesale selling price of copies in excess of 200,00 and not exceeding 500,00; plus ...% (in no case, however, less than 15%) of wholesale selling price of copies in excess of 500,000.

*This is a sliding scale of percentages that should increase the songwriters participation in revenues as the print sales increase. Here it is based on the wholesale selling price, and the percentages should be **twice** as large as if based on the retail selling price*

(c) ...% (in no case, however, less than 50%) of all net sums received by the Publisher in respect of regular piano copies, orchestrations, band arrangements, octavos, quartets, arrangements for combination of voices and/or instruments, and/or copies of the composition sold in any country other than the United States and Canada, provided, however, that if the Publisher should sell such copies through, or cause them to be sold by, a subsidiary or affiliate which is actually doing business in a foreign country, then in respect of such sales, the Publisher shall pay to the Writer not less than 5% of the market retail selling price in respect of each such copy sold and paid for.

*This clause deals with the publishing of arrangements of the work outside of the U.S. and Canada. If the publisher signing the agreement publishes the work, the writer is entitled to at least 50% of the **net** sums received. However, if the publisher sells or licenses the copies through an affiliate or subsidiary in the foreign country, the writer will receive not less than 5% of the market retail selling price for each copy sold and **paid for**. Make note of the inclusion of the phrase "paid for". With foreign publications it is sometimes very difficult to receive payment, and furthermore there is a time lapse between the sale and delivery of funds. Also, this clause does not specify if the payment will be made in U.S. or foreign currency. Many foreign companies hold funds collected until the currency exchange rate favors them, and there could be a different rate on the day the check* *is written than on the day of the sale.*

(d)   In respect of each copy sold and paid for in the United States and Canada, or for export from the United States, of orchestrations, band arrangements, octavos, quartets, arrangements for combinations of voices and/or instruments, and/or other copies of the composition (other than regular piano copies) the following royalties on the wholesale selling price (after trade discounts, if any):

...% (in no case however, less than 10%) on the first 200,000 copies or less; plus

...% (in no case, less than 12%) of all copies in excess of 200,00 and not exceeding 500,000; plus

...% (in no case, however, less than 15%) on all copies in excess of 500,000.

This clause pertains to orchestrations and other arrangements printed and sold in the U.S. and Canada, or printed and exported.

(e)   (i)   If the composition, or any part thereof, is included in any song book, folio or similar publication issued by the Publisher containing at least four, but not more than twenty-five musical compositions, the royalty to be paid by the Publisher to the Writer shall be an amount determined by dividing 10% of the Wholesale selling price (after trade Discounts, if any) of the copies sold, among the total number of the Publisher's copyrighted musical compositions included in such publication. If such publication contains more than twenty-five musical compositions, the said 10% shall be increased by an additional 1/2% for each additional musical composition.

    (ii)   If, pursuant to a license granted by the Publisher to a licensee not controlled by or affiliated with it, the composition, or any part thereof, is included in any song book, folio or similar publication, containing at least four musical compositions, the royalty to be paid by the Publisher to the Writer shall be that proportion of 50% of the gross amount received by it from the licensee, as the number of uses of the composition under the license and during the license period, bears to the total number of uses of the Publisher's copyrighted musical compositions under the license and during the license period.

    (iii)   In computing the number of the Publisher's copyrighted musical compositions under subdivisions (i) and (ii) hereof, there shall be excluded musical compositions in the public domain and arrangements thereof and those with respect to which the Publisher does not currently publish and offer for sale regular piano copies.

(iv) Royalties on publications containing less than four musical compositions shall be payable at regular piano copy rates.

This clause deals with song books and folios that are published by the publisher and/or licensed by the publisher. It is a given, that the writer wants the printed editions of the song published, however, there is no mention as to if the songs are going to be coupled with other writer's works. The songwriter may insist that the material in all folios published is exclusively his/hers, Also make note that all percentages and numbers are negotiable.

(f) As to "professional material" not sold or resold, no royalty shall be payable. Free copies of the lyrics of the composition shall not be distributed except under the following conditions: (i) with the Writer's written consent; or (ii) when printed without music in limited numbers for charitable, religious or governmental purposes, or for similar public purposes, if no profit is derived, directly or indirectly; or (iii) when authorized for printing in a book, magazine or periodical, where provided that any such use shall bear the Writer's name and the proper copyright notice; or (iv) when distributed solely for the purpose of exploiting the composition, provided, that such exploitation is restricted to the distribution of limited numbers of such copies for the purpose of influencing the sale of the composition, that the distribution is independent of the sale of any other musical compositions, services, goods, wares or merchandise, and that no profit is made, directly or indirectly, in connection therewith.

In this clause free copies and other professional uses are explained. The writer has the power to limit such uses, especially regarding religious and governmental purposes.

(g) ...% (in no case, however, less than 50%) of:All gross receipts of the Publisher in respect of any licenses (including statutory royalties) authorizing the manufacture of parts of instruments serving to mechanically reproduce the composition, or to use the composition in synchronization with sound motion pictures, or to reproduce it upon electrical transcription for broadcasting purposes, and of any and all gross receipts of the Publisher from any other source or right now known or which may hereafter come into existence, except as provided in paragraph 2.

All other rights are discussed here. And although the 50% is the standard split, the importance of all of these revenue producing areas probably merits more detailed descriptions.

(h) If the Publisher administers licenses authorizing the manufacture of parts of instruments serving to mechanically reproduce said composition, or the use of said composition in synchronization or in timed relation with sound motion pictures or its reproduction upon electrical transcriptions, or any of them, through an agent, trustee or other administrator acting for a substantial part of the industry and not under the exclusive control of the Publisher (hereafter sometimes referred to as licensing agent), the Publisher, in determining his receipts, shall be entitled to deduct from gross license fees paid by the Licensees, a sum equal to the charges paid by the Publisher to said licensing agent, provided, however, that in respect to synchronization or timed relation with sound motion pictures, said deduction shall in no event exceed $150 or 10% of said gross license fee, whichever is less; in connection with the manufacture of parts of instruments serving to mechanically reproduce said composition, said deductions shall not exceed 5% of said gross license fee; and in connection with electrical transcriptions, said deduction shall not exceed 10% of said gross license fee.

Here the Publisher administers licenses for the material through a licensing agent, any and all fees for the service accumulated by the Publisher will be shared by the writer.

(i)   The Publisher agrees that the use of the composition will not be included in any bulk or block license heretofore or hereafter granted, and that it will not grant any bulk or block license to include the same, without the written consent of the Writer in each instance, except (i) that the Publisher may grant such license with respect to electrical transcription for broadcasting purposes, ... A bulk or block license shall be deemed to mean any license or agreement, domestic or foreign, whereby rights are granted in respect of two or more musical compositions.

This is a particularly long clause (only partially reprinted here) that describes what a block license is. The Writer must give his/her consent before the Publisher is allowed to license two or more compositions together. It also includes exclusions, however, they are of standard practice.

(j)   Except to the extent that the Publisher and Writer have heretofore of may hereafter assign to or vest in the small performing rights licensing organization with which Writer and Publisher are affiliated, the said rights or the right to grant licenses therefore, it is agreed that no licenses shall be granted without the written consent, in each instance, of the Writer for the use of the composition by means of television, or by any means, or for any purposes not commercially established, of for which licenses were not granted by the Publisher on musical compositions prior to June 1, 1937.

The Writer must give consent for any television or new delivery system use.

(k)   The Publisher shall not, without the written consent of the Writer in each case, give or grant any right or license (i) to use the title of the composition, or (ii) for the exclusive use of the composition in any form or for any purpose, or for any period of time, or for any territory, other than its customary arrangements with foreign publishers, or (iii) to give a dramatic representation of the composition or to dramatize the plot or story thereof, or (iv) for a vocal rendition of the composition in synchronization with sound motion pictures, or (v) for any synchronization use thereof, of (vi) for the use of the composition or a quotation or excerpt therefrom in any article, book, periodical, advertisement or other similar publication. If, however, the Publisher shall give to the Writer written notice by certified mail, return receipt requested, or telegram, specifying the right or license to be given or granted, the name of the licensee and the terms and conditions thereof, including the price of other compensation to be received therefore, then, unless the Writer (or any one or more of them) shall, within five business days after the delivery of such notice to the address of the Writer herein designated, object thereto, the Publisher may grant such right or license accordance with the said notice without first obtaining the consent of the Writer. Such notice shall be deemed sufficient if sent to the writer at the address or addresses hereinafter designated or at the address or addresses last furnished to the Publisher in writing by the Writer.

This clause protects the writer against any unwanted licensing of his/her material.

(l)   Any portion of the receipts which may become due to the Writer from license fees (in excess of offsets), whether received directly from the licensee or from any licensing agent of the Publisher, shall, if not paid immediately on the receipt thereof by the Publisher, belong to the Writer and shall be held in trust for the Writer until payment is made; the ownership of said trust fund by the Writer shall not be questioned whether the monies are physically segregated or not.

(m)   The Publisher agrees that it will not issue any license as a result of which it will receive any financial benefit in which the Writer does not participate.

(n)   On all regular piano copies, orchestrations, band or other arrangements, octavos, quartets, commercial sound recordings and other reproductions of the composition or parts thereof, in whatever form and however produced, Publisher shall include or cause to be included, in addition to the copyright notice, the name of the Writer, and Publisher shall include a similar requirement in every license or authorization issued by it with respect to the composition.

6.   (a)   (i)   The Publisher shall, within ..... months from the date of this
contract (the "initial period"), cause a commercial sound recording of the
composition to be made and released in the customary form and through the
customary commercial channels. If at the end of such initial period a sound
recording has not been made and released, as above provided, then, subject
to the provisions of the next subdivision, this contract shall terminate.

*A new writer should negotiate for the shortest number of months that is agreeable,
however, it is customary to give the publisher 12 to 18 months to secure a deal.
The clause does not state which record labels would be acceptable, and there is a
major difference between a release on SONY Records and one on "DUMBELL." A
compromise might include "a commercial recording distributed by one of the five
major record distributors."*

   (ii)   If, prior to the expiration of the initial period, Publisher pays the
Writer the sum of $....(which shall not be charged against or recoupable
out of any advances, royalties or other monies theretofore paid, then due,
or which thereafter may become due the Writer from the Publisher pursuant
to this contract or otherwise), Publisher shall have an additional .... months
(the "additional period") commencing with the end of the initial period,
within which to cause such commercial sound recording to be made and
released as provided in subdivision (i) above. If at the end of the additional
period a commercial sound recording has not been made and released, as
above provided, then this contract shall terminate.

*Here there are two figures to be negotiated. The sum allows the publisher to buy some
additional time to secure a deal. This clause is included in case the publisher is working on a
record deal and it's beyond his/her control to close when s/he would like. The writer should not
give the publisher more than six additional months, and should receive a sum s/he feels
comfortable with.*

   (iii)   Upon termination pursuant to this Paragraph 6(a), all rights of any
and every nature in and to the composition and in and to any and all
copyrights secured thereon in the United States and throughout the world
shall automatically re-vest in and become the property of the Writer and
shall be reassigned to him by the Publisher. The Writer shall not be
obligated to return or pay to the Publisher any advance or indebtedness as a
condition of such reassignment; the said reassignment shall be in

accordance with and subject to the provisions of Paragraph 8 hereof, and, in addition, the Publisher shall pay to the Writer all gross sums which it has theretofore or may thereafter receive in respect of the composition.

This is a clause that the Publisher will have a difficulty signing as stated. S/he will want to participate in future revenues that may be generated due to agreements that s/he may have initiated but did not close. Sometimes there is a compromise that suggests that if any revenue is generated during the first ...months immediately following the termination date, the Publisher will receive ...% of the sums.

(b)   The Publisher shall furnish, or cause to be furnished, to the Writer six copies of the commercial sound recording referred to in Paragraph 6(a).

Remember that all numbers are negotiable.

(c)   The Publisher shall

(i)   within 30 days after the initial release of a commercial sound recording of the composition, make, publish and offer for sale regular piano copies of the composition in the form and through the channels customarily employed by it for that purpose;

(ii)   within 30 days after execution of this contract make a piano arrangement or lead sheet for he composition and furnish six copies thereof to the Writer.

In the event neither subdivision (i) nor (ii) of this subparagraph (c) is selected, the provisions of subdivision (ii) shall be automatically deemed to have been selected by the parties.

Since sheets are no longer manufactured for every song recorded (ii) would be sufficient.

9.   If the Publisher desires to exercise a right in and to the composition now known or which may hereafter become known, but for which no specific provision has been made herein, the Publisher shall give written notice to the Writer thereof. Negotiations respecting all the terms and conditions of any such disposition shall thereupon be entered into between the Publisher and the Writer and no such right shall be exercised until specific agreement has been made.

18.   Except to the extent herein otherwise expressly provided, the Publisher shall not sell, transfer, assign, convey, encumber or otherwise dispose of the compositions or the copyright or copyrights secured thereon without the prior written consent of the Writer. The Writer has been induces to enter into this contract in reliance upon the value to him of the personal service and ability of the Publisher in the exploitation of the composition, and

by reason thereof it is the intention of the parties and the essence of the relationship between them that the rights herein granted to the Publisher shall remain with the Publisher and that the same shall not pass to any other person, including, without limitations, successors to or receivers or trustees of the property of the Publisher, either by act or deed of the Publisher or by operation of law, and in the event of the voluntary or involuntary bankruptcy of the Publisher, this contract shall terminate, provided, however, that the composition may be included by the Publisher in a bona fide voluntary sale of its music business or its entire catalog of musical compositions, or in a merger or consolidation of the Publisher with another corporation, in which event the Publisher shall immediately give written notice thereof to the Writer; and provided further that the composition and the · copyright therein may be assigned by the Publisher to a subsidiary or affiliated company generally engaged in the music publishing business. If the Publisher is an individual, the composition may pass to a legatee or distributee as part of the inheritance of the Publisher's music business and entire catalog of musical compositions. Any such transfer or assignment shall, however, be conditioned upon the execution and delivery by the transferee or assignee to the Writer of an agreement to be bound by and to perform all of the terms and conditions of this contract to be performed on the part of the Publisher.

This clause does not allow the publisher to sell or trade any of the writer's songs without prior written consent of the writer. It protects the writer from being part of a package deal that the publisher may want to execute to obtain the rights to a song or catalog. However, if the publisher wells or is sold to another music publisher in the business, then the writer cannot stop his/her material from being assigned, provided that the contract between the writer and the new publisher contains all of the terms included in this contract.

Publishing

Record companies have taken over many of the responsibilities of the early music publishers, narrowing their role in exploiting the copyright. In fact, today virtually all record companies own publishing firms, and try to secure the rights to their artist's songs. So the main function of the independent music publisher is to generate "covers" of their clients catalog. This may include the following:

1. covering the song for other markets by having different artist record the song
2. completing several arrangements of the work ie. big band, piano arrangements, etc.

3.   licensing the song for use in advertising or promotional commercials

4.   licensing the song for print editions

5.   permitting the song to be used with time-related visuals (synchronization)

6.   sub-publishing the work for foreign income.

The consequences of these avenues of exploitation is the generation of income. The more ways a song is used, the better the chances that it wail generate income. And a publisher's strength is in the success of his/her catalog.

In the past decade, the size of the catalog has been of major concern. In the 1980's, bigger was better. Many catalogs were sold for what seemed like huge amounts of money. This was due to several reasons: Some companies were experiencing cash flow problems and needed revenue quickly; it was more cost effective to purchase an entire catalog than it was to purchase one or two hits; and lastly, with the development of new and different "delivery systems", it was advantageous to own the song rather than secure a license for one use. If you owned the song, it would be your option to license it or use it anyway you would see fit. The strength is in the catalog!

There is a joke in the business, the idea of it is that Paul McCartney and Michael Jackson own all the songs that were ever written! It's true that they both own large catalogs (Yoko Ono and Paul joined together to purchase the remaining Beatle songs that Paul didn't already own, but were out bid by Michael), however, they own them that only for their respective egos, but because the surest safest investment in the music business is owning a song catalog.

Sources of Income

Publishers (and songwriters) receive income from six basic song uses or licenses. They are:

1.   mechanical licensing
2.   performance licensing
3.   synchronization licensing
4.   print licensing
5.   foreign licensing
6.   special use licensing

1.   mechanical licensing   As a songwriter, if someone wants to manufacture (mechanically reproduce) a sound recording of your song, s/he must obtain a mechanical license from your publisher. In 1909, the statutory rate was $.02 per song and it cost $.03 to mail a letter. The current price for the license (the statutory rate) is $.066 per song or $.014 per minute, whichever is greater, on every record manufactured and sold, and it now costs almost eleven times as great to mail a letter! (Obviously the rate has not kept up with inflation, and has been quite a deal for the record companies.} The rate, now in effect, was set and adjusted according to the Consumer Price Index by the now disbanded U.S. Copyright Tribunal. If 500,000 copies of the recording were sold, the mechanical license would have generated $34,750 (500,000 X $.0695), which would have been split between the songwriter and the publisher. Once the initial recording is released, if anyone is willing to pay the current statutory rate, the song's owner must issue the license. Since the rate is set by law, many feel that it discriminates against successful songwriters. Is a song written by Paul McCartney worth the same price as one written by John Doe? Many feel that the licensing rate should be free to be negotiated on the open market. And in a way it is, and that is through the use of the negotiated license. If the copyright agrees, the manufacturer (record company), may pay a rate **lower** than the statutory rate. This negotiated mechanical license is used throughout the industry, especially when the artist is more famous than the songwriter. The record company may want to pay only $.02 on every recording manufactured and sold and may negotiate that rate with the song owner (publisher). Therefore on 500,000 copies sold, it would cost the company only $10,000 (500,000 X $.02) instead of $34,750.

In the U.S., most publishers issue mechanical licenses through one of the mechanical rights organizations. The largest is the Harry Fox Agency, who charges a fee (circa 3.5%) for its services. The services include the issuing of licenses, collecting royalties, and auditing record companies as well.

2 .   performance licensing   Another right the copyright owner is granted by law is the right to perform the copyrighted material in public. This includes the actual live performance of the work or the performance of a mechanical reproduction of the work. Consequently, the user of the work must obtain a license to broadcast a performance or have a live performance occur in his/her venue. Broadcast stations, wire services, auditoriums, arenas, and clubs throughout the world, all obtain various types of performance licenses. Because the issuing of these licenses would be an enormous task for individual copyright owners, performing rights organizations act as clearinghouses for their respective clients.

In the U.S. there are three performing rights organizations (PRO's): ASCAP (American Society of Authors, Composers, and Publishers), BMI (Broadcast Music Incorporated), and SESAC (Society of European Stage Authors and Composers). ASCAP and BMI are by far the largest and not for profit. A composer must exclusively belong to one of the three, however, a publisher may belong to all three. Their responsibilities include granting licenses, collecting royalties, and distributing the income to their clients.

The structure of the organizations include a broadcast licensing area, and a general licensing area. The broadcast license revenues are determined by a survey or logging procedure, where different broadcast performances are given a value (or weighted). A sophisticated formula determines how much revenue is produced by each performance.

The general licensing area issues licenses to venues. The fee for the license is determined by the capacity of the venue and various other factors. The revenue collected is distributed by the number of logged or surveyed **broadcast performance.** Therefore, songs that are performed a great deal live but have ceased (or never were) to be heard from broadcasts, lose out because they are disproportionately accounted for. The performing rights organizations are aware of the problems, however, a solution does not appear to be in the near future.

The PRO's distribute the income (after expenses) individually to the writers and the publishers (usually on a 50/50% share basis). Performance license royalties are the only license royalties that are not funneled through the publisher to be split and distributed to the writer.

3 . <u>synchronization licensing</u> Anytime music is combined with visual motion it becomes what is known as "time related" and require a "synch license." These uses include music in motion pictures (theatrical releases or made for TV movies), and music videos. The producer of the work must obtain the license form the publisher. Obviously, revenue from synch licenses can be very substantial. These revenues are collected by the publisher who in turn splits them (usually 50/50) with the writer.

4 . <u>print licensing</u> Before the recording industry took over, music publishers printed sheet music of the songs that they owned. This is what publishing meant! Today, only a few music publishers are in the print manufacturing business. Most license the rights to another company and receive a percentage of the revenue on music sold. They, in turn, pay the writer a small percent of what is received. Sheets or folios are not printed for every song recorded and for new artists, they are not printed until it is determined that the record has "some legs." However, big hits can produce substantial folio revenue.

5 . <u>foreign licensing</u> Foreign income is derive from licensing and subassignee throughout the world. The percentage of revenues realized from each license is substantively lower than revenue from similar domestic uses. Exchange rates, tariffs, and distribution costs play a major role in how much income is generated. Some songwriters are counselled to retain their foreign rights and issue their own licenses. Although this sounds great, it may prove to be disastrous because the hardest aspect of foreign licensing is receiving the revenues (getting paid), and an individual songwriter may not have the resources a publisher may have to track down money due to them.

6.   **special use licensing** These licenses include using the music in advertising jingles, greeting cards, and other merchandise. Sponsors who want music in their commercial notify their advertising agency who may produce the music in-house, or rely on the services of a music supplier. The commercials may run in a national television campaign or a 15 second local radio spot. The use of the music may vary from using the original recording of the song followed by a voice over, as a background "bed" under a voice over, or the use of the music with lyrics selling the product sung to the original melody. Therefore the special use release of the song usually a form of a synch license as well.

The chart below sums up the normal income distribution between the publisher and the songwriter. These figures can be only be used as a guide, either for one song contracts or long term agreements.

INCOME

License	Split
mechanical	publisher collects 100% and pays affiliated composer 50%
performance	PRO pays composer and publisher individual shares directly
synchronization	publisher collects and pays affiliated composer 50%
print	publisher collects 100% and pays composer small royalty at approximately $.10 per printed edition sold
foreign	when received from foreign or subpublisher, 50% of income is paid to composer
special use	publisher collects 100% and pays affiliated composer 50%

Performing

The record industry is such a product oriented business, that up until the past 25 years, the technology was not available to perform in the arenas and stadiums that are so common practice today. There is a great picture of the Beatles performing their now famous Shea Stadium Concert.

The two baselines of the baseball diamond are lined with five foot sound columns, with six or seven speakers in each. That was the sound reinforcement system for the fifty thousand fans seated (and screaming) in the stands!

There was also less emphasis placed the performance as another retailing opportunity for the artist. It was looked upon as another way of enhancing record sales, instead of a revenue generating experience. Today a worldwide concert tour takes years to complete and produces millions for top artists in ticket and merchandising sales revenues. Today, artists are totally aware of the potential and power of the live performance, and approach the live show creatively, to bring the consumer the most unforgettable experience possible. **CONCERTS DON'T SELL, EVENTS SELLOUT!** (A more in-depth discussion of the show appears in Chapter Nine.)

Video

How important is it? Should we spend the money? I don't know how to act anyway? Are se sure they sell recordings? Is everyone releasing videos now?

The video impact on the business is obvious. The Recording Industry Association of America (RIAA) has established the quotas for Gold and Platinum video awards. Figure 8.4 lists the number of units needed to be sold for video singles, long forms, and matchbox sets to be certified as gold platinum, and multi-platinum sellers.

GOLD & PLATINUM AWARDS CERTIFICATION LEVELS

	Gold	Platinum	Multi-Platinum
Video Single	25,000 units: max. running time of 15 minutes: two songs per title	50,000 units: max. running time of 15 minutes: two songs per title	100,000 units: max. running time of 15 minutes: two songs per title
Video Long Form	50,000 units	100,000 units	200,000 units
Video Multi-Box	50,000 units	100,000 units	200,000 units

Figure 8.4   Gold and Platinum Awards Certification Levels (Audio and Video). Statistical Overview 1991. Inside the Record Industry. RIAA, Washington DC p. 16.

Although they represent only one-tenth of the amounts needed for audio recording certifications, it should be noted that the configuration is still in its infancy stage.

Also, the sale of music videos has not come close to what was expected. In the early 1980's, it was thought that consumers would no longer purchase audio recordings. Their sales would be replaced by videos of entire albums that would be watched as well as listened to. That has not yet become a reality. Consumers seem to still want the freedom to do what they want when they want to, and use music in a variety of ways. Therefore, personal listening has continued to rise and the purchasing of entire video albums has yet to blossom.

Promotional videos have become an industry staple. MTV recognized this in the mid 1980's and offered to pay major record companies for the exclusive right to show new releases. The radio industry was astonished that MTV would be willing yto pay for a service that radio stations have always received for free. However, MTV gambled that the way to stifle competition form other video presenters was to gain exclusivity to new releases and was willing to pay for that access. It proved to be a brilliant decision as MTV is now a worldwide video presenter.

The forerunner to the modern videos were called "**soundies"**. They surfaced in the 1940's, and "were an ambitious attempt to merge the jukebox concept with three-minute filmclips."[11] They were made by the Mills Novelty Company in Chicago who in 1941, also began manufacturing Panorams. The Panorams were the hardware (viewing and listening machines) that were used to play the soundies. The screens were the size of two pieces of letterhead stationery, and selection were changed twice a month. Because racism prevailed, two separate catalogs were issued and distributed along color lines. Customers paid a dime to see a clip, almost entirely made of close-up shots with crude lip syncing. Because reels became outdated in a matter of days, the idea suffered from a built obsolescence.[12]

The early modern videos were basically concert footage (either live or staged) of the group performing. During the early 1980's the concept video appeared. In some related loose form, the story told in the lyrics was acted out by members of the group. The concept was usually a nonlinear approach, where certain scenes and symbols would appear and reappear without any simple storytelling logic.

The nonlinear concept was new, exciting, and fresh to television. Up until that point, TV shows used a linear approach. For example, in a detective show, a crime would be committed and then solved. A situation comedy would set up a dilemma (situation), and then act out the solution. Soap operas would do the same thing, only they would add a few twists and turns to unravel the story over time.

The first network show to use the nonlinear approach over any length of time was NBC's Miami Vice. The fashion statements were perfect for the 1980's video viewing age group, and the quasi nonlinear concept with rock stars making guest appearances, gave the show a long run.

The concept music video is commonplace today. Video producers and directors must consciously develop concepts that compliment the artist's image. If it is so unbelievable that its down right silly, it could spell trouble for the artist. Even video king, Michael Jackson was criticized for (and quickly pulled) the smashing of the cars scenes from the <u>Dangerous</u> album's initial video.

Record companies realize the promotional importance of videos and the possibility that their sales or licensing may become strong revenue producers. Therefore, what was once a few paragraphs of a recording contract, now encompasses several pages. Below are key video clauses and commentary from a recent recording contract. Use it as guide. **Do not** negotiate video rights without consulting an entertainment attorney.

Video Clauses

1. (a) In addition to ARTIST's recording and PRODUCTIONS' production and delivery commitments as set forth in Paragraph # of this Agreement, PRODUCTIONS and ARTIST shall comply with requests, if any, made by COMPANY in connection with the production of Pictures. In this connection, PRODUCTIONS shall cause ARTIST to appear on dates and at places requested by COMPANY for the filming, taping or other fixation of audiovisual recordings. PRODUCTIONS and ARTIST shall perform services with respect thereto as COMPANY deems desirable in a timely and first-class manner. PRODUCTIONS and ARTIST acknowledge that the production of Pictures involves matters of judgment with respect to art and taste, which judgment shall mutually exercised by COMPANY and PRODUCTIONS in good faith, it being understood that if agreement cannot be reached, COMPANY's decisions with respect thereto shall be final.

In this contract, the artist's works are being produced by a company called PRODUCTIONS, and the COMPANY is requiring the artist to appear for "pictures" when asked. It also states that the record company will have the final word on the release of the audiovisual work, eventhough it plans on discussing the matter with the artist in good faith.

(b) (i) Each picture produced during the Term of this Agreement shall be owned by COMPANY (including the worldwide copyrights therein and thereto and all extensions and renewals thereof) to the same extent as COMPANY's rights in master recordings made under this Agreement.

(ii)   COMPANY will have the unlimited right to manufacture Videoshows of the Picture and to rent, sell, distribute, transfer, sublicense of otherwise deal in such Videoshows under any trademarks, tradenames and labels; to exploit the Picture by any means now or hereafter known or developed; or to refrain from any such exploitation, throughout the world.

(c) (i)   Following COMPANY's receipt of invoices therefor, COMPANY agrees to pay all costs actually incurred in the production of Pictures made at COMPANY's request hereunder, provided such costs have been previously approved by COMPANY in writing.   In this connection, prior to commencing production of any Picture, PRODUCTIONS shall submit to COMPANY, in writing, a detailed budget for each Picture.   Said budget shall include the following information: (i) the musical compositions and other material to be embodied thereon (ii) the general concept therefor and (iii) the producer, director, and any other key personnel therefor. Following PRODUCTIONS' receipt of COMPANY's approval of said budget, PRODUCTIONS' shall commence production if the Picture.   All costs incurred in excess of the applicable approved budget shall be PRODUCTIONS' sole responsibility and PRODUCTIONS agrees to pay any such excess costs on PRODUCTIONS' behalf, PRODUCTIONS shall, upon demand, reimburses COMPANY for such excess costs and/or COMPANY may deduct such excess costs from any and all monies due to PRODUCTIONS pursuant to this or any other agreement between the parties hereto. All sums paid by COMPANY in connection with each Picture shall be an advance against and recoupable by COMPANY out of all royalties becoming payable to PRODUCTIONS pursuant to this or any other agreement, provided that COMPANY shall not recoup more than fifty (50%) percent of such sums from royalties becoming payable to PRODUCTIONS pursuant to Paragraph # of this Agreement.

These clauses specify ownership and how production costs will be paid. It also addresses COMPANY's right to cross-collateralize up to 50% of sum stated in an earlier paragraph. Remember that almost all percentages are negotiable.

(ii)   Each of the following sums, if any, paid by COMPANY in connection with each Picture shall be an advance against and recoupable by COMPANY out of all royalties becoming payable to PRODUCTIONS pursuant to this or any other agreement, provided that COMPANY shall not recoup more than fifty (50%) percent of such sums from royalties becoming payable to PRODUCTIONS pursuant to Paragraph # of this Agreement:

Fifty percent is the standard sum.

(A)   All expenses incurred by COMPANY in connection with the preparation and production of the Picture and the conversion of the Picture to Video Masters that are made to serve as prototypes for the duplication of the Videoshows of the Picture;

(B)   All of COMPANY's direct out-of-pocket costs (such as for rights, artists (including ARTIST), other personnel, facilities, materials, services, and the use of equipment) in connection with all steps in the production of the Picture and the process leading to and including the production of such Video Masters (including, but not limited to, packaging costs and the costs of making and delivering duplicate copies of such Video Masters); and (COMPANY) If in connection therewith COMPANY furnishes any of its own facilities, materials, services or equipment for which COMPANY has a standard rate, the amount of such standard rate or if there is no standard rate, the market value for the services or thing furnished.

(iii)   All sums that COMPANY in its sole discretion deems necessary or advisable to pay in connection with the production of Pictures and the exploitation of COMPANY's right therein in order to clear rights or to make any contractual payments that are or may become due on the part of COMPANY, to PRODUCTIONS, ARTIST or any other person, form or corporation by virtue of the exploitation of COMPANY's rights therein, in order to avoid, satisfy or make unnecessary any claims or demands by any person, firm or corporation claiming the right to payment therefor, including, but not limited to, any payment to an actual or alleged copyright owner, patent owner, union, union-related trust fund, pension plan or other entity, and any payment for an actual or alleged rerun fee, residual, royalty, license fee or otherwise shall constitute advances against and recoupable out of all royalties becoming payable to PRODUCTIONS pursuant to this or any other agreement between the parties hereto. No payment pursuant to this subparagraph shall constitute a waiver of any of PRODUCTIONS' express or implied warranties and representations.

(d)   Conditioned upon PRODUCTIONS' and ARTIST's full and faithful performance of all of the terms and conditions of this Agreement, COMPANY shall pay PRODUCTIONS the following royalties with respect to Pictures:

(i)   In respect of COMPANY's commercial exploitation, if any, of Videoshows solely embodying Pictures subject hereto which are sold through normal retailer channels for the "home video market" (as such term is commonly understood in the music and video industry):

(A) (1)   With respect to Album Videoshows sold through normal retailer channels in the United States, full priced as initially released, a royalty rate at the rate equal to applicable Basic U.S. Album Rate;

The rate should be negotiated, and the basic album rate should not be accepted.

(2) The royalty rate set forth in the last paragraph is hereinafter sometimes referred to as the "Basic U.S. Home Video Rate".

(B) (1)   With respect to Album Videoshows sold through normal retailer channels outside the United States, full priced as initially released, the royalty rate shall be the applicable Basic Foreign Album Rate;

(2) The royalty rate set forth in the last paragraph is hereinafter sometimes referred to as the "Basic Foreign Home Video Rate".

As a reminder, all rates are negotiable.

(C)   Except as otherwise set forth in this Agreement, the applicable Basic U.S. Home Video Rate and the applicable Basic Foreign Home Video Rate shall be calculated, computed, determined, prorated, reduced, adjusted (but not escalated) and paid in the same manner and at the same times (e.g., configurations other than Albums, "free goods", reserves, percentages of sales, price, number of units for which royalties are payable, calculated, computed, determined, prorated, reduced, adjusted (but not escalated) pursuant to Paragraph # of this Agreement

(ii)   (A)   The applicable Basic U.S. Home Video Rate and applicable Basic Foreign Home Video Rate shall be applied against COMPANY's wholesale price, as hereinafter defined (less COMPANY's container deductions, distribution fees, excise taxes, duties and other applicable taxes) for Videoshows sold which are paid for and not returned. The term "wholesale price" as used in this Paragraph # shall mean that amount which COMPANY received from COMPANY's distributor(s), whether or not affiliated with COMPANY, for each such Videoshow. In computing sales, COMPANY shall have the right to deduct all so-called "free goods" and all returns made at any time and for any reason. COMPANY may maintain reasonable reserves against returns. Videoshows distributed in the United States by any of COMPANY's affiliated branch wholesalers shall be deemed sold for the purposes of this Agreement only if sold by any such affiliated branch wholesaler to one of its independent third party customers.

Here the company is attempting to define what is meant by wholesale price, free goods, and returns. It also is attempting to maintain "reasonable" reserves against returns. These reserves should not be greater than the reserves held against the audio recording returns.

(B)   COMPANY's container deductions in respect of Videoshows shall be a sum equal to: (i) twenty (20%) percent of the wholesale price of the applicable Videoshow for Videoshows in COMPANY's standard packaging for one cassette, disc, cartridge or other unit, and (ii) thirty (30%) percent of the wholesale price of the applicable Videoshow for Videoshow in packaging for more than one cassette, disc, cartridge or other unit, or packaging with special materials, components, inserts or elements, or in any form of package, container or box other than COMPANY's standard packaging for one cassette, disc, cartridge or other unit.

Wow! These percentages are high and should not be accepted.

(iii)   With respect to sales and uses of Pictures hereunder other than Videoshow sold through normal retailer channels for the home video market, COMPANY shall pay PRODUCTIONS royalties equal to fifty (50%) percent of COMPANY's Video Net Receipts with respect to COMPANY's exploitation of Pictures subject to this Agreement, unless otherwise elsewhere provided to the contrary in this Agreement Monies earned and received by COMPANY form any licensee (rather than monies earned and received by the licensee) in respect of exploitation from Pictures shall be included in the conjunction of Video Net Receipts.

(iv)   No royalties shall be payable to PRODUCTIONS hereunder in respect of

Videoshows comprising so-called "video magazines", sampler or other promotional formats, or in respect of Pictures or Videoshows used or distributed for promotional purposes, whether or not COMPANY receives payment therefor.

(v) The royalties provided in subparagraphs (d) (i) and (iii) include any royalty obligations COMPANY may have to any other person, firm or corporation who supplied services or rights used in connection with pictures, including, without limitation, producers, directors, extras, and music publisher, and any such royalties shall be deducted form the video royalties otherwise payable to PRODUCTIONS.

(vi) With respect to records embodying Pictures made hereunder together with other material, royalties payable to PRODUCTIONS shall be computed by multiplying the royalties otherwise applicable by a fraction, the numerator of which is the amount of playing time in any such record of Pictures made hereunder and the denominator of which is the total playing time of all material in any such record.

(vii) As to Pictures embodying performances of ARTIST together with the performances of another artist or artists, the royalties otherwise payable hereunder shall be prorated by multiplying such royalties by a fraction, the numerator of which is one and the denominator of which is the total number of artists whose performances are embodies on such Pictures. COMPANY shall not require ARTIST to so perform with other artists without PRODUCTIONS' consent, however, if ARTIST does perform with other artists, such performance shall constitute consent.

The formula stated in vi and vii is okay for a short form video where the artist is the star of the picture. However, in a long form video, if the artist is the biggest star on the video and his/her performance does not constitute the majority of the playing time, then this formula would have to be negotiated.

(e) COMPANY shall have the right to use and allow others to use each Picture for advertising and promotional purposes with no payment to PRODUCTIONS or ARTIST.

(f) (i) During the Term of this Agreement, no person, firm or corporation other than COMPANY will be authorized to make, sell, broadcast or otherwise exploit audiovisual materials unless: (A) PRODUCTIONS first notifies COMPANY of all of the material terms and conditions of the proposed agreement pursuant to which the audiovisual materials is to be made, sold, broadcast or otherwise exploited, including, but no limited to, the titles of the compositions covered by the proposed agreement, the format to be used, the manner of exploitation proposed and the identities of all proposed parties to the agreement, and (B) PRODUCTIONS offers to enter into an agreement with COMPANY containing the same terms and conditions described in such notice and otherwise in the same form as this Agreement. If COMPANY does not accept PRODUCTIONS' offer within sixty (60) days after COMPANY's receipt of same, PRODUCTIONS may then enter into that proposed agreement with the same parties mentioned in such notice, subject to subparagraph (f) (ii) hereof and provided that such agreement is consummated with those parties within thirty (30) days after the end of that sixty (60) day period upon the same financial terms land condition set forth in PRODUCTIONS' notice and latter thirty (30) day period, no party except COMPANY will be authorized to make, sell, broadcast or otherwise exploit such audiovisual materials unless PRODUCTIONS first offers to enter into an agreement with COMPANY as provided in the first sentence of this subparagraph . . . .

(ii) If COMPANY does not accept an offer made to it pursuant to this subparagraph (f), such nonacceptance shall not be considered a waiver of any of COMPANY's rights pursuant this Agreement. Such rights include, without limitation, the right to prevent PRODUCTIONS from exploiting audiovisual material featuring ARTIST in the form of Videoshows, and the right to prevent PRODUCTIONS from authorizing any use of masters owned by or exclusively licensed to COMPANY unless COMPANY so agree. PRODUCTIONS shall not act in contravention of such rights.

COMPANY is exercising a right to first refusal by asking for notice and a time period to respond. It also is stating that it is not given up any of its rights to masters.

(g) Not withstanding anything to the contrary contained in subparagraph (f), ARTIST shall have the right to perform as an actor in motion pictures or other visual media, the contents of which are dramatic and substantially non-musical.

(h) In all other respects (e.g., the times for accounting to be rendered, and warranties . . . .

Media Check!   Live vs. Audio vs. Video

It is often said that artists that land a recording deal and don't make it, fail because of one of two reasons: poor management (read this book) or a lack of understanding of the differences between live performance and recorded performance. So many artists have said "we don't know what happened man, we sounded so great on stage, but the excitement was not captured on our record." Demo recordings of many great young bands do not sound as good as the band does in a club.   On the other hand, occasionally, bands that sell a whole bunch of records, are a disappointment when seen in concert. One of the reasons is that young bands that play in   clubs night after night become really proficient at playing in the live medium. And some bands with record deals make records that are produced by producers who understand the medium of recording make great records, however, when they play in front of 10,000 people for the first time, they don't sound so hot because they have yet to master the arena performance medium.

Some things that work great on stage for a live performance can not be captured in the audio (recorded) medium. However, on the record, something different takes the place of the stage happening to generate excitement. For example, listen to a Rolling Stone's record, the excitement that is generated by Mick Jagger prancing across the stage making faces at the audience, is somehow compensated for in the studio medium to develop that excitement. Secondly, The Stones are not intimidated by the physical characteristics of the recording studio. They do not let the isolation of the studio hinder their performance. To capture their sound they layer tracks, double themselves, and use every studio trick ever invented (I'm certain that they invented quite a few themselves). The record is produced with the clear understanding that it must generate the excitement of the visual effects of their show without being scene. The producer understands the recording medium and its uniqueness.

Over the last ten years, a third, yet different medium has become important. Artists must have an understanding of the what is successful in the video medium. Television and computer screens (video) wash colors and make one appear to be heavier than s/he really is. The illusion of movement can be created by moving the camera or background scenery. Lyrics and solos can be lipsynced to allow for exaggerated acting. Producers and directors make videos work. Again, it is the understanding of the uniqueness of the medium that is important.

As a manager, it is suggested that if an artist has not had experience in the recorded medium, the making of an entire album master (rather than a demo) should be discouraged. More often than not, a great deal of expense is incurred, and the end result of the ego trip is a record that does not capture the live excitement of the band's club performances. The same must be said for the budget video. Leave it the pros. In the end money will be saved.

Guiding The Creative Talent

What is the manager's role in guiding an artist? On page 63 in Guiding Creative Talent, Paul Torrance lists both general and specific goals in guiding creative talent. He lists the general goals as:

1. encouraging of a healthy kind of individuality
2. developing of conditions which will permit creativeness
3. regressing in the service of the ego and
4. counteracting pressures of regression to the average.

In order to achieve the general goals, he suggest obtaining the following specific goals as essential:

1. reward diverse contributions
2. help creative persons recognize the value of their own talents
3. avoid exploitation
4. accept limitations creatively
5. develop minimum skills
6. make use of opportunities
7. develop values and purposes
8. hold to purposes
9. avoid the equation of divergent with mental illness or delinquency
10. reduce overemphasis or misplace emphasis on sex roles
11. help them learn how to be less obnoxious
12. reduce isolation and
13. help them learn how to cope with anxieties, fears, hardships, and failures.[13]

And who said management wasn't fun!

SUMMARY

1.   The creative process is a function of the right hemisphere of the brain.

2.   The creative process is different for different people and different for the same individual at different times.

3.   Traits of the creative individual include being intuitive, open-minded, spontaneous, sensitive, flexible, and original.

4.   Traits of the creative product include, unusualness, appropriateness, newness, and compactness.

5.   Unless in a coma, everyone has a degree of creativity.

6.   Research has found that the greatest contribution to their field were made by musicians between thirty and forty years old.

7.   Factors that accompany age change bring about a reduction in creativity.

8.   Creativity cannot be taught, but creative uses of a craft can.

9.   Creativity can be evaluated by some quantitative measure.

10.   Songwriting is both an art and a craft.

11.   Songs that have a potential of being successful have certain characteristics.

12.   Money is made from songwriting by exploiting the copyright.

13.   The Songwriter's Guild of America publishes a Popular Songwriter's Contract that contains clauses describing all revenue producing areas.

14.   The music publisher's role of exploiting the song's copyright includes many functions.

15.   Publishers receive income form six basic song uses.

16.   The publisher and songwriter usually split income on an equal basis.

17.   The RIAA now lists criteria for Gold and Platinum Video Awards.

18.   The first videos were called soundies and were viewed on panorams.

19.   Many modern music videos use the nonlinear concept of story evolution.

20.   Record company video clauses have grown larger and more complex.

21.   Many artist with record contracts are not successful because they do not understand the differences between the live vs. audio and now video media.

22.   Management must play a role in guiding creative talent.

PROJECTS

1. Think of someone you know who you feel is very creative. List his/her personality characteristics.

2. Analyze why a song is successful. List the characteristics that make it successful.

3. Discuss whether songwriting is an art or a craft.

4. Compile a songwriter/publisher agreement that is fair for both parties.

5. Discuss the nonlinear approach of story evolution in a current music video.

6. List the different characteristics of live vs. audio vs. video performance.

7. Discuss the role of management in the nurturing of creative talent.

NOTES

1.   John S. Dacey. Fundamentals of Creative Thinking. Lexington Books. Lexington, MA. 1989, pg. 7-8.

2.   Gudmund J. Smith & Ingegerd M. Carlsson. The Creative Process.
International Universities Press, Inc. Madison, CT. 1990. pg. 1.

3.   Edward Buxton. Creative People at Work. Executive Communications, Inc. New York, 1975. pg. x.

4.   Op. Cit., Fundamentals of Creative Thinking. pg. 5.

5.   E. Paul Torrance. Guiding Creative Talent. Prentice Hall, Inc., Englewood Cliffs, NJ, 1962. pg. 100.

6.   Op. Cit., Creative People at Work. Interview with Marvin Honig of Dole, Dane, Bernback Agency. pg. 17.

7.   Morris I. Stein. Stimulating Creativity Vol 2. Academic Press Inc., New York, 1973, pg. vii.

8.   Ian Whitcomb. After The Ball. Penguin Books Inc. Baltimore, MD. 1972. pg. 3.

9.   David Baskerville, Music Business Handbook. Sherwood Publishing, Los Angeles, 1990. pg. 28-29.

10.   Ibid. pg. 29.

11.   R. Serge Denisoff, assisted by William Schurk. Tarnished Gold. Transaction Books, New Brunswick, NJ. 1986. pg. 330.

12.   Ibid. pg. 331.

13.   Op. Cit., Guiding Creative Talent. pg. 63.

CHAPTER NINE

TOURING

"I've made seven albums and two babies in the last five years, but it's not the same as touring. There's something so positive about it . . . Not that you're adulated, but that you feel euphorically encouraged and completely whole." Tina Weymouth, formerly of Talking Heads . . . Rolling Stone Magazine: RS 491

By the end of this chapter your should be able to:

1. Discuss the five basic tour objectives
2. Draw a timeline, listing the approximate deadlines for specific tour-related procedures
3. Discuss the most productive routing for most tours
4. Discuss the procedure for securing a concert performance
5. Discuss the various concert performance fee structures
6. Discuss the basic budget lines for an artist's tour
7. Discuss the various categories of a concert contract rider
8. Discuss tour publicity
9. Discuss all aspects of staging and production
10. Discuss how to evaluate a tour's objectives
11. Discuss the manager's role before, during, and after the tour.

<u>ITS HISTORY</u>

Touring has always played a role in musicians' lives. From the eleventh to the end of the thirteenth centuries, many poet-musicians traveled the southern regions of France, singing lyric poetry. In America, during the nineteenth century, minstrel shows with singers, musicians and variety acts combed the south daily. Around 1900, vaudeville entertainers visited the newly developed industrial urban centers, playing one nighters. In the early 1920's, jazz musicians traveled from New Orleans, up the Mississippi toward Chicago, performing in every city along the way.

The big bands of the 1930's and early 1940's really solidified the idea of musicians being "married" to the road. We hear most stories about the effects of travel on a musician's physical and emotional well being from this era. But, although the players have changed and our transportation systems have improved, the road is still an essential part of a musician's life.

_____

Rock musicians and rock bands have taken on the role of the 1930's and 40's big bands. Each metropolitan area and region of the country had its own favorite big bands in those days. They included the nationally famous bands of the era. . . The Benny Goodman Band, The Glen Miller Orchestra, The Duke Ellington Orchestra, and others. Today, local and regional rock bands hope to gather a following of fans who are as loyal but who will allow them to perform their own material. Eventually they hope this will lead to a recording contract with a nationally distributed record company.

The live performance has been and continues to be a form of artist-to-consumer retailing. When someone purchases a ticket to see an artist perform, he or she is the consumer. The concert promoter is the retailer. The music is the product. And the live performance is a way of selling the artist's product. For this reason, performances, and touring remain very necessary aspects of an artist's career.

Fortunately, for most modern musicians, "the road" no longer means an old bus, cheap hotels, junk food, and beer joints. Most musicians have a strong desire to experience the rewards that an immediate response from an audience provides. As a manager, you'll need to know why, when, and where to tour. Some guidelines follow. A timeline is included, showing, when certain aspects of tour preparation should be completed. Take note of the objectives you will want to accomplish during the tour. Finally, you will be given some pointers on how to evaluate the tour's success. In our tour example, the artist on tour holds a recording contract with a major label and performs in arena venues of approximately 10,000 seats or more.

TOUR OBJECTIVES

Why tour at all? It's very expensive, and it consumes a great deal of time and energy from the artist and the manager. A successful tour can meet useful objectives. Several of these are:

ONE: To increase the artist's visibility in a given market.

Obviously, the artist's presence in a market increases the likelihood that the concertgoer will buy his or her record. In turn, the concertgoer will introduce the music to other people who might also buy the record. A concert provides the opportunity for an audience to see the artist perform in person, and to identify with him or her. While videos capture some aspects of an artist's personality, this "cool" medium does not have the same impact as the artist's physical presence does on the emotions of the fan. No video can really capture Bruce Springsteen's charisma!

TWO: **To increase the number of industry workers on the artist's team and win their loyalty.**

When an artist arrives in a city for a concert performance, he or she should spend time wisely. The artist should make contact with the record company's local representatives (which generally include the promotion and sales representatives), radio stations and other media personnel, the local record retail community, and anyone else who might prove useful in furthering his or her career. These meetings, although sometimes tiresome and repetitious to the artist, pay off "down the road." These individuals appreciate the opportunity to meet the person behind the music.

THREE: **To make the artist's performance "*an event*" on a performance by performance basis.**

Unless an artist is well-known enough to receive immediate national media exposure via "Entertainment Tonight," "The Today Show," or other news and information programs, a ground swell effect must be created on a market-by-market basis. The objective is to develop a ripple effect that will extend to additional markets. Creating a media event pays off! They almost always sell out; most ordinary performances or concerts do not. Contests, give-aways, tie-ins with local sponsors, will help to distinguish your artist's concert as special. The same promotional "gimmicks" maybe used throughout the tour. But they must be tailored to every individual stop so they seem fresh and exciting.

FOUR: **To provide an opportunity for the artist to perform in a major market when the record is reaching its "stride."**

A release usually reaches its "stride" about twelve weeks after its release. At that point, it hasn't peaked yet, but has gathered enough momentum so that it's beginning to sell itself. By this time, the ripple effect should have reached enough people, given the artist has the opportunity to perform in a major market and make a profit. (A performance should <u>not</u> be scheduled in a major market if enough tickets won't be sold to make any money!) According to the 1992 Rand McNally Commercial Atlas and Marketing Guide, over forty percent of the American population live in the twenty major markets. Selling product in these markets is critical to an artist's success.

FIVE: **To make a profit.**

An artist may derive a tremendous amount of creative fulfillment from performing. And you may get personal satisfaction from managing. But the bottom line is the artist is a business.

Below is a brief summary of an article that appeared in <u>Rolling Stone Magazine</u> on November 28, 1996. It ran just after the group, *Pearl Jam,* made a goal line stance for its fans and challenged the monopoly that Ticketmaster has on the entertainment industry. The band was upset with the high service charges that Ticketmaster was demanding for tickets to its shows. It estimates that the band might have given up over $30 million.

"If *Pearl Jam* simply plugged into the established summertime concert system both this year and last - playing approximately 40 shows each summer at mostly Ticketmaster-controlled amphitheaters - they could have earned $20 million from ticket sales. The band could have raked in an additional $5 million from merchandising and $6 million from corporate sponsorships.

Assuming that *Pearl Jam* had sold out 20,000 seat capacity venues at $23 a ticket, generating $460,000 in revenues each night the band would have taken home $330,000 from each of the 40 performances, or $13.2 million each summer. After deducting for eight-week production costs ($800,000), an agent's 6 percent commission ($792,000), and a manager's 15 percent commission ($1.7 million), that would have left *Pearl Jam* with $9.9 million each year."[1]

According to the New York Times, other more successful situations were reported at year's end by <u>Performance Magazine.</u> *The Rolling Stones'* "Bridges to Babylon" was the top-grossing tour of 1997, taking in $90 million, and continuing to hold its top-grossing record from its 1989 and '94 tours. *U2* grossed $78 million, followed by *Metallica*, with $37 million. Overall, the top 50 touring acts took in $781 million.[2]

RAND McNALLY METRO AREAS
1990
RANKED BY POPULATION

RMA		POP. EST
1.	New York, NY-NJ-CT	17,359,700
2.	Los Angeles	11,989,200
3.	Chicago, ILL-IN-WI	7.851,000
4.	San Francisco	5,435,900
5.	Philadelphia, PA-NJ-DE-MD	5,417,900
6.	Detroit, MI-CAN	4,351,300
7.	Boston, MA-NH	4,170,900
8.	Washington, DC-MD-VA	3,854,500
9.	Dallas	3,624,200
10.	Miami	3,530,300
11.	Houston	3.334.700
12.	Atlanta	2,676,400
13.	Seattle	2,610,200
14.	Minneapolis, MN-WI	2,047,600
15.	SanDiego, CA-MEX	2,269,300
16.	St. Louis	2,220,600
17.	Cleveland	2,138,200
18.	Phoenix	2,129,800
19.	Baltimore	2,099,500
20.	Pittsburgh	2,047,600
21.	Denver	1,578,000
22.	Cincinnati, OH-KY-IN	1,554,600
23.	Milwaukee	1,408,600
24.	Portland, OR-WA	1,408,500
25.	Kansas City, MO-KS	1,397,500
26.	Riverside, CA	1,348,000
27.	Sacramento	1,193,700
28.	San Antonio	1,180,500
29.	Indianapolis	1,156,300
30.	New Orleans	1,114,800

Source: 1992 Rand McNally Commercial Atlas & Marketing Guide, Pg. 126 Figure 9.1

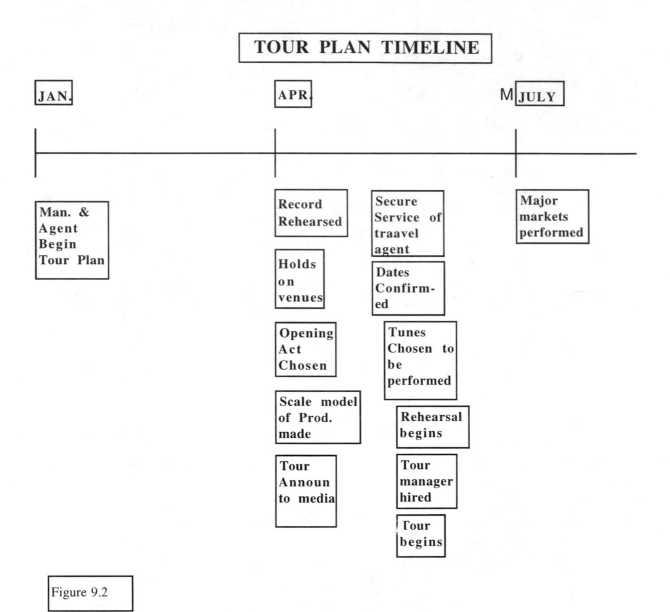

TOUR PLAN TIMELINE

JAN.   APR.   M JULY

Man. &
Agent
Begin
Tour Plan

Record
Rehearsed

Secure
Service of
traavel
agent

Major
markets
performed

Holds
on
venues

Dates
Confirm-
ed

Opening
Act
Chosen

Tunes
Chosen to
be
performed

Scale model
of Prod.
made

Rehearsal
begins

Tour
Announ
to media

Tour
manager
hired

Tour
begins

Figure 9.2

PREPARING FOR THE TOUR

WHEN AND WHERE TO START

Deciding where to begin a tour depends upon a number of factors. The tour should begin far from media attention and industry visibility. This insulation gives the artist a chance to iron out unforeseen problems before moving into a major market. Problems may occur in the actual stage /performance, the technical production preparation, or the performance publicity. Any media attention at this point might focus on them, and could damage the tour.

A rule of thumb is to begin a tour approximately eight weeks after the release of the record. By this time, the album's first single should be getting airplay, and album should be coming into its "stride." The artist should play the secondary and tertiary markets (metro areas numbers 16-30 in Figure 9.1) for three or four weeks, and then perform in the major target markets about twelve weeks after the release (see Figure 9.2).

ROUTING

In which secondary market should the tour begin? In which secondary market will the artist draw a large enough audience to show a profit? Where is a good place to try out the material and warm up the show? Should the tour begin in the east or someplace in the midwest?

The key to a successful tour is flexibility. As manager, you must be willing to add additional dates and reroute the artist at any time. The tentative routing of the tour should begin several months prior to its start (see Figure 9.2). It makes good business sense to begin near the artist's home. People and equipment will only need to travel a short distance. If the artist lives in Atlanta, why cart the equipment across the country to begin in Boise, Idaho? Sketch out where (in which major market) you would like to be when you anticipate the record hitting its stride. Use the weekend nights as cornerstones for the routing and build the rest of the tour around these dates. It's feasible to play markets that are starved for entertainment on weekday nights; however, the dates in major markets should be booked for weekends. Of course, if the artist is very popular, it doesn't matter if the concert is on a weekday or a weekend. However, if the venue attracts audiences from great distances, attendance at a weekday concert might be hampered by people needing to go to work the next day. If the artist has toured before, use the results of previous tours to rationalize why this routing should be successful.

Some variables may decrease the size of the anticipated audience. First, be aware of the other "traffic" in the market (traffic refers to concerts by competing artists). If an artist that draws the same audience that your artist does has performed in the market within two weeks prior to your artist's show, it may seriously hurt ticket sales. This is especially true if your artist's audience has a limited disposable income, or the market's population cannot with stand a heavy concert schedule.

Second, be aware of the economic conditions of the market. A depressed economy may seriously decrease the expected number of ticket sales in a geographic area, no matter what you may do to help the publicity. An example of this would be the effect the bargain price of oil has had on Houston, Texas.

PROCEDURE

The process of securing a concert performance involves the artist's manager, the booking agent, and the concert promoter. The following is a typical sequence of events:

Step 1: The manager and agent arrive at a price the artist is seeking for its performance.

This price is based on the tour budget, and the artist's worth in the marketplace. The price may be represented in three different forms:

1.   A flat guarantee
2.   A guarantee vs. a percentage (whichever is greater) after verified expenses
3.   A percentage after verified expenses

1. <u>A flat guarantee</u>

Today, even though a headlining artist usually does not perform solely for a guaranteed price, it is still an option. A flat guarantee is most often the price offered to an opening act. For example, **"The artist will perform one 45 minute set for $1500 flat guarantee."**

2. <u>A guarantee vs. a percentage</u>

Many headlining artists require a concert promoter to guarantee them a sum of money to perform, and will also want to share in the profits from the number of tickets sold. This option assures them a sum of money to cover expenses in case ticket sales don't meet their expectations. For example, **"The artist will perform for $60,000 guarantee vs. 85% of the Gross Box Office Receipts after verified expenses, whichever is greater."** In this case, if the gross potential from the ticket receipts after taxes is $400,000, and the promoter has incurred expenses of $220,000 (the artist's guarantee would **not** enter the calculations), the remainder would be $180,000. The artist would receive 85% of the remainder or $153,000. The concert promoter would receive the rest -- $27,000.

$400,000 GP

-$220,000 Expenses

$180,000 Remaining

$180,000

x .85

$153,000 Artist receives

$27,000 Promoter receives

3. A percentage after verified expenses

On occasion, a headlining artist may not require a concert promoter to guarantee a performance fee, but demand a higher percentage of the net receipts (after verified expenses). These are artists who are in demand at showtime because of a long awaited release of an album, or are just simply hot. The contract would read **"90% of the Gross Box Office Receipts after verified expenses (including taxes, if required)."** In this case, if the gross potential from the ticket sales after taxes is $400,000, and the promoter has incurred expense of $220,000, the remaining $180,000 would be split $162,000 for the artist and $18,000 for the concert promoter.

$400,000 Gross Potential

-$220,000 Expenses

$180,000

$180,000

x .90

$162,500 Artist Receives

$18,000 Promoter Receives

This method works out better for the artist and is demanded by management when a sellout is almost assured.

_____

Some headliners may demand a graduated scale of the compensation agreed upon. As an example, this clause might read:

"85% of the Gross Box Office Receipts up to 80% capacity,

87.5% of the Gross Box Office Receipts from 81-90% capacity,

90% of the Gross Box Office Receipts from 91% capacity and over.

All Percentages are after verified expenses."

So if we use these percentages in our example, we still have a Gross Potential of $400,000 and expenses of $220,000. However, if the show is not a sellout, the actual ticket sales will not reach the gross potential, but the expenses will remain the same. (In fact, expenses usually rise because additional advertising is needed that was not originally budgeted, and thus becomes an added expense.) So at 80% capacity, the revenue from ticket sales is only $320,000. $320,000 - $220,000 expenses leaves only $100,000. The artist would receive only $85,000 and the promoter $15,000. (The artist would probably never perform for the promoter again!)

At 80% capacity:

$320,000 Gross

$220,000 expenses

$100,000 net

$100,000

  x .85

 $85,000 Artist receives

 $15,000 Promoter receives

At 90% capacity:

$360,000 Gross

$220,000 expenses

$140,000 net

$140,000

 x .875

$122,500 Artist receives

$17,500 Promoter receives

At sellout, the split would be the same as our first example in this section. The artist would receive $162,000 and the promoter $18,000.

In both circunstances numbers two and three, when there is a sellout, the promoter expects to receive to receive around 5% of the concert's gross after all expenses, including the artist's share. As stated in an article about Pace Concerts, one of the largest promoters in the country: "Pace Concerts expects to net 4 percent to 7 percent of a concert's gross after accounting for expenses and settling with the band."[3]

Step 2: **The agent solicits concert promoters in each region of the country, or calls venues in each region to inquire about available dates.**

The booking agent calls each concert promoter with the artist's price requirement and other details to determine if the promoter will buy or "pass" on the act's package. Even at this early stage, some negotiations occur concerning the selling price of tickets, and the scaling (how many seats at what price) of the house. In fact, some managers insist that every item is thoroughly discussed. However, now the promoter must decide if he or she can deliver a sellout show.

Step 3: **The promoter or agent puts a tentative hold on a venue for a specific date (or dates).**

Professional and college sports, circuses, ice shows, auto shows, trade shows, etc. are held in arenas. So they are booked very heavily all across the country. At times, very few dates that allow for concert setup and breakdown are available to the promoter. So tentative holds on specific dates should be placed as early as possible.

Step 4: **Dates are confirmed with weekend nights as cornerstones.**

As the manager accepts the offers to perform, the dates are confirmed with each venue. Using the weekend nights as the basis for building the rest of the tour, the routing begins to take shape. As this occurs, the manager and agent make decisions as to how many miles they want the artist and the entourage to travel between performances in each region. Obviously, the number of miles between performances will differ in the west as compared to the northeast. After this decision has been made, the rest of the performance dates are accepted to complete the tour itinerary.

The confirming of the dates means that a decision has been made as to the selling price of the admission tickets. The concert promoter in each region must negotiate an admission price that matches the economic conditions of his/her region, and still meets all expenses, including a profit for him/herself. According to John Scher, concert promoter, part-owner of Metropolitan

----

Entertainment, and then head of Polygram Diversified Entertainment, the factors entering into the decision concerning how much to charge include: the artist guarantee and the cost of media advertising space and time.[4] Both have risen significantly in recent years, and the concert business has suffered. Scher goes on to say that the ticket price a consumer will pay is rarely established by the promoter or the artist; but by the ticket scalper.

> ". . . for hot attractions people are willing to pay very large sums of money for the best tickets. A high ticket price minimizes the difference between what these tickets are ultimately being sold for by scalpers and what the box office is getting for them."[5]

Then why aren't ticket prices for super attractions higher in general? Richard Thayer, an economist at Cornell says that "those with businesses cannot afford the "perception of unfairness." He argues, "if you gouge skiers at Christmas, they won't come back in March."[6] Consequently, because the concert promotor's business is at risk, the ticket price is extremely important.

BUDGET

A manager can never be too conservative in estimating a tour budget! If an artist is "going out" for a guarantee against a percentage, the tour budget should be based roughly on the guarantee with only a small percentage of potential additional earnings being anticipated.

Begin "costing out the show" based on the expenses of the artist's last tour, or compile actual estimates for every budget line. Be sure to take special notice of the budget line allocated for miscellaneous expenses. Include travel agents, truck leasing firms, etc. Below (see Figure 9.3) is an actual budget form used by a major booking agency. The deal is called a "**Gross Split Point**" deal, which is a form of the "a percentage after verified expenses" deal. In this case, the promoter budgets in a percentage of the breakeven point or his/her expenses as his/her cut (or in other words, the promoter is guaranteed a percentage). The remainder is the amount when the percentages agreed upon kick in.

The top category is the **gross potential** for the show. The calculations are simple multiplication, and notice that the taxes must be included as an expense, however, not an expense that can be controlled and therefore they are not listed in the expense category. The **adjusted gross potential** for this example is $54,817.54

The second category is **expenses**. The artist guarantee is listed here, as well as all the fixed expenses that the promoter is responsible for. The promoter is guarranteed 15% of the breakeven point. These are the expenses that will be "verified" at the show settlement by the receipts collected by the promoter. In this example the **expense category** totals $45,156.79

The next category are the **variables*** or the costs that are directly related to the number of tickets sold. The venue rental fee is the only variable that has a guarantee attached to it. The other fees are adjusted according to the number in attendance.

The **summary** lists the total projected costs for the show, both fixed and variable and the **breakeven point** (in this case, $17050. + 8106.79 + 20000 = $45156.79). The computation for the breakeven point is complicated:

1. Add the total of all fixed expenses: $20,000 + 17,050 = $37,050.
2. Add the variable expenses: (13% rent + 6.88% tix, insur, & cre.cd. commisions)
3. Subtract total (.1988) from 1.00 = (1.00 - .1988 = .8012)
4. Divide the fixed expenses by step 3 result: (37,050 / .8012 = 46,243.14)

(This is only an approximation because it doesn't show flat fees + % for these variable costs.)

Anything above the $45000+ amount is split between the artist and the promoter. The profit differential - variables is the sum of the ticket commission, insurance, and credit card rates, or 6.88%. Adding the $6773.52 + 500.45 + 45156.79 = $52430.76, the **split point at which percentage amounts kick in**.

The last category, **earnings potential** includes the **overage** or the difference between the concert gross and the split point. Here the artist's share is 75.4% of $2386.78 and the promoter takes 18.75%. The artist's potential for a sellout show is $21799.63 and the promoter may earn a maximum of $7221.06. The variable share of the overage is the extra cost of the additional variable costs. This type of **"Gross Split Point"** deal is a conventional method for costing out a show and is used almost exclusively when the venue it not arena size, or the artist is not a guarantee sellout. It is necessary to learn these calculations and the computations should be practiced.

* These amounts are calculated on a flate rate plus a per head basis (see "insurance" in contract addendum below). The insurance is there to protect the artist, promoter and arena from damages.

GROSS SPLIT POINT DEAL

Event: **City:**
Date: TBA
Shows:

_____ POTENTIAL _____

	Seats	Price	Gross		Taxes	TOTAL
RES	600	28.50	17,100.00	5.50%	$3,014.96 Tax	
RES	600	24.50	14,700.00			
RES	1,335	19.50	26,032.50			
	2,535		**57,832.50**	less	$3,014.96	

Adjusted Gross Potential...$54,817.54

_____ EXPENSES _____

TALENT GUARANTEE	$20,000

 T O T A L...$20,000.00

FIXED

ADVERTISING	7,500.00
ASCAP/BMI	375.00
BOX OFFICE	500.00
CATERING	2,500.00
CLEAN-UP	500.00
DOOR/TIX/USHERS	375.00
INSURANCE	125.00
PAYROLL	500.00
RUNNER	125.00
SECURITY T-SHIRT	800.00
SPOTLIGHTS	200.00
STAGE HANDS	2,750.00
STAGE MANAGER	300.00
TELEPHONE	100.00
UTILITIES/ELECTRICAL	400.00

 T O T A L...$17,050.00

VARIABLES	Rate	@ Sellout	Guarantee	Ceiling
RENT	13.00 %	5,000.00	2,500.00	5,000.00
TICKET COMMISSION	2.00 %	1,000.00	.00	1,000.00
INSURANCE	2.38 %	1,376.41	.00	.00
CREDIT CARD	2.50 %	1,370.44	.00	.00

_____ SUMMARY _____

Total PROJECTED **SHOW COSTS----FIXED**..	17,050.00		
VARIABLE COST at Breakeven...................	8,106.79		
Talent and Production..	20,000.00.		
BREAKEVEN...	45,156.79	(2,007 seats)	79% (of hse.)
Promoter Profit @ Split........................ 15.00 %	6,773.52		
Profit Differential - Variables................. 6.88 %	500.45		
SPLIT POINT...	**52,430.76**		

_____ EARNINGS POTENTIAL _____

Concert Gross (less taxes)...............................	54,817.94........................		
Less Split Point..	52,430.76.		
O V E R A G E..	**2,386.78**....................		
Artist's Share of OVERAGE.................75.4 %.......	1,799.63.......+ 20,000.00 =	21,799.63	
Promoter's Share of OVERAGE........... 18.75%.....	447.54....... + 6,773.52 =	7,221.06	
Variable Share of OVERAGE.............. 5.85%.......	139.61......................		

Once a manager has sketched out a budget, he or she should develop a sense of how many concerts per week and per month must be performed in order to meet expenses and make a profit. Remember -- one of the objectives of a tour is to make a profit.

TRAVEL AND ACCOMMODATIONS

Secure the services of a competent, reliable travel agent for booking hotel rooms, public transportation, local car rental, and agent's services do not cost anything, and an efficient one allows the manager to concentrate on the other pressing tour issues. Trailer trucks and a band bus (provided the artist has agreed to this mode of travel) are usually leased separately.

CHOOSING AN OPENING ACT

All consumers respond to value for their money. When they purchase their tickets, many concertgoers are aware of who is the opening act. Therefore a hot opening act should increase ticket sales. A smart manager looks for an opening act that has had a level of success which will create name recognition with the audience. An opening act should have an established image that complements the headliner. An act that has already toured should have a small base of ticket buyers already established. However, nothing <u>guarantees</u> that the opening act will help sell tickets. A manager must rely on his or her own intuition plus any hard data concerning the prospective opening act's performing ability.

Once the manager chooses the act, he or she must "buy" the act before some other act's manager does. The term "buying an act" means that the headliner's manager offers the act a series of performance dates for a flat guaranteed price per show. In return, most often, the opening act may use the headliner's sound system and lights. In special cases, the offer to the opening act is negotiated to include a guarantee and a bonus based on the number of tickets sold per concert. However, this occurs only when the opening act's career has such momentum that it is in a position to demand it, or the competition for the opening act's participation amongst several other headlining acts requires it.

THE CONTRACT

The agreement that is normally issued for a live engagement is a form of the American Federation of Musicians's live engagement contract. Because booking agents are licensed by the A F of M, it appears on the booking agency's letterhead, and is a standard agreement that contains the name and place of the engagement, the name of the artist, the date and time of the performance, how much and how the artist will be compensated for the appearance, and other important information. The signatures that appear on the contract are the buyer of the show, usually the concert promoter, the artist (or representative of the artist), and the booking agent's; however his/her role is only as a conduit or middleman.

The buyer or concert promoter is not recognized as an employer of the musicians, but rather a **purchaser**. As a purchaser, s/he is not libel for any occurrences that the musicians might encounter, and has very little responsibility concerning the personal welfare of any of the performers. If the concert promoter was considered an employer, then the musicians performing would be subject to workman's compensation insurance, and all other employee benefits bound by law. As the contract reads, the musician is considered an **independent contractor** and is responsible for declaring the net revenue of the proceeds on his/her income tax form.

Figure 9.4a&b is an actual engagement contract issued by a booking agency to the headlining act. The name of the artist and the date of the event has been omitted, however, the other information is as it appeared on the original document.

AMERICAN FEDERATION OF MUSICIANS OF THE UNITED STATES AND CANADA
(THERIN CALLED FEDERATION)
CONTRACT
(FORM T-2)
FOR TRAVELING ENGAGEMENTS ONLY

Whenever The Term "The Local Union" Is Used For This Contract It Shall Mean The Local Union Of The Federation With Jurisdiction Over The Territory In Which The Engagement Covered By This Contract Is To Be Performed.

THIS CONTRACT for the personal services of musicians on the engagement described below is made this 20 day of October 1997 between the undersigned purchaser of music (herein called Purchaser) and the undersigned musician or musicians.

1. **Name and Address of Engagement:** _____
   Name of Artist:_____

   Number of Musicians: 4   Number of Vocalist: 1

2. **Date(s) of Engagement, Daily or weekly schedule and daily clock hours:** Wednesday   1997
Doors: 6:30 PM   Opening Act: 7:30PM   Opening Act: 8:00PM   Headliner:9.15PM   Capacity: 14,612
Ticket Scaling: 8,087   @ $65.00   6,525   @ $35.00   Gross Potential: $754,030 00 .   There is an additional $2 00
Facility Fee to patrons at the box office TicketMaster patrons are subject to Ticket Master service fees. On Sale Date:

3. **Type of Engagement**: Concert   3a. Merchandising Deal: 60/40 Venue Sells

4. **Compensation Agreed:** $300,000   All   Inclusive Guarantee vs. 85% of the gross box office receipts after verified expense whichever is greater.   (Headliner to receive $187,500 Guarantee plus a $15,000 Production Fee.   Opening Act to receive $97 500 Guarantee.   Headliner to pay any overages due Opening Act.)

5. **Purchaser Will Make Payments As Follows:**   50% ($93,750)   Due upon on sale via certified check money order or bank wire. Balance Due immediately prior to performance via, cash certified check or money order.

6. No performance on the engagement shall be recorded, reproduced, or transmitted from the place of performance in any manner or by any means whatsoever in the absence of a specific written agreement with the Federation relating to and permitting such recording reproduction or transmission.

7. It is expressly understood by the Purchaser and the musicians who are parties to this contract that neither the Federation no the Local Union are parties to this contract in any capacity except as expressly provided in & above and, therefore, that neither the Federation nor the Local Union shall be liable for the performance or breach of any provision hereof.

8. A representative of the Local Union, or the Federation, shall have access to the place of engagement covered by the contract for purposes of communicating with the musicians performing the engagement and the Purchaser.

9. The agreement of the musicians to perform is subject to proven detention by sickness, accidents, riots, strikes, epidemics, acts of God, or any other legitimate conditions beyond their control.

10. Attached addenda and Artist's Rider are made part of this contract herein.

IN WITNESS WHEREOF, The parties hereto have hereunto set their names and seals on the day and year above written.

PURCHASER: _____   ARTIST: _____
Figure 9.4a

203

09/ 12/97

<FIXED EXPENSES>

/97 WEDNESDAY

CAPACITY: < 14,612>
POTENTIAL: $754,030.0

TOTAL: $615,275.00

New York, NY 10001

Expense Categories	Ind.	Budget Amt	Notes
FLAT RENT/BLDG EXP.	F	216,000.00	INCL. SPOTLIGHTS, PHONE/LINES
ADVERTISING	F	70,000.00	CLEANING, MEDICAL, POLICE, FIRE
ASCAP/BMI	F	925.00	SECURITY, STAGEHANDS, USHERS,
CATERING	F	7,000.00	TIX TAKERS & BOX OFFICE
ADDT'L PHONE LINES	F	600.00	$300 PER LINE
INSURANCE	F	9,000.00	$321 + $0.57 PER HEAD
PRODUCTION MANAGER	F	750.00	
RUNNERS (3)	F	450.00	
SECURITY	F	1,200.00	
TOWELS	F	200.00	
FURNITURE RENTAL	F	1,200.00	
CREDIT CARD CHARGES	F	1,200.00	
MISCELLANEOUS	F	750.00	
TRANSPORTATION	F	2,500.00	
* INTENTIONALLY OMITTED	F	3,500.00	
ARTISTS GUARANTEE	F	300,000.00	
		$615,275.00	

Expenses must be documented on the night of the engagement and approved by Artist's representative. Any expenses not documented shall be the Purchasers sole responsibility. Producer requires notarized affidavits from all sources with whom commercials are placed including, but not limited to, radio stations, television stations, and print media, to be presented at settlement. If the Purchaser has other or greater expenses than those indicated above, the break figure shall not be affected. However the bona fide aggregate paid bills relating to any of the above listed costs shall total less than breakeven stated above, the break Figure will be reduced accordingly.

ACCEPTED and AGREED TO:

PURCHASER: _____   ARTIST: _____

Figure 9.4b

Line 2 expresses the date of the performance, and also includes the time the doors will open, the time any support act will begin, the time the headliner will go on, and the capacity of the house. It also states the price of the ticket, excluding any service charge, the type of ticket (general admission or reserve), the gross potential for a sellout (including taxes), and the date tickets will go on sale.

Line 3 includes the type of engagement and 3a the merchandising arrangement. 3a may list the company that will handle the merchandising, or the percentage arrangement, ie. 60/40 if the venue concessionaires are to be involved with the physically selling the merchandise.

Line 4 contains the terms of how the compensation will occur. For this performance, the headliner is receiving **a guarantee vs. 85% of the gross box office receipts after verified expenses whichever is greater.** The percentage is based on the amount of tickets the promoter sells. A sellout will reap the artist and the promoter considerably more money than less than a sellout, as discussed earlier in this chapter. The list of verifiable or fixed expenses appears at the end of the contract as an addendum and has been agreed upon by the buyer and the artists' representatives. If the concert revenue moves the deal into the splits, the artists' guarantee of $300,000 does not enter the calculation of expenses, because they stand to earn a considerably larger amount of money. This example is rare, as the opening act is performing for a very high guarantee and will take part in the splits.

Line 5 states how the payment will be made. Artists usually demand about 50% upon the signing of the contract. Should the promoter really screw up, this amount is non-refundable . It also locks in the performance date. Without a considerable amount of money upfront, the artist might be asked to perform somewhere else and have to decline the offer believing that s/he is already booked for a performance that may never happen.

Line 6 states that the performance may not be recorded or transmitted with a specific agreement allowing such to occur. The A F of M has insisted on this language since commercial recordings began.

THE CONCERT CONTRACT RIDER

The most important reason for the existence of a contract rider is to inform the promoter of the artist's expectations and requirements, and to protect the artist against any unforeseen difficulties. Is there a way to react to a problem legally? Is there some language in the written agreement that will allow the artist to cancel the performance? Do we really need twelve cases of French wine in the dressing room after every show?

Of course, there are other reasons for attaching a rider to a contract. Some artists want to feel as at home on the road as they possibly can, and they expect the concert promoter to see that they do. Others carry a spectacular visual production and massive sound systems that have extraordinary technical needs. Specific requirements for this sophisticated equipment should be listed in the rider. Most concert riders include the following categories. Some artists require more details on some categories than others. For the concert promoter, the technical requirements are most important since they will insure the promoter's preparedness with everything from electrical power to the number of stagehands needed.

Rider Categories

The following are the usual categories found in a concert rider..

1.   Billing and Advertising

Headlining artist require "100% sole star billing" in all advertising and publicity for the show. This means that nothing else connected with the performance will be larger than the artist's name.

2.   Cameras/VCRs/Recorders

Cameras or recorders of any type are not permitted by the artist (with the exception of the press) unless specific arrangements have been made.

3.   Financial Considerations (including ticket sales, merchandising requirements and insurance)

Specifics concerning the guest list and other box office requirements are listed.

Concert gate receipts and expenses not detailed in the actual contract are also listed. The purchasers obligations as to the sale of concert merchandise, and the artist's rights are also specified. On some tours, the official concert merchandise is sold by the venue's concessionaires, and on others, the artist has personal vendors.

The purchaser (concert promoter) must provide for full public liability insurance coverage to protect against any accidents during the load in, operation, and load out of the equipment. The purchaser must also carry insurance that excludes any of the artist's entourage from any claims that may arise due to the personal injury of an audience member.

4. Backstage Accommodations, Catering, and Security

Although this section of the rider makes for the most humorous reading, the essential aspects of these three areas cannot be ignored.

Specifics concerning backstage accommodations are not only important to the artist, but also the crew and management. Some "legs" of tours last six to eight months. The road becomes home! Hassle free comfort is important in maintaining one's sanity and concentration.

The same is true for the catering requirements. Everyone in the crew must eat a nourishing, balanced, diet. Energy levels must be maintained and fatigue must be kept at a minimum. Dietary requirements such as beefless meals, or special diets due to medical needs must be honored.

Limited access, security, and safety are the responsibility of the purchaser. It is here that details are specified.

5. Crew Arrangements

Accommodations and catering requirements must be specified for the crew as well. Meals must be served at the times specified and other essentials, such as showers and restrooms must be available. Space for truck and bus parking must be reeserved as well as information concerning medical emergency facilities.

6. Productions and Technical Requirements

As previously stated, this is the most important aspect of the concert rider. Specific electrical requirements, and the purchaser's responsibility for hiring carpenters, electricians, spotlight operators, stagehands, riggers (climbing and ground), truckloaders, and forklift operators are listed. Remember, the actual success of the artist's presentation relies heavily on the total compliance with this section of the rider.

Figures 9.5 and 9.6 are articles that appeared concerning the 1992 U2 tour and the 1997 Rolling Stones tour respectively. Make note of the elaborate production requirements of each show. Although these are far from the ordinary arena shows that take place daily throughout the world, it is clear the because of the rising admission prices, fans are demanding more and more show.

7. Cancellation and Force Majeure

Usually the artist states that if any member of the act or production staff becomes ill (or incapacitated), the artist maintains the right to cancel and not be obligated to reschedule the show. The force majeure clause also includes other events beyond the control of the artist, such as civil unrest or Acts of God.

----

8.   Legal Remedies

In case of any breech of the contract by the purchaser or any damages, this section specifies the legal remedies available.

Originally, concert riders were initiated because promoters agreed to supply certain production requirements and then didn't. For example, the artist would request a stage with dimensions of 64'x 48'x 8' high. The promoter would say "no problem" and then deliver a stage that was only 4' high! However, today this is the exception. Delinquent or unprofessional concert promoters do not stay in business.

Cutting extraneous expenses can be critical to the profitability of a tour. As mentioned earlier, most headlining artists perform for a percentage of the profits. While the artist receives a percentage of every $20 ticket sold, it is also true that the artist looses a percentage for every $20 spent on expenses!

Technology Update

Rock Band U2's Zoo TV Tour: A Marvel in Stadium Staging

by MARK FORMANEK

Before rock band U2 took the stage on its recently completed stadium tour of the United States, a small army of technicians descended to rig and wire 52 tractor-trailer loads of "Zoo TV Outside Broadcast" equipment.

This was a mind-boggling array of high and low technology—ranging from live phone lines available on stage to giant video screens suspended in banks inside each venue.

"We've drawn on everything: Disneyland, advertising from Coca-Cola to McDonald's, TV evangelism, pornography, election ad campaigns, and television in general," lead singer Bono told *USA Today.*

Indeed, it seems U2 upped the ante after its 30-city, sold-out arena tour by bringing in more of everything to this wild rock and roll stadium party. There were more bright lights, four mega-video screens, four Phillips Vidi-Walls and 36 video monitors.

There was more sound—Zoo TV used more than one million watts of power driving 176 speaker enclosures, 312 18-inch woofers, 592 10-inch mid-ranges and 604 high-frequency drivers. And, of course, a stadium tour means plenty of spontaneous action. On this tour, Bono made telephone calls during the show, ordering pizza for the entire audience, calling the Home Shopping Club and live sex lines, and placing calls to the White House and British Prime Minister John Major to protest the Sellafield Nuclear Fuel Reprocessing Plant.

High-Tech Zoo An Apt Description

Zoo TV is an appropriate name for this roving caravan of rock and roll abandon. On a stage measuring 248-feet wide and more than 80-feet deep (designed by Fischer Park of London), several radio masts, reaching to 110 feet above the venue, were erected. Some of these structures are so tall, in fact, that they required FAA-approved aircraft warning lights at their summits.

Spread on and around the stage were more than 30 tons of equipment. For sound, Zoo TV used two separate monitor mix positions, each with two consoles providing 160 channel input capacity and 26 on-stage mixes and 60 separate monitor speakers. Front-of-house had three 40-channel consoles with a total input capacity of 120 channels, all constructed by Clair Brothers Sound Systems. As concert goers can attest, the volume of this sound was amazing.

Move First, Party Later

But before all of these systems could begin to function, the little matter of moving equipment and personnel from stadium to stadium arose. In addition to more than 200 locally supplied laborers, Zoo TV used more than 180 traveling crew in 12 buses (provided by Four Seasons) and a 40-passenger chartered jet. Two catering companies fed the personnel each day.

Along with the manpower, the show carried almost 2.5-million pounds of equipment. Twelve forklifts and a 120-foot, 40-ton crane helped with the heavy lifting. Four generators were carried to power the show, using in excess of three miles of cable and throwing off enough power to light two city blocks.

Under the stage was a tangle of wires and TV equipment. A mini-TV station was set up below the boards in each city. In this command post Carol Dodds, video director, used a custom system, called CDI, developed for this tour by Phillips Interactive Media. During the show live satellite broadcasts were televised on stage—Bono made his choices with a channel changer. This is the first live tour in which this system has been employed. It featured 12 laser-disc players, monitors containing the live TV feeds, and five cameras that Dodds mixed on site during each performance. The laser-disc players contained footage created by Kevin Godly, Brian Eno, Mark Pellington, Peter Williams, Dodds, and Pearson-Post Industries of New York. The tour also used 18 video projectors. A video crew of 18 assisted Dodds in bringing an avalanche of images to the stadium video screens.

Back on top, the stage set included 11 specially decorated Trabant cars, two of which were suspended over the stage and were illuminated inside and out. The Trabants, which were made from compressed cardboard in East Germany prior to the fall of the Eastern block, originally weighed 400 pounds and cost around $300 each. They were the people's car of East Germany, each owned and used by private families. Today

they have been structurally modified and each now weighs more than a ton. Two of the cars were on cranes and others were on hydraulic systems. They were decorated with art by Catherine Owens, Rene Castro and Williams.

Stage Set Up And Design

This U2 show took more than 40 hours to set up and required 12 mobile office trailers. Once the stage was up and running, the band made full use of it—including an innovative runway system that moved out into the audience for mid-show "unplugged sets." The staging was designed by Up-Front Staging of Austin, TX and the lighting by Light & Sound Design. The band's public address system was placed behind the staging area on this tour—another technical accomplishment.

The stage was set up in the "zone" of a stadium, a move that tour officials say cut down on transporting heavy equipment within the stadium. A 100-foot tower flied

about one-third of the lights, requiring about 25 tons of ballast and a heavy crane. There were also 28 production trucks and two steel systems that required 13 trucks each.

According to tour officials, for set-up the crew arrived between noon and 4 p.m. the day before the show and worked straight through to opening. Take-down went more swiftly, averaging about five-to-six hours.

Zoo and U2

What was the total production cost for Zoo TV? About $6 million, according to tour managers. The crew has strong engineering and computer backgrounds; roughly 30% are from overseas, mainly Australia, New Zealand, England, Ireland and Norway. The transportation and steel people are largely American.

In the end, however, all the lights and gadgetry in the world cannot make up for an average performance. With Zoo TV, U2 has found a unique showcase in which to display its formidable talents. Its tour was a first in stadium staging. ❐

Zoo TV added technological punch to U2's recently-completed tour

Behind the Stones' High-Tech Curtain

Since they began touring in the early 1960's, the Rolling Stones have turned the concept of a concert into an event. The Stones' latest tour, "Bridges to Babylon," continues their tradition of employing the technology of the age. From lighting to sound to video to pyrotechnics, the scene behind the stage is abuzz with the sounds of keys clicking and hard drives grinding. Here is a look at what makes the Stones' show roll.

Lights
The light show is choreographed by a computer. With the click of a mouse, all of the lights, except spotlights, can run without an operator.

Mick Jagger

Cameras
Footage from five onstage cameras is fed into a video editing room. Editors mix the live video with preprogrammed special effects to create the look of a music video.

Lyrics
Mick Jagger is assisted by two large monitors, which display the song list and the first lines of each song. The monitors are run by an I.B.M. laptop off the stage.

Movies
The centerpiece of the stage is a gigantic Sony Jumbotron, which uses digital television technology to create a clear image.

Dolls
The stage, which the architect Mark Fisher describes as "a lost city in the desert," uses inflatable scenery to minimize set up time and travel size.

Speakers
Built for the Stones, X-Array speakers are much smaller and require less power than traditional speakers.

Source: Rolling Stones

Photographs by Paul Natkin (stage); Associated Press (Mick Jagger)

Virtual Satisfaction

Software Runs a Special Effects Extravaganza on the Concert Tour

BY ANDREW ROSS SORKIN

Booming "Can't get no satisfaction," beneath the blank gaze of two guely sphinx-like and unambigusly suggestive statues, Mick Jager strutted and pranced onto the age in front of more than 55,000 ns at Giants stadium late last eek.

But underneath the music of the nd and the cheers of the crowd, an most inaudible hum continued thout letup — the sound of the ndreds of computers and whining rd drives that controlled this spectular stage show, all gyrating to tune of 1's and 0's.

The Rolling Stones latest world ir, "Bridges to Babylon," comes ore than 35 years since Mick Jagr and Keith Richards began belt-g out blues: it is a showcase for the olution of high technology in the ncert business.

There is the audio system custom lt for the tour controlled by two gital sound boards. There are the reless microphones which use HF frequencies. There is the computer controlled light show, powered software that synchronizes 3,000 watts of light with the beats more than a dozen Stones songs. They may still be looking for satisfaction, but the Stones are already red.

"You know, there are rarely any antum leaps in anything," Mr. gger, who is 54, said in interview fore the Rolling Stones' first concrt in New York last week. "And ien you're doing this all the time, u don't notice it. But if you look ck even 10 years ago, technology s changed everything."

Indeed, technology has affected almost every facet of the stadium concrt. Today, computers — the personal kind and others built specifically for the concert industry — control ery aspect of what an audience...

stadium concerts have become spectaculars. Singing no longer suffices in an age of MTV and $60 tickets.

The rise of the electronic spectacular has its costs, some feel. "It's a double-edged sword," said Jim Henke, chief curator of Cleveland's Rock and Roll Hall of Fame and Museum. "There is this expectation to turn the concert into this exciting spectacle. But at the same time, you lose that magical intimacy."

But TNA International Ltd., a privately held company based in Toronto, does not make its money from intimacy. While the company refused to disclose the cost of putting on the Stones' concert series, it did say that the Rolling Stones 1992 world tour, grossed $121.2 million in ticket sales in North America. Executives familiar with the current tour estimate the cost of leasing lighting and sound equipment during the 35-...

Perhaps the most vivid example of technology's influence in the Stones latest tour is a gigantic self-illuminating screen that serves as the centerpiece to an expansive 200-foot-wide stage. The screen — which consists of 100,224 pixels that create crisp images like those on digital TV — is similar to the Sony Jumbotron that once hung in Times Square, but is almost twice as big and twice as sharp.

"It shrink-a-sizes the stadium," said Michael Cohl, the tour director for the Rolling Stones. "Obviously, it makes it a lot better for the people in the back."

Mark Fisher, the electronic impresario who built the stage and assembled the effects for this tour as well as for other tours by the Stones and U2, said: "Back in the late 1960's we were using General Electric projectors designed to be used in U.S. military situation rooms. You'd get these...

of them together and bounce them off a mirror to get some illumination. But it still looked awful."

Today, what appears on this monstrous screen is the equivalent of a two-hour long live music video. Five wandering cameramen, tethered only by their long power cords, capture the show on the stage video cameras. The images are fed to computers — where the video is mixed with programmed special effects using special digital editing equipment made by Arti, and Apple Macintosh computers — and then sent back to the Jumbotron.

Framing celebrities and politicians with super-large images of themselves is hardly new. But in a twist on the high-tech video experience, the Rolling Stones also have a World Wide Web site where users can vote for a song request. The winning song is then displayed on the Jumbotron and played by the band.

The stage is illuminated by what the lighting designer, Patrick Woodroffe, called "intelligent" or "obedient" lights, run by software which took three weeks to program.

Much of the preproduction and staging is also computerized. Before the tour, Mr. Fisher had gotten approval for his plans based on a three-dimensional, virtual design for the stage created in Autocad, an Autodesk software program used by architects.

The stage itself is an engineering feat. Mr. Fisher has created a second stage in the middle of the arena that emerges in mid-crowd during the concert. A self-propelled bridge then emerges from the main stage and vaults 140 feet over the audience to connect both stages so the band can get to what is called "B Stage."

But does all the technology render the band almost secondary? No, Dick Carruthers, the video director, said. "It's still the Rolling Stones. People are still coming out to see Mick's bony knees."

Dave Moss, the assistant video engineer for the Rolling Stones, uses a laptop computer to prepare video images for a recent concert.

Bill Kramer for The New York Times

RECORD COMPANY SUPPORT

In some instances, record companies contribute tour support money to new artists recently signed to the label. This is sometimes negotiated into the artist's contract and then administered by the artist development department. However, for an established artist, record companies offer any financial support very reluctantly. They support their artists in terms of promotion and merchandising in each market where the artist performs. But money is another story.

Record companies want to determine the fan support for the artist in each market. They want to keep track of how the record is selling in the performance market and they'll want to do whatever is needed to increase sales.

Record companies may also want the act to perform in markets where the record isn't selling. Since the concert promoter and the agent would like to sell as many concert tickets as possible, they want the artist to perform where the record is doing well. This dilemma must be resolved by the manager.

CHOOSING MATERIAL FOR THE PERFORMANCE

Another question facing the artist and the manager is what to perform on the tour. The audience wants to hear songs that are familiar. The artist may be tired of performing hits that are often years old and wants to perform new material. How many songs should be included from the new album? How many songs should be repeated form the last tour? When should the hits be performed? Should any cover material such as rock classics be included?

When deciding what to perform, one rule of thumb is to choose material that works well in the live setting. Songs that rely on sound production techniques may not "come off" on stage as well as on the recording. Simpler tunes may work best. A good rule is to give the audience as much familiar material as possible and save the biggest hit for the encore. The old show business adage still holds true: "Leave them wanting more!"

TOUR REHEARSAL

Each artist sets his or her own rehearsal schedule for the tour. The schedule is based on how long it's been since the band has played together or how many new players will be on the tour. Most bands rehearse for only a few weeks as a group before the tour begins. The material to be performed should be chosen before rehearsals begin for the sake of efficiency.

Before the start of the tour, it's useful to hold the final tour dress rehearsals in the opening arena. An artist's manager will book the arena for three days to a week before the beginning of the tour, and rehearse the music and production. These dress rehearsals benefit the production crew. However, they also give the artist an opportunity to rehearse different stage

_____

moves and any choreography.

PRODUCTION PREPARATION

As a tour headliner, the artist is responsible for the concert staging. Stage production design should be completed as far in advance of opening night as possible to allow for competitive bidding for the actual construction of the staging, lighting, etc. The manager and the tour production manager should estimate the production budget and then meet with a designer for the actual design. A drawing to scale or an actual scale model should be completed at least two months before the beginning of the tour. Unless the artist knows exactly what he or she wants, or has had some experience in stage design, the artist won't view the model until this point.

The production development budget for a headlining act is currently $100,000 to millions depending on the design. Artists generally own the stage production rather than lease and, most often, use it for only one tour. Consequently, keep in mind that <u>what is spent is only used once</u>!

TRANSPORTATION

The vehicles used to transport tour equipment are usually leased. Because if a highway breakdown occurs, the leasing company is responsible for transporting the equipment to the arena. It is important to work with reputable leasing companies that offer commercial leasing agreements.

TOUR PUBLICITY

The tour should be announced to the media no earlier than two months before the opening date (see Chapter Four). There are mixed opinions as to the importance of any announcement that doesn't publicize a specific date. However, most managers do release a press announcement with details about the entire tour. The release is then disseminated to various publications throughout the country. If the artist retains the services of a publicist, then the publicist uses his or her influence to get the information published. Posters and other tour paraphernalia which uses the artist's name and likeness is usually licensed to a merchandising company. This will be covered in the next chapter.

ENTOURAGE

The number of people that travel with the artist varies. They include: musicians, support crew, and guests. The concert rider contains the list of entourage members that travel with the band and the crew members that are hired locally for each specific site. Refer back to Figure 9.5, the article concerning U2's Zoo TV Tour. The traveling crew numbered 180 people, transported in 12 buses, and a 40 passenger chartered jet, plus an addition 200 locally hired laborers.

ROAD CREW

A road crew consists of sound people, lighting people, stage construction people, drivers, etc. The production manager usually hires the crew for the entire tour. A simple rule is "Don't pay people until you need them!"

TOUR MANAGER

The tour manager (road manager) is responsible for the logistics of transporting the artist during the tour, and for the daily activities of the entire tour entourage. He or she must be organized, articulate, and able to make decisions under stress. The tour manager sometimes acts as the tour "accountant." His or her responsibilities include "settling" the show with the promoter and receiving payment for each performance, as well as handling the weekly petty cash needs. The tour manager usually begins receiving a salary two weeks before the tour begins. During these two weeks he or she begins advancing the initial concert dates with the promoters, and reviewing the transportation and hotel arrangements. He or she also meets with the manager and accountant to determine what bookkeeping and other duties will be expected.

SECURITY

Some artists, like Madonna, contract their own security personnel for the entire tour. Other artists rely on the security personnel contracted by each concert promoter for each performance.

INSURANCE

The entire tour must be covered by the various forms liability insurance (refer back to the budget section). Sometimes artists also contract performance cancellation insurance. This means that if a performance is cancelled for any reason, the artist receives a percentage of his or her fee. Performance cancellation insurance premiums are very expensive. The manager usually budgets the fee into the artist's performance price. However, a reputable insurance agent that handles performance insurance must be contacted. Promoters carry weather insurance for outdoor events. Lloyds of London writes this type of protection.

DURING THE TOUR

Manager's Responsibilities

As a manager, you must carry on the daily activities of the management office, and handle the maintenance and execution of all unforeseen emergencies! Since every tour date is a major financial transaction involving thousands of dollars, it's your responsibility to see that every date is as successful as possible.

_____

Typically, there are ten to twenty performances on sale simultaneously, and five or six different concert promoters presenting the shows. You should telephone every promoter daily. You should also arrange for and monitor 90% of all details for each show. So you must keep track of the artist on the road, as well as promotional materials, ticket sales, radio spots, and any media coverage for each performance. This requires good organizational skills. Managers use computers to organize their jobs or create working forms for specific tasks. Forms are designed to help keep track of all the promotional materials, press interviews, and concert production details.

A calendar should also be kept for each performance date of the tour. The calendar information should include the artist's itinerary and the daily advertising schedule. The calendar will remind you when every radio spot on every station will be aired, and when the other pieces in the advertising mix are scheduled.

ARTIST FATIGUE

Fatigue can lead to sloppy performances while touring. That's why it's important to schedule periodic days off for the artist and make certain they remain days "off" rather than just days without a performance. The artist should not give interviews or attend rehearsals on these days (unless it is absolutely necessary). And, it's important to keep all tour problems away from the artist as well. Problems should be solved by the tour manager. Lastly, proper diet and rest are essential to the artist's health. An artist who is in good shape will be in a better frame of mind with a more positive attitude.

SETTLING WITH THE PROMOTER

The artist representative (usually the tour manager) and the concert promoter make the financial settlement for the date on the night of the performance. When the box office has tallied the evening's receipts, the financial transaction takes place. Most often it occurs after the first few songs of the headliner's set. The promoter submits his or her expenses incurred in producing the performance, and the figures are totaled per the written contract. If the expenses appear to be in excess if what was anticipated, they are negotiated. However, most artists work with concert promoters on more than one occasion and a mutual respect is reached. Figure 9.7 is a show **settlement form**. You may plug in the amounts from the budget worksheet discussed earlier to create the completed settlement form.

From time to time, a mathematical error may occur. To avoid this, is important for the tour manager/accountant to check and recheck all accounting. A 2% error on a $240,000 performance fee is $4800. The same error could cost the artist $96,000 if it was multiplied over 20 shows!

<u>AFTER THE TOUR</u>

After the tour ends and everyone has rested, the entire experience should be evaluated to see if the objectives have been met. The obvious question is: Did the tour make money and how much? However, the other tour objectives are important as well. Did the artist increase his or her visibility in a given market? Have any new industry personnel been added to the artist's support system? Have any left? Why? On a market-by-market basis, did any concert reach the status of being recognized as an event? Did the artist perform in the major markets while the record was peaking? Does the artist consider the tour successful? Do you? What was learned from the total experience?

TOTAL TICKETS SOLD _____ PLUS COMPS _____ TOTAL ATTENDANCE _____

GROSS $ _____ _____
TAX $ _____ SOLD AT DOOR
NET $ _____

NIGHT OF SHOW SETTLEMENT | FINAL SETTLEMENT

ARTIST RECONCILIATION

NET GROSS	$ _____	CONT. HELD	$ _____
LESS EXP.	$ _____ ____ % GROSS	SPENT	$ _____
LESS OTHER	$ _____)	FOR	_____
TO BE SPLIT	$ _____		_____
% TO ARTIST	_____ %		_____
DUE ARTIST	$ _____		_____
VS. GUAR.	$ _____		_____
		RETURNED	$ _____

DUE ARTIST	$ _____
LESS DEPOSIT	$ _____
LESS OTHER	$ _____
SUBTOTAL	$ _____
LESS CASH	$ _____
LESS OTHER	$ _____
LESS OTHER	$ _____
PLUS OTHER	$ _____
CK TO ARTIST	$ _____

ARTIST RECONCILIATION

CONT. RET.	$ _____	
% DUE ARTIST	_____ %	
DUE ARTIST	$ _____	
PD. NOS	$ _____	
TOTAL PD.	$ _____	____ % GROSS
PLUS PROD.	$ _____	____ % GROSS
TOTAL	$ _____	____ % GROSS

FEE TO ARTIST	$ _____	____ % GROSS
PLUS PROD.	$ _____	____ % GROSS
TOTAL ARTIST	$ _____	____ % GROSS

PROMOTER RECONCILIATION

CONT. RET.	$ _____
% DUE. PROM.	_____ %
DUE PROM.	$ _____
DUE CO-PROMO	_____ % $ _____
DUE MONARCH	_____ % $ _____
PLUS NOS	$ _____
TOTAL PROM.	$ _____ % GROSS

PROMOTER RECONCILIATION

TO BE SPLIT	$ _____	
% TO PROM.	_____ %	
DUE PROM.	$ _____	____ % GROSS
DUE CO. PROM.	_____ % $ _____	
DUE MONARCH	_____ % $ _____	

FOR CO-PROMO _____ FOR FACILITY _____
FOR MONARCH _____ FOR B.O. _____
FOR ARTIST _____ PROD. MGR. _____

COMMENTS _____
_____
_____
_____
_____
_____
_____
_____
_____
_____
_____
_____
_____
_____
_____
_____
_____
_____
_____

SUMMARY

1.   The main objectives for any tour are: to increase the artist's visibility in a given market; to increase the number of industry players on an artist's team and win their loyalty; to make the artist's performance an "event" on a performance-by-performance basis; to provide an opportunity to perform in a major market when the record is reaching its stride; and to make a profit.

2.   A tour should begin in a secondary market close to the artist's home.

3.   The booking agent and manager should work closely to arrive at all the specifications for the tour.

4.   The procedure for booking a tour entails: the manager and agent arrive at a price the artist is seeking for the performance; the agent solicits concert promoters in each region to inquire about bookings; the promoter or agent puts a tentative hold on a venue for a specific date; and dates are confirmed.

5.   Tour budgets should be based on conservative estimates.

6.   An opening act should be chosen on its ability to generate ticket sales.

7.   A concert rider should protect the artist against any unforeseen difficulties. The categories should include: billing and artist approval; recording; financial considerations; backstage accommodations and catering; crew arrangements; cancellation; and legal considerations.

8.   Material for concert performance should be familiar to the audience and should work well in a live setting.

9.   Production preparation should include the actual staging specifications.

10.   The entire tour should be announced to the press no earlier than two months in advance.

11.   During the tour, the manager must monitor 90% of all details for each show on a daily basis.

12.   After the tour, the experience should be evaluated.

PROJECTS

1. Cost out a three day regional tour, including a budget (with real cost figures) for expenses.

2. Draw up a production budget, including a sound system, lights, and staging.

3. Formulate a fair and meaningful concert rider, including the categories listed in this chapter.

4. Write a press release announcing an artist's tour.

5. Role play the job of a concert promoter; negotiate a contract for a performance, and submit a realistic list of expenses using the Gross Split Point Deal method.....do the math!

NOTES

1.   Eric Boehlert. "Road Woes: What It Costs." Rolling Stone. November 28, 1996. Pg. 53.
2.   Neil Strauss. "Stones Tour Ranks No. 1." New York Times. December 18, 1997. Pg. E7.
3.   Rick Mitchell. "The Music Mogul" Houston Chronicle. March 19, 1995. Pg. 8.
4.   John Scher. "Why are Ticket Prices so High? Musician Magazine. January, 1994. pg. 12.
5.   Ibid.
6.   Peter Passell. "If scalpers can get so much, why aren't tickets costlier?" Economic Scene. New York Times. 23 December 1993. pg. D2.

CHAPTER TEN

MERCHANDISING, ENDORSEMENTS, & SPONSORSHIP

"The Woodstock generation has gone away. In the end, this business is really not so different from Xerox or General Motors." Larry Stersel, Director Merchandising, Epic, Portrait & Assoc. labels, NY Times, October 2, 1983.

By the end of this chapter you should be able to:
1. Discuss the differences between merchandising, endorsements, and sponsorship.
2. Discuss the five basic ingredients in a merchandising deal.
4. Discuss how the revenues are shared.
5. Compute the average revenue splits in a merchandising deal.
6. List the factors that contribute to the size of the artist's advance   money.
7. Discuss the procedures for prosecuting offenders.
9. Discuss four issues a manager should discuss concerning product endorsements.
10. Discuss the important areas of an endorsement deal.
11. Discuss the two types of sponsorships that exist in the business.

The areas of merchandising, endorsements, and sponsorship are very lucrative for many of today's artists. Merchandising and sponsorship are relatively new to the entertainment business. Nevertheless, to some stars, the exploitation of their name and/or likeness as a property right now represents not only an important promotional vehicle, but substantial income as well. Endorsements, on the other hand, have been a revenue producing aspect of the entertainment business for many years.

THE DIFFERENCE

Merchandising

In general terms, merchandising is the buying and selling of goods for profit. In the entertainment industry, these goods feature the name or likeness of the artist (and the artist's recordings) on every good produced. The owner of the artist's name or likeness has the legal right (property or "personality" right) to exploit it for either promotional reasons or as a means of generating income.

Endorsements

When an artist endorses a product he or she gives support or approval to the product for a set fee for a limited time. Usually, this represents a relationship between the artist and the product.

Extreme caution must be used when choosing a product to endorse. No endorsement deal is worth the possibility of deteriorating the artist's image.

Sponsorship

A business (or corporation) that pays an artist a fee for the right to associate its name or logo with the artist's appearance is a sponsor. The name may blatantly appear on a banner hung behind the stage in a concert hall or on merchandise sold, or it may be tastefully incorporated into posters advertising the event. Today, nonrecord company sponsorship is reserved only for the most successful stars.

MERCHANDISING

Its History

Artist merchandising seriously began in the rock business in the early 1970's. Winterland Productions, which is one of the biggest merchandising companies in the business, began in the early 1970s by selling Grateful Dead T-shirts at one of their concerts at the Winterland Ballroom in San Francisco.[1] However, not many people recall any substantial exploitation of an act's name prior to the Peter Frampton "Live" tour in the mid-1970's. In any case, merchandising was more or less a dirty word to the Woodstock generation, and was not a factor in the exploitation of the counterculture of the 1960's. A former employee of the Filmores East and West could not recall any act selling T-shirts or other paraphernalia in either hall.

Now it's big business. According to Debra J. Graff, Esq., revenue from merchandising in the music industry exceeded 1/2 billion dollars in 1980, and it had doubled by 1985.[2] Worldwide revenues are now in the billions of dollars, and on some tours, an average of $10-$20 a ticket is generated from the sale of tour merchandise.

How Does It Work?

Tour merchandising is the primary source of merchandising revenue. Except for a cultural phenomenon such as Michael Jackson, or an act that has had a fanatic following, such as the New Kids On The Block (who incidently, had over 500 items licensed for the marketplace), the retail market is still a hard sell. Fan club and direct mail merchandising are growing, but revenue depends on the loyalty of the group's fan base. As a whole, the industry is only waking up to direct to consumer marketing and a few independent companies have convinced record companies to use their services.

The merchandising procedure is as follows:

Three months prior to the start of a tour, the manager will contact the three major rock music merchandising companies and ask them to bid for on merchandising the tour. If the artist does not have any product value in the marketplace (even though he or she may have a recording contract), the merchandiser may pass on the tour, or may offer to merchandise the tour without offering any advance money. If the artist has a proven merchandising track record, the merchandiser will examine the tour dates and determine a projected "**per-head gross**."

The manager and merchandiser agree on the terms of the contract.

The merchandiser designs the graphics for the products and brings the designs to the manager for approval. If the tour coincides with the release of a recording (and it usually does), then the recording jacket's graphic should be incorporated into the merchandising graphics.

The merchandiser and the manager decide which products are to be manufactured. This decision is fairly simple. T-shirts are mandatory. Some groups estimate that they sell shirts to a quarter of their fans. The other products should be priced to cover the spending power of the audience. In other words, there should be something for every pocketbook. Common items include: T-shirts, baseball shirts, sweatshirts, visors, caps, posters, and buttons. However, towels, undergarments, sheets & pillowcases, and soccer balls have also been offered!

The manager approves all of the items to be merchandised accepting only high quality pieces.

The Deal

There isn't a standard merchandising deal in the music business. The power of the artist in the marketplace plays a major role in determining who receives the biggest piece of the pie. Some merchandisers will take a smaller share of the revenue to have the prestige of merchandising a superstar's tour. The number of dates on the tour and the number of countries covered are also factors.

Usually, a manager will give the merchandiser the right to exploit the name and likeness of the artist for the purpose of selling merchandise for a negotiated royalty . . . with a minimum guarantee or an advance against the royalty. The royalty for the license is negotiated and computed on either the wholesale or retail prices of the products, based on the number sold.

For an established act, the length of the deal usually coincides with the length of the tour. If the deal is with a new artist, the merchandiser will specify that the length of the deal run until the monies are recouped, for fear of not making any profit.

The revenue splits are roughly as follows:

<u>Cost</u> of the goods (including freight, security, etc.) 25-35%.

<u>Venue</u> (arena) receives 20-40% commission. This arrangement may vary depending on whether the merchandiser works the concessions or the venues's concessionaires are used.

<u>Merchandiser</u> receives 5-30%.

<u>Artist royalty</u> is 15-35% or higher, depending upon his or her status.[3]

For example:

$30.00 shirt

<u>10.50</u> cost (35%)

$19.50

-<u>$7.50</u> venue (25%)

$12.00

-<u>$2.70</u> merc (9%)

$9.30 artist (31%)

<u>Advance money</u>: A number of factors come into play when negotiating the artist's advance. Obviously, the size of the advance is based on the volume of business expected. This may be calculated by the number of dates on the tour and the volume of business transacted on previous tours. Advances may range from $10,000 to $1,000,000+. The manager may negotiate a higher royalty rate in lieu of an advance if he or she is sure the artist's products will sell well and cash is not needed.

Normally, the agreement will contain a personal guarantee by the performer that minimum tour obligations will be met. If they are not met, unrecouped advances (unlike record company advances) will be repayable, with interest, by the performer.

Because the concert business has been so risky recently, advances have been given in increments throughout the tours.[4]

<u>Selloff.</u>   The merchandiser will want to selloff unsold goods. The manager should negotiate a time limit that extends beyond the tour for the selloff to occur. The merchandiser should not be permitted to **manufacture** any additional merchandise. This prevents merchandise to be sold for an unlimited time under the old contract.

Ownership

Since the mid-1980's, record companies have not allowed new artists ownership of the recording jacket's artwork or graphics. They have made it clear that they intend to take part in all merchandising that bears the name or likeness of the artist. It may be stated in the contract as follows: **"If __ Records receives any payments for any use of your name or picture in connection with merchandise other than Phonograph Records, your royalty account will be credited 50% of the net amount of those receipts, after deduction of the following expenses."** The manager may negotiate the ownership (or a bigger share) from the record company to the artist for a price.

Record/Entertainment companies now own merchandising companies and offer new artists the opportunity to do business with them. (Since 1987, MCA Music has owned Winterland, Labatt Brewing of Canada is a shareholder in The Brouckum Group, Giant Merchandise is a joint venture with Warner Bros. Records and Time Warner Inc., and Polygram Diversified Entertainment has recently acquired Great Southern Co.)[5]

Bootlegs And Counterfeits

During a major artist's tour, products featuring the tour logo are in such demand and sell so well that bootleg and counterfeit products are big business. Since official tour merchandise is marketed outside the arena as well as inside, a concert-goer has no way of knowing if the product he or she buys in the parking lot is "official" or not. Nor does he or she really care! Therefore, the bootlegger doesn't care if the products he or she sells are exact replicas of official products. If a bootlegger incorporates the artist's name, the latest recording's graphics, and the tour specifics, the product will sell as well as the "official" product. In fact, some claim that at times the bootleg products are designed better!

Stopping Them

Obviously, it's disturbing to the artist and manager to see bootleg and counterfeit products sold at a concert. However, it's usually the merchandiser's responsibility to police the tour.

There are several ways to curtail the sale of bootleg and counterfeit products. According to Graff, suits may be filed based on trademark infringement under the Federal Lanham Act; copyright infringement under the Federal Copyright Act; and unfair competition and misappropriation of the right of publicity under common law.[6] An enforcement procedure is important, although many merchandisers do not always find it cost effective.

Until the 1980's, the best procedure is to obtain a court order prohibiting the sale of unauthorized merchandise. However, the merchandiser had to bring the bootlegger into court before a judge would grant the injunction. However, with the result of the **Matter of Vuitton et Fils, S.A.606F.2d.1 (2d Cir. 1979**) case, an ex parte temporary restraining order (TRO) can be obtained from a court without notice to the defendant. This allows the plaintiff to obtain an injunction, without first notifying a bootlegger, and restrains the unauthorized activities for a limited time period, usually ten days, after which the court will consider granting a preliminary injunction which will remain in effect during the pendency of the case.[7] Because some bootleggers don't really have legal addresses, the courts have allowed "John Doe" TROs to be served by marshals. These TROs are enforceable during specified times and areas, usually within a three-mile radius of the concert hall, during several hours before and after the concert. This has been very helpful in curtailing the business of bootlegging.

ENDORSEMENTS

Product endorsement has long been a part of the entertainment industry. Celebrities have endorsed products through TV and radio advertisements and print ads for years.

Others have allowed (licensed) their names or likenesses to be used in conjunction with product promotion. The royalties may be high, but caution should be taken before consenting to an endorsement deal.

An endorsement represents a relationship between the product and the artist. Potentially, it can damage the artist's image, and no endorsement is worth that risk. The manager should exercise caution and investigate the following before signing an agreement.

Is the product valid one. How effective is it? Is it harmful? Will certain interest groups be against its use? Will the artist's fans believe the artist uses the product?

How accurate are the products claims? Does it do what it claims to do?

Has it been tested by an independent laboratory and given its seal of approval?

Does the artist use the product? If not, he or she should live with it to see if he or she feels comfortable with it.

The endorsement must be evaluated in terms of its effect on the long range career goals.

The Deal

An ad agency will usually approach a manager inquiring about the possibility of an endorsement. As a manager, if you are seeking an endorsement deal, a big fan in an account services department can be helpful in working a deal.

The important areas of the contract are:

The length of time a commercial will appear or a printad will run.

2.The region or number of regions of the country where the commercial or printadwill appear.

3.The media for which it is intended.

4.Advances against a royalty deal.

5.Residuals from the airing of a commercial

6. Creative control. Does the artist have any input?

7. Rights. Who will own what?

Bill Cosby is a good example of overexposure. At one time, it seemed that he appeared in every advertisement on TV and in print. A good rule is <u>don't endorse anything and everything</u> . . . be selective!

SPONSORSHIP

There are two methods of nonrecord company sponsorship active in the industry. The first involves a nonrecord company that pays for advertising in exchange for the right to associate its name or logo with an artist's appearance. It's reported that the Rolling Stones received over $3 million in advertising from Jovan (a subsidiary of Beecham Group LTD.) in the early days of sponsorship, during the 1981 tour. Rod Stewart received $4 million from Canada Dry, the Jacksons received over $5 million from Pepsi, Julio Iglesias received over $30 million from CocaCola in a multitier deal, and the list goes on. Other nonrecord companies that have sponsored tours include: Jordache (Air Supply), Schlitz (ZZ Top and The Who), and U.S. Tobacco (Charlie Daniels)[8]. But according to Jay Coleman of Rockbill, a company that coordinates sponsorships and is now called <u>Entertainment Marketing Communications International</u>, the idea of a company putting up several hundred thousand dollars just because it sounds like a good public relations move are over.[9] Presently, it is not as easy for an artist to acquire sponsorship as it has been in the past.

The second form of sponsorship involves media companies and nonrecord companies teaming up. For example, MTV or Westwood One Broadcasting contributes a certain amount of tour support for the right to an exclusive broadcast performance of an artist. Westwood One, with the nonrecord company support, sells the show to radio station affiliates who sell air time to local advertisers. The artist is supported by the media company as well as the nonrecord company. This arrangement is only offered to major stars.

Sponsorship can get the artist millions in advertising. If appearances in commercials are included in the deal, several million dollars can be guaranteed. Obviously, sponsorship deals can represent a great deal of money and be very lucrative for an artist. Therefore, companies, such as Entertainment Marketing, usually take about a 15% commission from the party seeking a deal.[10]

Because the sponsor may want high visibility on the tour, a manager must be certain that any advertisements during or after the concerts are not offensive to the artist (*Pearl Jam* bans sponsors from their tours). A banner hung over the stage, or an ad with an artist guzzling a bottle of beer may not have a positive effect on long range career goals. As Herbie Herbert, the manager of Journey said back in 1983: "We are going to gross $30 million in ticket sales and $10 million more on record sales, so why go out there and sell our souls for a lousy million bucks?"[11]

SUMMARY

1. Merchandising is the buying and selling of goods with the artist's name or likeness on them for profit. An artist endorses a product by giving support or approval of it for a set fee. A business that pays an artist a fee for the right to associate with him or her is called a sponsor.

2. Merchandising's largest expansion in the rock music field occurred in the mid 1970's.

3. Revenue from tour merchandising averages over $1 billion a year.

4. The procedure for acquiring a merchandising deal is as follows: The manager calls merchandisers and asks them to bid on merchandising the tour. The terms of the contract are agreed upon and the merchandiser designs the products. The manager approves all of the items to be merchandised.

5. The revenue from the merchandising is split between the maker of the goods, the venue, the merchandiser, and the artist.

6. Advance money is based on the volume of business expected.

7. The record company shares in the merchandising revenue unless the artist buys the ownership of the graphics and artwork from the record company.

8. Bootleggers and counterfeits are difficult and time consuming to prosecute.

9. Several issues should be investigated before endorsing a product. Namely, is the product effective? How accurate are its claims? Does the artist use the product?

10. Poor endorsement choices can have a negative effect on the artist's image.

11. Several areas of importance in an endorsement contract include: The length of the advertising run, audience reach, media, advances, residuals, creative control, and rights.

12. Tour sponsorship is only reserved for major acts.

13. The two types of sponsorships are nonrecord company sponsorship and nonrecord company sponsorship in conjunction with a media company.

PROJECTS

1. Design a logo for a group that incorporates the group's image.

2. Locate a local silkscreen company that will create a silkscreen for the artist's merchandise.

3. Locate a local company that would like your artist to endorse a product and negotiate a deal.

4. Do the same for a sponsorship deal

NOTES

1. Larry Rohter. "Pop-Music Fashion Becomes a Sales Hit." <u>New York Times</u>. 8 January 1991. pg. D9.
2. Debra J. Graff Esq. "Merchandising in the Music Industry," <u>The Musicians Manual: A Practical Guide</u>. Beverly Hills Bar Assn., Beverly Hills, CA. 1986, pg. 379.
3. Paul B. Ungar, ESQ. "Negotiating Concert Agreements During a Recessionary Period," <u>Agent & Manager</u>. March 1992. pg. 51.
4. Ibid.
5. Op. Cit., <u>New York Times.</u>
6. Op. Cit., <u>The Musicians Manual</u>, pg. 381.
7. Barry I. Sloctnick, Esq. "Are Bootleggers Walking Away With The Performance Profit Center?" <u>Agent & Manager</u>. April 1992. pg. 53.
8. Michael J. Specter. "Rock Puts On a Three-Piece Suit," <u>New York Times</u>. 2 October 1983. Section Three.
9. Steve Gett. "One to One," <u>Billboard</u>. 23 May 1987. pg.32.
10. Ibid.
11. Op. Cit., <u>New York Times</u>. 2 October 1983.

CHAPTER ELEVEN

BUSINESS MANAGEMENT

"The business manager's primary function is to maximize client's earnings while safeguarding their capital."   Marshall M. Gelfand and Wayne C. Coleman in The Musician's Business & Legal Guide. Mark Halloran (ed.) Prentice Hall, 1991. Pg. 153.

By the end of this module you should be able to:

1.   Describe the role of the business manager.
2.   Describe the various functions s/he performs.
3.   Discuss the various fee structures.
4.   Discuss how to choose a business manager.
5.   Using your knowledge of project management, discuss in detail
         how to prepare a funding proposal.

_____

There are a million stories in the rock business about artists and their money. And there are a two million stories in the business about artists without their money! When money comes quickly it sometimes gets "lost in the shuffle." Take *Kiss* for example, as reported in the New York Times: a former employee said that "she was told by an accounting firm that about $700,000 in cash had somehow fallen through the cracks."[1] The financial woes of Mick Fleetwood from *Fleetwood Mac* are also well documented (see "There's No Stopping Tommorrow" by Geraldine Fabrikant, New York Times, November 30, 1997 Bus. Sec. Pg. 1), as are Marvin Gaye's, Jerry Lee Lewis', and Wayne Newton's.

One of the saddest tales is that of Stanley Kirk Burrell, a.k.a. "Hammer." Hammer's "Please Don't Hurt Me" sold 18 million copies. He won three Grammys, had a private jet, movie offers, his own record production company, and a cartoon show. According to *Forbes,* he earned $33 million in 1990 and 91. By 1996 his income totaled over $50 million. If Hammer had invested conservatively, he could have enjoyed an annual income of $3 to $5 million for the rest of his life.

Instead, he spent over $11 million to build a house, while on tour, he stayed at the best hotels, travelled by private jet, and bought 17 cars. Consequently, his debts now total $13.7 million and he has only $9.6 million in assets. One business associate owed money by Hammer summed it up by saying, "In this business you have overnight-success stories, but they tend to go down very quickly. They think it will always be as good as it is now."[2]

BUSINESS MANAGER

The Role:

Business managers play an important role in the artist's career. Their relationship, as with the personal manager, is a fiduciary one, and the artist must have total confidence in their judgement. Many business management firms also act as accountants, and play a greater role in the daily fiscal activities. Therefore, the breath and depth of their role may vary depending on their function(s).

Functions

Accounting: One should expect reports (balance sheet, etc.) completed on time (on an agreed upon schedule), and accurate to the penny.

Collecting of funds: Receipts from appearances, merchandising deals, and royalty agreements, should be designated with the artist's appropriate account number, and deposited **IN FULL**, in the artist's account. Funds should be drawn against, if needed. Audits should be conducted in a timely manner, especially record company royalty account audits, which are very tedious, but unfortunately, necessary.

Budgeting: If needed, and it usually is, budgets for projects, as well as living expenses, should be generated by the artist and the personal manager, in consultation with the business manager. The responsibility of the business manager is to notify the personal manager when a budget is not being adhered to.

Tax Advising: If the business manager is also the artist's accountant, s/he should be a Certified Public Accountant (CPA) and knowledgeable about the <u>current</u> state, federal, and international tax codes. Should any project be as complicated as to require special attention, the business manager should recommend a tax specialist.

Investment Advising: True business managers (not simply accountants) are also investment advisors. Since anyone has the ability to give advise (and they usually do), as a form of protection, the artist should look to any one of the various types of licensed financial investment advisors. However, there aren't any guarantees that anyone with or without a license has the ability to give sound financial advise AND make money. Therefore, the general advise from the investment community is to be aware of investments that can't be explained properly ("I think it's a form of plastic . . ."), are hard to understand ("It's a device that allows your computer to . . ."), and are so new that no one really knows what earnings will be ("You can get in on the ground floor!").

Fees

Fees will vary, depending on location and reputation of, and the licenses and academic degrees held by the business manager, as well as the and extent of the role s/he will play. Fees are computed based on any one (or more) of the following factors:

1. time: A rate per hour charged while s/he is conducting business (spending his/her time) on your behalf.

2. a percentage of income: Especially when the business manager is investing the artist's income, s/he is likely to charge a percentage (usually around 5%). The artist should make certain to understand whether income from <u>investments</u> (passive income) is included in determining the fee due, or only on funds received from career endeavors.

3. retainer: A retainer is a fee charged per week, month, or quarter for the normal accounting activities. An additional fee, along with the retainer, may be charged when additional functions are being carried out. If the additional fee is an hourly rate for performing a huge task such as auditing a royalty account for example, because s/he is on a retainer, the hourly rate should be lower than if the business manager was not.

CHOOSING A BUSINESS MANAGER

Reputations are usually built on word of mouth recommendations. As stated in Chapter One, a good personal manager will suggest to his/her client the names of several reputable business managers, and then allow the artist to make the choice. A good personal manager will also emphasize to his/her client, that this is an important decision, and will effect many short and long term goals of the career.

FINANCING A PROJECT

It would be a wonderful world if everyone had enough capital to fund any creative idea. But it isn't. Some say, it would be a wonderful world if we still worked on the barter system of trade. But we don't. Although people outside the entertainment industry think performers make "money for nothing," at the beginning of a career, there just doesn't seem to be enough available. Since robbery is against the law, attempts at raising capital for a project must be completed in an organized, convincing, businesslike manner.

Assuming that the artist is signed with a record label, the most often vehicle for borrowing money is a draw against the artist's royalty account. Assuming the artist is successful, another source of funds is a bank. However, assuming that both these resources are not available to the artist, a capital funding proposal needs to be developed.

The Deal

The are many ways to structure capital investment deal. Below are three such possibilities. Before any deal is structured a business manager should be consulted.

1. A loan The simplest and easiest way to get money is for someone to loan it you and you pay s/he back. You can draw a loan agreement describing the amount of money that is being borrowed and how and when it is will be paid back (a promissory note).

2. A limited partnership As described in Chapter Two, a limited partnership is sometimes setup so that the person loaning money becomes a partner that will share in income resulting from the project. S/he risks only the sum being borrowed, and takes on no additional liability.

3. A corporation Someone may loan money in return for a number of shares in a corporation. The amount of shares received in exchange is based on the amount of money loaned in relation to the number of shares outstanding. Similar to a limited partner, the only risk is the amount invested (loaned), and no additional liability is assumed.

The Plan

Adapting the tools of project management discussed in Chapter One to a capital seeking proposal is one method of organizing the plan. Figure 11.1 lists the categories that should be included. A discussion follows.

I. Problem Statement An explanation of what is perceived to be needed, what this project entails, and why it has been determined to be a solution.

II. Background Statement This section usually begins with a description of the artist and his/her organization, his/her financial condition, the current status of his/her career, successes and any special attributes or awards that may persuade someone to believe that the artist is someone special. A description of similar situations and how the successful completion of the project solved a similar problem, must be included. This section should also include a thorough description (including statistical information) of the music business.

FUNDING PROPOSAL
(based on Project Management)

I.	Problem Statement
II.	Background Statement
III.	Goals & Objectives

IV.	Procedures
V.	Plan
VI.	Schedule
VII.	Budget
VIII.	Financing Structure
IX.	Success Indicator
X.	Executive Summary

Figure 11.1

III. Goals and Objectives The goals and objectives, (both long an short term) of the project must be clearly stated.

IV. Procedures It is sometimes helpful to list what has to be completed before the actual plan is presented. This is especially true when the plan is very complicated and contains steps that are unique to the music business. For example, if one is seeking funds to support a tour, production, security, and catering requirements might seem elaborate to someone outside the industry.

V. The Plan It is here that how the steps of the plan are to completed is clearly described. Who is responsible for doing what is clearly listed. If a marketing plan is needed, it should be included here. All aspects of the plan must be able to be explained easily, and no aspect of the project should be left to chance.

VI. The Schedule Describing when the steps are to be completed is the main function of this section. Critical path analysis, a method to determine what aspect of the project will take the longest, should be performed first, so that unrealistic deadlines are not proposed. The schedule should remain flexible.

VII. The Budget The budget should also include the financial statement showing the present financial condition of the artist's company requesting funding. If the artist has been in business for three years or more, the financial condition of the past three years should also be included.

VIII. Financing Structure The financing requirements are included in this section. The structure and responsibilities of the company loaning the funds, such as the formation of a limited partnership are described here. How and when the funds will be paid back are included. The projected time it will take to payback the loan is also described. The business manager must known the current "going rate" for such a project so that the artist does not pay too much for the deal.

IX. Success Indicators Projected sales should be described in intervals to act as progress report. Inherent risks and possible problems should be indicated.

X. Executive Summary This should be a one page description of the deal including all the basic requirements and financial conditions. It is intended for executives that do not have time to read the proposal. It should be concise and businesslike with an eye-catching appeal.

The old saying "you can't make money without spending money" is true than ever. What seems also to be true today, is the saying "to make a lot you need to risk a lot."

SUMMARY

1. The role of the business manager varies from artist to artist.
2. The basic functions are: accounting, collecting funds, budgeting, tax advising, and investment advising.
3. Any funds collected should be deposited in the artist's account in full and then drawn against when needed.
4. One should make certain how the gee for services is to be collected and what it is based on.
5. Business managers work on hourly fees, percentage of income, and retainers.
6. The artist's business manager has a fiduciary relationship with the artist, and should be chosen by the artist and not the manager.
7. The financing of a project will come forth easier if the funding proposal is organized, convincing, and businesslike.
8. The procedures used in project management can be adapted to be used in a capital seeking proposal.

PROJECTS

1. Develop a funding proposal for a project using actual cost estimates and a realistic time-line.

2. Ask the class to develop a funding proposal and have individuals role play as investors by examining each other's proposals.

NOTES

1.   Geraldine Fabrikant. "The Bad Boys Start Watching Their Pockets." New York Times.   February 23, 1997. Sec. Pg. 7.

2.   John Cassidy. "Under The Hammer." New Yorker Magazine. August 26, 1996. Pg. 62.

CHAPTER TWELVE

CASE STUDIES---LEGAL BATTLES

"The first thing we do, let's kill all the lawyers."
Shakespeare, Henry VI, Part 2
Act IV, Scene II

[The author thanks students from his personal management classes for their research in updating information concerning the cases listed in this chapter. Further information on these and other cases can by easily found at the Court TV website **www.courttv.com/library**.]

The following are selected cases of artist manager disagreements that resulted in very publicized law suits. In the entertainment industry, when a substantial amount of income is achieved over a relatively short period of time, it is not unusual for allegations evolving around the misappropriating of funds to arise. Although the law suits may result in large attorney fees, this is an "ego driven" business based on relationships, where emotions play an major role, and when someone is suspected of a misappropriation, the usual response is "I don't care what it costs, I'm going to get that sucker!" The truth in many settlements is that the attorneys are the real winners.

In reality, many artists young or old, fail to read or fully comprehend the artist-manager agreement, and consequently set themselves up for misunderstandings. Secondly, most contracts use terms like "reasonable effort" or "best effort" to describe the behavior expected by the parties, which are obviously open to a broad range of interpretation. What follows are lawsuits that were filed for a variety of reasons. They were chosen as a representation of the various misunderstanding that occur. They are meant to be used as learning tools for students, and not intended to be partial to the artist or manager involved.

TABLE OF CHAPTER CONTENT

BeeGees vs Robert Stigwood

The Background

The Bee Gees, Barry, Robin, and Maurice Gibb are pop singers from Australia who became one of the most successful recording groups in the world in the late 1970's. As a result of the overwhelmingly successful movie "Saturday Nite Fever," their soundtrack album, recorded for RSO Records, sold over twenty million records worldwide, and is considered by most as one of the crowning achievements of the disco era. Barry's falsetto vocals became a familiar sound on radio, television, elevators, supermarkets, and health clubs All accounts support that the BeeGees were on top of the industry.

Robert Stigwood, an entertainment mogul also from Australia is the principal owner the Robert Stigwood Group. Under the umbrella of the RSO Group are a number of companies that encompass many aspects of the business. In addition to RSO Records, there is a personal management firm, and a number of music publishing companies. Stigwood is considered a giant in the worldwide entertainment industry.

The Dilemma

In October 1980, the Bee Gees filed suit in a New York State Supreme Court that Stigwood had cheated the act out of more that $16 million through a pattern of fraud, breach of trust, and conflict of interest. Filed on behalf of the three, the suit asked for upwards of $75 million in damages and other costs from a host of Stigwood related companies.[1] They sued for release from all their ties with Stigwood, and charged that he deliberately mismanaged them to his own advantage and withheld millions of dollars in royalties

Details of the claim asked for $75 million from Stigwood; $75 million from Polygram, which owned half of the Stigwood Group companies; $50 million in punitive damages; and additional millions in interest and back royalties. They also asked for the return of all the Bee Gees' master recording and copyrights, and a release from all their many contracts with Stigwood.[2] The suit alleged that Stigwood diverted millions of dollars from them by creating self-servicing corporate entities that hid money and delayed royalty payments.[3] The three brothers hired Paul McCartney's brother-in-law, John Eastman, to represent them, who negotiated Paul's release from the Beatles and from Allen Klein.

On the emotional level, the Bee Gees became insecure about the monopoly Stigwood had on every aspect of their career. He was their personal manager since 1968, and head of their record company. They were also signed to his publishing firm. In 1980 they questioned, as their manager, why Stigwood didn't solicit them deals from any other record companies or publishing firms. After all, as a manager, he took twenty-five percent of their gross earnings for twelve years. Weren't they entitled to negotiate deals through competitive bidding?

The suit continued to allege that Stigwood fraudulently failed and refused to account properly for royalties and other income and hid the fact that he owed them large sums of money[4]. In fact they conducted their own audit and found that they were owed millions in unpaid royalties dating back to 1968.[5]

The Stigwood group called the suit "revolting" and countered by claiming the whole suit was just a way for the three to renegotiate a better contract. Stigwood appealed in London England for an injunction against anyone who tried to usurp his interests in the group. Stigwood denied all charges and executives at RSO Records claimed that the group was being paid "excessively high royalties" and owed their careers to Stigwood.[6]

The Resolution

Although it was widely speculated that the case would be very difficult and last for quite a number of years, the suit was settled out of court and all charges dropped. Details of the settlement were not revealed, however, an industry representative claims that Stigwood gave up his rights to the group and released them from their RSO Records deal but retained their catalogue.

Billy Joel vs Frank Weber
Index No. 20702/89
Supreme Court of New York, New York County

The Background

Billy Joel is one of the biggest record selling artists in the world. Starting out as a songwriter/piano player, his first shot at the big time, came as the singer/songwriter/ keyboards player in a keyboard and drum duo called "Attila". Recording solo albums for Columbia since the 1970's, Joel has gained the attention of the college age. In fact, he is tied with the Beatles as having the largest number of platinum albums. Several worldwide tours have grossed him hundreds of millions of dollars as well.

Joel's rise to stardom did not come overnight nor without setbacks. His history as a singer in piano lounges in Los Angeles is public knowledge. His lose of ownership to many of his songs to various "parasites" in the industry is also a common hazard of this industry.

His career is bigger than ever. His marriage and subsequent divorce to supermodel Christie Brinkley has added to the aura of his public persona. He gained superstar status in the 1980's and continues to enjoy the status in the 1990's.

Frank Weber is Joel's ex-brother-in-law who began managing him in 1979. Also named in the suit were his wife Lucille, his brother-in-law Richard London, and two other in-laws. Weber's prior experience in the industry is not known.

The Dilemma

On September 25, 1989, Billy Joel filed a $90 million lawsuit against Frank Weber, accusing him of misappropriating recording royalties and tour funds over a period of ten years.[7] According to the papers filed in New York State Supreme Court, Weber "maliciously defrauded" Joel while being paid millions of dollars annually in management commissions, and funds from Joel's tours and record royalties.

Details of the allegations include:

1. misappropriation of $2.5 million in unauthorized, interest-free loans,

2. $10 million loss from risky investments,

3. double-billed Joel for production costs for music videos shot by a Weber controlled company,

4. and obtained loans from CBS Records for Joel,

using his copyrights as collateral.[8]

Joel also asked to void his 1980 agreement with Weber and block him from any further compensation.

Weber moved to have the claims dismissed at the start of the hearings. He claimed he was innocent. Rumors in the industry suggested that Joel's new wife at that time, Christie Brinkley, convinced Joel that his former wife's family was unfaithful to his career, and the suit was filed with a great deal of ill feeling and mixed emotions.

The Resolution

The court ruled against Weber on counts of fraud and embezzlement, and awarded Joel $2 million as compensation for funds that were allegedly drawn from Joel's bank account.[9]

Although Joel was awarded $2 million in the Spring of 1990, as of May 1991, Joel collected only $250,000 from Weber. Weber has filed for bankruptcy. Consequently, Joel pursued Weber's accountants and attorney claiming they had a role in the improper transfer of $1.5 million of Joel's assets![10]

On February 25, 1993, Judge Lehner of the New York Supreme Court awarded Joel $675,670.68 in a summary judgement concerning two real estate partnership distributions.[11] The remaining claims have yet to have hearings scheduled.

Weber filed an $11 million suit against Brinkley alleging that she induced Joel to terminate the management agreement. A New York judge has moved a dismissal of the complaint as a spouse is unnamed against a claim of interference and cannot be forced to testify against his or her spouse or reveal details about private conversations.[12]

In April, 1995, Joel's attorney, Leonard Marks, filed a motion in the Supreme Court of the State of New York to discontinue action without prejudice from the case so that the plainiff is free to file a new suit on the same claim. However, at this time further action would be a waste of time and money.

Lisa Marie Presley vs. Tom Parker & RCA Records
Probate Court, Memphis TN.

The Background

(This suit was filed on behalf of Elvis' daughter, Lisa Marie in 1980.)

Elvis was (and might still be) **THE KING**. He was one of the biggest stars in the entire entertainment business, attracting audiences whose ages ranged from "eight to eighty." For years, his records represented one-half of RCA Records' sales. He has over 700 hundred charted

----

songs recorded on dozens of hit albums to his credit.

Colonel Tom Parker had been Elvis' personal manager since 1956. Legend has it that the colonel and Elvis didn't have a written agreement. A handshake and trust held their relationship together on a 50%-50% basis for those many years. Many consider Parker the brains behind Elvis' enormous success. After all, it was Parker's idea to convince RCA Records to buy his contract from Sam Phillips at Sun Records in Memphis for the total sum of $40,000.

Parker was once a carnival barker. He was known to have no problem with saying anything to anyone. In fact, he was known as one of the industry's biggest practical jokers.

RCA Records is one of the oldest continuously operating record labels in the USA. RCA is a subsidiary of BMG a major international entertainment company with facilities throughout the world. Historically, their emphasis has been in the recording and releasing of country and classical music.

The Dilemma

A court-appointed guardian of Lisa Marie Presley, then twelve years old, filed a report on July 31, 1981 accusing Col. Tom Parker and RCA Records of "collusion, conspiracy, fraud, misrepresentation, bad faith, and overreaching" in their business dealings with Elvis.[13] Central to the charges was the 1973 sale of royalty rights to Presley's entire catalog to RCA for $5 million, to be split equally between Elvis and the colonel. With Elvis in the 50% tax bracket, his net would only be $1.35 million, and he would forfeiture of all future rights![14] This was certainly not a sound business decision on Parker's part for Elvis, however, it did provide a nice income for the 63 year old Parker.

The report also cited a number of side deals that the Colonel made with RCA, the Hilton International Hotel in Las Vegas, and Management III. Blanchard E. Tual, the court appointed attorney filing the suit, also claimed that Elvis lost considerable revenue by never playing outside the U.S.

Tual claimed that he never performed outside the country because Parker was never naturalized as an American citizen, and was really Andreas Cornelus van Kuijk, born in Holland on June 26, 1909.[15]

Elvis tended to ignore any attorney's advice and put his entire fate in Parker's hands. Elvis went along with the buyout by RCA that was suggested by Parker, even though the contract was not due to expire until 1975. Furthermore, RCA Records had not purchased any of its other artists' master catalogs.[16] The new 1973 seven year contract called for a royalty rate of 10c per single and 50c per album for U.S. sales, half of which was to paid to "All Star Shows," the Colonel's company. At the time, other stars such as the Rolling Stones and Elton John were getting twice the royalty and paying half the commission rate to their management.[17]

Some of the side deals cited were the agreement that RCA Records would pay All Star Shows $675,000 over seven years, and RCA Records Tours would additionally pay the same for "planning, promotion, and merchandising." Parker would also receive 10% of RCA Tours profit. RCA agreed to pay Parker a $50,000 consulting fee and another $350,000 of All Star Tours for planning, promotion, and merchandising. Tual reported that with these deals, Elvis would gross $4.65 million, while Parker would make $6.2 million, plus 10% of all tour profits.[18]

The contract contained a "no audit clause" which did not allow an Elvis representative to examine the books! By 1972, Elvis physical and emotional condition did not allow him to evaluate any agreements, and it seems obvious that Parker was interested in cashing in before the King's inevitable early expiration.

Another side deal was with the Hilton. Parker was provided with a year-round suite of offices and hotel rooms, all the food and beverages for his home in Palm Springs, and free transportation to Las Vegas anytime that he requested it. Parker was also a notorious gambler, good for $1,000,000 per year at the hotel tables. Included in this deal was the services of Elvis at $100,000 to $130,000 per week. A fee that was surpassed by acts of far less value.[19]

The Resolution

A settlement was made on behalf of Lisa Marie. However, the Colonel never was convicted of enough crimes to spend any time in jail.

Laura Branigan vs. Susan Joseph

The Background

Laura Branigan is a pop singer that enjoyed a number of hit records on the Atlantic label in the 1980s. Her personal manager at the time was Susan Joseph, a partner of Henry Marx in Grand Trine Management. Marx is also a partner in Ram Promotions, an independent record promotion company. Branigan is married to Laurence Kruteck who is also her business manager.

The Dilemma

In 1985, Branigan sued Joseph for failing to fulfill her obligations of the personal management agreement. Branigan then terminated her agreement with Joseph. Specifically mentioned in the suit was the use of $125,000 of Branigan's money for independent promotion of

----

her records.   Also at issue was the claim that Joseph misrepresented the role offered to Branigan in an Australian film.[20]

Branigan claimed that the $125,000 spent on independent promotion was improperly spent by Ram Promotions, the company hired by Joseph to do the job. Branigan also claimed that Joseph was a partner in the company. Over $1 million was spent on independent promotion of Branigan's records over a two year period.

The testimony revealed that Branigan had reservations about the role in the Australian film. However, she already committed herself to the project when she filed suit in 1985.[21]

According to Joseph's attorney, Branigan's husband, Kruteck, induced her to breach the contract with Joseph.

The Resolution

Branigan lost her suit against Joseph. A jury granted Joseph's counterclaim filed in federal court on November 30, 1987. They found that Joseph had not breached the contract or her fiduciary duty to the singer. Also she was not a partner in Ram Promotions. They awarded $509,238.74 to Joseph, and levied $100,000 punitive damages against Kruteck, as they believed he induced Branigan to breach the agreement. This settlement was very unusual because juries do not normally award punitive damages against a third party.[22]

Michael Lang vs. Joe Cocker

The Background

Joe Cocker is a blues oriented singer with an usual stage presence. When he performs in his raspy voice, he contorts his body and releases spasms with his hands and arms that make him appear to be suffering from a crippling disease. Cocker hit the international scene in the early 1970's with a cover version of the Beatles' "A Little Help From My Friends." His career has had its ups and downs, however, he does sell records and makes concert hall appearances.

Michael Lang and Better Music Inc. began managing Cocker in 1977. The agreement expired in 1980 but the parties agreed to continue under its terms and conditions. In 1984 they entered into a new agreement.

The Dilemma

On March 26, 1992 Michael Lang and Better Music Inc. filed suit in federal court in New York City against Joe Cocker and Adaven Productions, which sometimes acts as Cocker's agent, claiming that Cocker agreed to pay Better Music 15% of his gross earnings from recordings, concerts, merchandising rights, song royalties, and TV appearances during the term of the 1977 agreement. The suit names several albums made under the original agreement as well as singles from the soundtracks of "An Officer And A Gentleman" and "An Innocent Man."[23]

The suit claims damages of $1 million for breach of contract and $1 million for the plaintiffs' services, 15% of the net from Cocker's recordings and concert appearances, as well as court costs.[24]

Better Music continued to manage Cocker until August 19, 1991 when they were notified by the singer that he no longer required Lang's services and would no longer pay him.[25]

The Resolution

Cocker attorney denies Lang's claims and said Cocker will countersue.

Prince vs. Cavallo, Ruffalo, & Fargnoli

Los Angeles Superior Court

The Background

Prince is considered one of the most innovative performers in the business. His creative endeavors in addition to performing include producer, songwriter, screenwriter, moviestar, and multi-instrumentalist. His mixture of raw sexual appeal with rhythm and blues has made him a huge success with crossover appeal.

The Dilemma

His former managers Robert Cavallo, Joseph Ruffalo, and Steve Fargnoli reportedly filed suit against him in Los Angeles Superior Court February 1, 1991 claiming that he owes them $600,000 that he agreed to pay when he released them from their responsibilities. The three assert that they were able to collect potential earnings when he ignored their career advice. They further claim that the disagreement arrised when Prince decided to release his records "in competition with one another."[26]

The Resolution

A settlement has not been reached.

Anita Baker vs. Sherwin Bash, David Braun, & Randy Bash
Los Angeles Superior Court

The Background

Grammy-winning artist Anita Baker is one of the greatest r & b singers of the 1990's. As an Elektra artist, her records have sold consistently well and she is recognized as one of today's most enduring female stars. Ms. Baker possesses great crossover appeal, as she is popular with the pop and jazz audiences as well.

The Dilemma

Ms. Baker has filed a breach-of-contract cross-complaint against former manager Sherwin Bash, former attorney David Braun, and Randy Bash, who administered her catalog through Big Heart Music. The filing occurred on May 14, 1996, claiming "fraud and deceit, breach of fiduciary duty, breach of contract, defamation and slander, intentional infliction of emotional distress, civil conspiracy, and attorney malpractice."[27]

Her action stems from a default judgment filed by Sherwin Bash in February, 1996, for "damages, back royalties, unpaid commissions, other revenue sources and court costs."[28] Baker stated: "Management firms and large labels don't pay you. [Bash] thinks that he should live off me the rest of my life."[29]

The suit follows another action against Bash that was filed before the labor commission of California that alleges that Bash's BNB Associates acted as a talent agent without being licensed in that state. Baker entered into a 5 year personal management contract with BNB at a commission rate of 15% in 1983 and again in 1988, with an option to terminate in 1991. Baker terminated the agreement but retained BNB on a as needed basis for 10%. On December 13, 1994, Baker advised Bash that the management contract was terminated. Therefore, her agreements with BNB are unenforceable because BNB was unlicensed and that claims on existing and future commissions, royalties, or other sums arising from previous contracts be voided. Baker's suit claims that the defendants "knowingly and willfully conspired and agreed among themselves to further their own self-interest at Baker's expense."[30]

The Resolution

A settlement has not been reached.

PROJECTS

1. Lawsuits involving some of the biggest stars in the music business were purposely omitted from this chapter so that students would have the opportunity to investigate the cases as a project. Two of those cases involved the following people and should be researched: Bruce Springsteen vs. Mike Apel, and Bob Dylan vs. Albert Grossman.

2. Pick any suit from the chapter and role play the two sides of the argument. Draw logical solutions.

3. Further investigate any of the above cases.

4. Examine the trade papers for current artist-manager suits and investigate.

_____

NOTES

1.   Irv Lichtman, Peter Jones, and Mike Hennessy. "Stigwood Responds," Billboard Magazine. 18 October 1980. pg. 1.

2.   Marc Kirkeby. "Bee Gees sue Stigwood, charge mismanagement," Rolling Stone Magazine. 13 November 1980. pg. 22.

3.   Op. Cit., Billboard Magazine.

4.   Op. Cit., Rolling Stone Magazine.

5.   Ibid.

6.   Op. Cit., Billboard Magazine

7.   Larry Flick. "Billy Joel Sues Former Manager For $90 Mil," Billboard Magazine. 7 October 1989. pg. 96.

8.   Ibid.

9.   Larry Flick. "Billy Joel Gets $2 Mil In Suit," Billboard Magazine. 7 April 1990. pg. 94.

10.   Irv Lichtman. "Inside Track," Billboard Magazine. 25 May 1991. pg. 80.

11.   Melinda Newman. Billboard Magazine. 20 March 1993. pg. 12.

12.   Billboard Magazine. 14 March 1992. pg. 92.

13.   Roman Kozak. "Parker, RCA Accused Of Fraud In Elvis Dealings," Billboard Magazine. 15 August 1981. pg. 1.

14.   Ibid.

15.   Ibid.

16.   Ibid. pg. 15.

17.   Ibid.

18.   Ibid.

19.   Ibid. pg. 90.

20.   Ken Terry. "Branigan Loses Lawsuit," Billboard Magazine. 12 December 1987. pg. 69.

21.   Ibid.

22.   Ibid.

23.   Trudi Miller. "Ex-Manager Sues Joe Cocker," Billboard Magazine. 18 April 1992. pg. 34.

24.   Ibid.

25.   Ibid.

26.   Irv Lichtman. "Inside Track," Billboard Magazine. 2 March 1991. pg. 79.

27.   J.R. Reynolds. "Anita Baker Suing Her Former Manager, Lawyer, And Publisher." Billboard Magazine, 8 June 1996. Pg. 6

28.   Ibid.

29.   Ibid. pg. 15

30.   Ibid.

INDEX

257

DR. STEPHEN MARCONE

Stephen Marcone graduated from Syracuse University with a B.A. and a Master of Music Education. As a trumpet player, he joined an Epic Records' recording group and toured the country taking an active role in the creative and managerial aspects of the ensemble.

In 1973, he joined the faculty of the School of Music at Syracuse University as an adjunct lecturer and continued his performance activities as a free-lance player and fourth trumpet with the Syracuse Symphony.

In 1976, he became a full-time member of the faculty as Program Developer-Director of the Bachelor of Music, Music Industry emphasis degree, and was also elected Vice-President of Syracuse Musicians Association (Local #78 of the A.F. of M.)

In 1979, as an Associate Professor of Music, Marcone became the chairperson of the Music Industry Department and the director of the jazz area.

He has written several articles for such publications as: Music Educators Journal, The Instrumentalist, NAJE Journal, and Musician Magazine. Marcone has lectured at The Hartt School, NYU, College of the Finger Lakes, MENC National and Regional Conferences, College Music Society Annual Meetings, National Association of Schools of Music Annual Meetings, New Jersey Music Educators Association, NJ Artist-Teacher Institute, Music and Entertainment Industry Educators Association, and the New Jersey Committee for the Humanities.

Professor Marcone holds an ED. D in Instructional Design, Development, and Evaluation from Syracuse University and is currently Chairperson of the Music Department, and Program Director of the Bachelor of Music, Music Management Program at The William Paterson University of New Jersey. He is responsible for the installation of the department's Center for Electroacoustic Music, and the updating of the audio recording studio. Every summer Marcone directs the WPU Summer Jazz Ensemble.